THE
BREWPUB
EXPLORER
OF THE
Pacific Northwest

Salùt!

THE BREWPUB EXPLORER OF THE Pacific Northwest

2nd Edition

•

Ina Zucker
Hudson Dodd
Matthew Latterell

DISCLAIMER

Although diligent efforts have been made to confirm the completeness and accuracy of information contained in this work, neither the publisher nor the authors are responsible for errors or inaccuracies, or for changes occurring after publication. This work was not prepared under the sponsorship, license, or authorization of any business, attraction, or organization described, depicted, or discussed herein.

The Brewpub Explorer of the Pacific Northwest, Second Edition
© Copyright 2000 by Ina Zucker, Hudson Dodd and Matthew Latterell

ISBN 1-881409-16-3
Book design and layout by Gray Mouse Graphics

JASI
P.O. Box 313
Medina, Washington 98039
(425) 454-3490; fax: (425) 462-1335
e-mail: jasibooks@aol.com

Printed in the United States of America
Library of Congress Cataloging-in-Publication Data
(To come)

CONTENTS

ACKNOWLEDGMENTS   7

INTRODUCTION   9

Craft Brewing Terminology: What's in This Book   10
Contract Brewing: Why Isn't That Beer With the Green Label in
Here?   11
Beer Styles: Why Are There Different Beers?   11
The Brewing Process: What's in This Stuff Anyway?   12
How to Use This Guide   14

OREGON   15

Region 1: The Oregon Coast   18

Region 2: Southern Oregon   25
Sidebar: Southern Oregon Brew Tour   25

Region 3: The Willamette Valley and Portland Metro   33
Sidebar: The Eugene Brewpub Scene   33
Sidebar: Portland, Beervana of the Northwest   45
Sidebar: McMenamins Brew Tour   55

Region 4: Central and Eastern Oregon   69
Sidebar: McMenamins Pubs & Breweries, "A Neighborhood Place for
Family & Friends"   79

WASHINGTON 85

Region 1: Olympic Peninsula & Southwest Washington   88
   Sidebar: Greater Puget Sound Brew Tour   95

Region 2: Seattle/Tacoma & Metro Area   104
   Sidebar: The Seattle Alehouse Scene   111

Region 3: San Juan Islands & Northwestern Washington   145
   Sidebar: Washington's "Fourth Corner" Brew Tour   150

Region 4: Southeastern Washington   159
   Sidebar: Yakima Valley Brew Tour   159

Region 5: Northeastern Washington   169

BRITISH COLUMBIA 177

Region 1: Vancouver/Lower Mainland & Vancouver Island   180
   Sidebar: Victoria's Charm   183
   Sidebar: Vancouver, B. (Beer) C. (City)   196

Region 2: Interior & Eastern British Columbia   213
   Sidebar: Okanagan Valley Brew Tour   213

GLOSSARY 226

APPENDICES 242

Pacific Northwest Alehouses   242

Recommended Reading   250

INDEX 251

ACKNOWLEDGEMENTS

We, the authors would like to express our thanks to:

Our families and friends for their support, advice and encouragement, especially Mary Kurlinski for her integral support and editing expertise;

The brewers, principals, and staff members of the brewpubs and microbreweries gracing these pages for their generous sharing of time and information, without which these pages would be blank;

The craft beer enthusiasts across the Pacific Northwest who have made the whole brewing renaissance a reality by buying, drinking, and enjoying all the new beer that has become available;

Thanks also go, in no particular order, to: Ravi Myers and family for the epic B.C. trips; Tom Lehmann, Rob Nelson, and Howard Koon for the glossary advice; Roger Hull and Greg Seeligson for the reconnaissance; Alan Moen and Tom Dalldorf for their support; Ed Bennett for his good nature; and the brewers of beer everywhere.

Visit our website: brewpubexplorer.com

DRINK RESPONSIBLY

When consuming alcohol, you assume responsibility for your own health and safety, and should take steps to ensure the safety of others. You must be of legal age to consume alcohol, and the responsibility for knowing the laws in the area in which you are drinking is yours alone.

Travel safely. At the outset of any brewery tour select a designated driver who will not drink. Drinking and driving is simply not an option, so if you're going to drive to and from the establishments listed in this book, make sure the person behind the wheel is not sampling brews along the way.

INTRODUCTION

A revolution in brewing and beer drinking has been sweeping North America since the early 1980s. The flavors, quality, and local charms of microbrews, ales, and lagers, produced in limited batches by small breweries, are re-educating our palates and redefining what we think of as good beer. Nowhere is this more true than in the Pacific Northwest, widely regarded as the birthplace of the microbrewing revolution.

Prior to Prohibition, local breweries were common throughout the United States. Small-town breweries and brewpubs served ales and lagers to friends and neighbors, and workers would fill up buckets of beer on their way home in the evening. Prohibition shut down nearly all these operations by the early 1920s. The repeal of Prohibition a short time later gave rise to a legacy of large regional and national breweries that still exists in the U.S. and Canada today. The small neighborhood breweries, seemingly, were gone forever.

In the late 1970s, however, local brewing got two much needed jumpstarts. First, President Carter signed the bill that legalized homebrewing in the U.S. for the first time since before Prohibition. Fritz Maytag took over the then-failing Anchor Steam Brewing Company of San Francisco and began to expand its brewing operation and distribution. Its growth and success inspired others, especially brewers in the Pacific Northwest, to bring local brewing back to the neighborhoods. In 1982, Bert Grant's Yakima Brewing Company and Redhook Ales of Seattle both rolled out their first kegs. British Columbia's Horseshoe Bay Brewing, now consolidated with Whistler Brewing Company, also opened in 1982.

The Pacific Northwest brewing culture is setting the standards for microbrews across the continent, with annual production of regional brewers increasing nearly fifty percent a year. This is supported by the wild enthusiasm of the highest per capita population of microbrew drinkers in North America.

The revival of local brewing in the Pacific Northwest has also produced a diversity of styles and brewing approaches that vary widely within the region. Oregon state has the most breweries and brewpubs per person anywhere outside Europe. Washington is home to two of the largest microbreweries in North America: Redhook Ales and Pyramid Brewery, Inc. While the brewers south of the border primarily brew ale, British Columbia has refined the art of lagering, reviving the smooth, rich flavors produced at the dawn of the twentieth century.

It is this exciting and dynamic brewing culture that inspired the creation of this book. We offer it as a celebration of the outstanding beers produced throughout the region, and of the brewers and breweries that produce them. Use it in that celebratory spirit as you start out on your educational, fun, and flavorful tour of the microbreweries and brewpubs of the Pacific Northwest.

CRAFT BREWERY TERMINOLOGY: WHAT'S COVERED IN THIS BOOK

The overall content of this book covers craft breweries, as distinct from industrial "mega" breweries. Explained below are some terms and working definitions that you'll hear throughout the beer scene (see also Glossary, page 226).

Craft brewery is a catch-all term for any size brewery producing "hand-crafted" beers, a term that connotes attention to the finer points of brewing without compromising quality in the name of quantity—though several craft breweries are now producing large quantities of beer. What differentiates these beers from industrial beers is the attention to the brewing process and the more-or-less strict adherence to tradition in utilizing only the ingredients of malted barley, hops, yeast, and water without adjuncts or pasteurization.

Within this overall field are the two subsets referred to throughout the book: *microbreweries* and *brewpubs*. The term *microbrewery* is most widely recognized by the general public and is used as a synonym for craft brewery. Technically, a microbrewery is a craft brewery of limited size, commonly categorized by less than 20,000 barrels in annual production. However, in this book we have included some of the larger craft breweries under this umbrella.

A *brewpub* is a drinking establishment that serves beers brewed on the premises. Generally these establishments also serve food in a restaurant atmosphere, as well as beverages other than beer. The term *brewhouse* is technically the area where the actual mashing and brewing occurs and consists primarily of the mash tun, lauter tun, and kettle. However, this term has also become synonymous with "brewpub."

Within these already blurry definitions, however, there are even grayer areas. For instance, brewpubs theoretically are establishments that sell their beer only on the premises. But some also distribute their product to restaurants or pubs. In other cases, a microbrewery might have a deluxe tasting room which, though not a brewpub, has the feel of one, and offers a limited menu. In other cases, the brewery strictly sells kegs wholesale, but happens to reside in the same building as a restaurant or pub that buys and serves the brewery's beers, lending it a brewpub-like feel.

CONTRACT BREWING: WHY ISN'T THAT BEER WITH THE GREEN LABEL IN HERE?

Contract brewing is the perfectly logical result of a burgeoning demand for craft beer. With a seemingly ever-increasing market, for anyone who knows how to make a decent beer there is ample opportunity to sell it. The main hindrance to entering the nouveau beer marketplace is the capital required to build a modern brewery. Several brewing ventures have bypassed this obstacle by striking deals with industrial breweries to brew their recipes, and then market the beer as "micro-brewed." Similarly, all of the major industrial breweries have targeted microbrew drinkers with phantom craft brews, often sporting local-sounding names as the brewery of origin.

Since this is a guidebook to establishments that brew craft beers, it does not include information on contract beers. You won't find information on Emerald City Ales, Oregon Ales, Jet City Ales or Pete's Wicked Ales (all of which have brewing contracts in the Northwest), because they are beers without a brewery. Their absence is in no way a judgement on the merits of these products.

However, several of the breweries in this book have contracts to brew "house beers" for other establishments, commonly restaurants. This is a different phenomenon altogether, in which the brewing establishment is its own brewery and just happens to brew special lines of beer for other venues.

BEER STYLES: WHY ARE THERE DIFFERENT BEERS?

Beer styles such as Pilsner, stout, and best bitter originated centuries ago in European regions which, to a great extent, remained remote from one another until the modern era. These isolated hamlets and valleys had their own wild yeast strains that caused the actual fermenting process, though early brewers were unclear about yeast's properties. Varying grains, malting facilities and hop types led to diverse recipes for making beer. In this way, regions gave birth to different beer styles.

With increased trade in Europe, these original European styles evolved over time and blended together somewhat. When the brewing process was brought to the New World, traditional styles soon took on unique twists, partly due to the differences between indigenous grains and yeasts, and partly due to the independent nature of North American settlers. Many of the new American styles survive to this day, including such old favorites as cream ale and mild brown ale. Though many European and American beer styles are distinctly different from one another, this book offers basic working definitions for most recognized styles and reflects the most enduring traditional characteristics.

In the nineteenth century, when yeast was isolated as the actual cause of fermentation, brewing began evolving into the scientifically defined endeavor it is today. Along with this important discovery came the realization that there are many strains of yeast, each lending very different characteristics to the finished beer, and each behaving differently during fermentation. The two main branches of yeast strains are *ale yeasts* and *lager yeasts*.

The isolation of lager strain yeasts created a revolution in brewing. By the turn of the twentieth century, the lighter bodied, crisper lagers had become the beer of choice throughout much of the world. And the revolution just kept growing, fueled by the spread of modern cooling equipment necessary for lager brewing. Though Great Britain was the last holdout of devout ale drinkers, today, thanks largely to the Campaign For Real Ale (CAMRA), there is an ale renaissance throughout many parts of the world, most notably North America.

THE BREWING PROCESS: WHAT'S IN THIS STUFF ANYWAY?

The basics of brewing are just that—pretty basic. While this is not a book on how to brew, here's a brief description of the process. For use as a tool during beer tastings and discussions, this simple, straightforward description, along with the glossary at the end of the book, is intended to give you a good, fundamental understanding of all aspects of the beer world, from the malted grains entering the grist hopper through to the finished product's style characteristics and the container in which it is delivered.

Beer is made from fermented grain, with barley being the grain of choice. Before the grain is fermented, it's turned into malt by means of a subtle and intricate process developed over centuries of experimentation. To start the process, the grain is soaked in water, then allowed to begin germination. Just after germination begins, the grains are whisked into a roasting oven called a *kiln*. Here the barley is roasted to varying degrees. The resulting product is called *malted barley*, or just *malt*.

Breweries purchase the malt, then crack the intact husks in a *mill* at the brewery. The cracked malt or grist is poured, either by hand or, more commonly, via an auger system, into a large vessel called a *mash tun*. The grist is cooked or *mashed* in water, and the temperature is held steady in order to extract the enzymes and proteins. The soupy mix is then pumped into the *lauter tun* where the spent grains are rinsed with hot water or *sparged* and removed from the liquid, which is called *sweet wort*.

The *sweet wort* is pumped into a kettle and boiled. Hops are added at various times during the boil, depending on what properties the brewer wants. Many kettles are equipped with a whirlpool mechanism, which collects the hops and undissolved proteins at the end of the boil and flushes them out of the finished wort.

The wort is now ready to ferment, which will occur when the yeast metabolizes

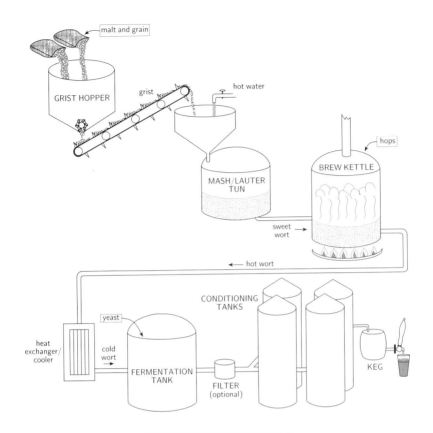

THE BREWING PROCESS

the sugars and converts them into alcohol and carbon dioxide. However, the wort is still much too hot from the long boil for yeast to survive. So it's cooled in a *heat exchanger* before being sent to the fermentation tank. Once in the fermentation tank, the yeast is added or *pitched* to the wort.

The length of fermentation time is determined by the strain of yeast and the recipe for the finished beer, however it is roughly a week. At the end of fermentation, the beer is transferred or *racked* to the *conditioning tank*, leaving the unwanted sediment behind. Here the yeast is allowed to finish metabolizing as high a percentage of sugars in the wort as possible, and the remaining sediment is allowed to settle out of the beer. Again, the time a brew spends in a conditioning tank depends on the kind of beer being made, as well as the recipe.

The beer is now ready for consumption, although it can be filtered to achieve greater clarity than the natural clarification that conditioning generally yields. The beer is racked into a *bright tank* from which it can be served directly to customers or held before bottling or kegging.

HOW TO USE THIS GUIDE

I n this book, each listing describes a given brewpub or craft brewery in two ways: the "write-up" and the "thumbnail sketch." The write-up consists of a descriptive, non-technical examination of the establishment's setting and ambiance, its standard and seasonal beers, and a ranging discussion that touches on everything from menu highlights to outdoor adventure opportunities nearby. We have tried to give an unbiased and noncritical overview of the brewpub or brewery as a whole. We leave it to you to rate the beers according to your tastes. Directions are worded to get you to the brewpub or brewery as directly as possible from the nearest main highway.

The "Established" year listed with the brewpub name is the first year of house-brewed beer sales. Note that in many cases establishments were long-operating restaurants or bars that added brewing operations later.

The thumbnail sketch section of each listing gives the hard facts about each brewpub or craft brewery. The areas covered are:

Hours: If different for separate sections of an establishment, the differences are indicated; if different by season, the various seasons are indicated

Children: If different for separate sections of an establishment, the various times are indicated; if different by hours of the day, the limitations are indicated

Food: One-phrase description, such as: upscale pub fare or steaks, pastas, seafood

Entertainment: Anything that qualifies as a form of entertainment provided by the establishment, including: pool and darts, live music, televised sports events, volleyball courts, monthly brewmaster dinners, etc.

Smoking: If different for separate sections of an establishment, the various limitations are indicated

Payment: Cash is accepted by all, and is therefore not indicated; other categories listed include: checks, debit/Interac, Visa/Mastercard, American Express, Discover, Diners Club

Beer to go: An indication of the availability of beer for sale retail, with draft and/or bottles indicated

Oregon is doubly blessed in that it has both incredible beauty and an abundance of hand-crafted beers. With more breweries per capita than anywhere else outside of Europe, the state is a leader in the microbrewing revolution, influencing styles, flavors, and the brewing culture throughout North America.

By the mid 1990s, the craft-brewing scene in Oregon was already quite mature, aided in no small part by the Oregon Brewers Guild, a trade association representing the majority of Oregon breweries, both large and small. Founded in 1992, the Oregon Brewers Guild has become an important resource for brewers,

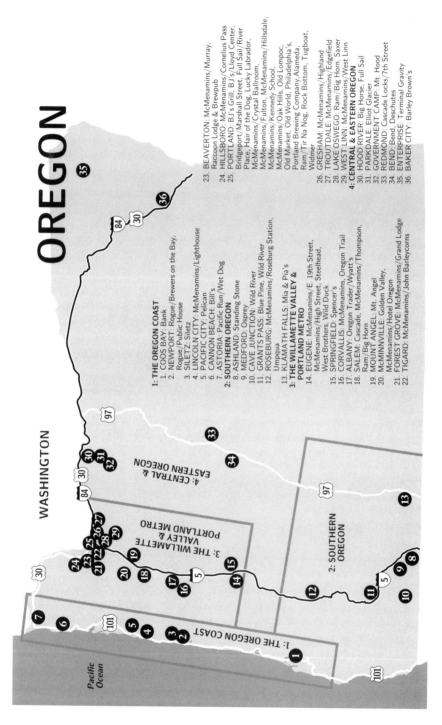

OREGON

WASHINGTON

Pacific
Ocean

1: THE OREGON COAST
1. COOS BAY: Bank
2. NEWPORT: Rogue/Brewers on the Bay, Rogue/Public House
3. SILETZ: Siletz
4. LINCOLN CITY: McMenamins/Lighthouse
5. PACIFIC CITY: Pelican
6. CANNON BEACH: Bill's
7. ASTORIA: Pacific Run/Wet Dog

2: SOUTHERN OREGON
8. ASHLAND: Standing Stone
9. MEDFORD: Osprey
10. CAVE JUNCTION: Wild River
11. GRANTS PASS: Blue Pine, Wild River
12. ROSEBURG: McMenamins/Roseburg Station, Umpqua
13. KLAMATH FALLS: Mia & Pia's

3: THE WILLAMETTE VALLEY & PORTLAND METRO
14. EUGENE: McMenamins/E. 19th Street, McMenamins/High Street, Steelhead, West Brothers, Wild Duck
15. SPRINGFIELD: Spencer's
16. CORVALLIS: McMenamins, Oregon Trail
17. ALBANY: Oregon Trader/Wyatt's
18. SALEM: Cascade, McMenamins/Thompson, Ram/Big Horn
19. MOUNT ANGEL: Mt. Angel
20. McMINNVILLE: Golden Valley, McMenamins/Hotel Oregon
21. FOREST GROVE: McMenamins/Grand Lodge
22. TIGARD: McMenamins/John Barleycorns
23. BEAVERTON: McMenamins/Murray, Raccoon Lodge & Brewpub
24. HILLSBORO: McMenamins/Cornelius Pass
25. PORTLAND: BJ's Grill, BJ's/Lloyd Center, Bridgeport/Marshall Street, Full Sail/River Place, Hair of the Dog, Lucky Labrador, McMenamins/Crystal Ballroom, McMenamins/Fulton, McMenamins/Hillsdale, McMenamins/Kennedy School, McMenamins/Oak Hills, Old Lompoc, Old Market, Old World, Philadelphia's, Portland Brewing Company, Alameda, Ram/Tir Na Nog, Rock Bottom, Tugboat, Widmer
26. GRESHAM: McMenamins/Highland
27. TROUTDALE: McMenamins/Edgefield
28. LAKE OSWEGO: Ram/Big Horn, Saxer
29. WEST LINN: McMenamins/West Linn

4: CENTRAL & EASTERN OREGON
30. HOOD RIVER: Big Horse, Full Sail
31. PARKDALE: Elliot Glacier
32. GOVERNMENT CAMP: Mt. Hood
33. REDMOND: Cascade Locks/7th Street
34. BEND: Bend, Deschutes
35. ENTERPRISE: Terminal Gravity
36. BAKER CITY: Barley Brown's

16 THE OREGON COAST
4: CENTRAL & EASTERN OREGON
3: THE WILLAMETTE VALLEY & PORTLAND METRO
2: SOUTHERN OREGON

beer enthusiasts, and other brewing organizations throughout North America. Recent forays into brewer-initiated "quality testing" of Oregon ales and lagers, the display of a Guild seal on true Oregon-crafted beers, and a willingness to work cooperatively for the good of members have all contributed to bringing the breweries of Oregon much deserved attention.

In the late 1990s even more brewpubs and small breweries have continued to appear. Sadly, a few have closed. None closed more dramatically than Siskiyou Brewing in Ashland, washed out (literally) one winter day by a swollen Ashland Creek. Siskiyou has since returned as a pub, and two former brewers, Ross Litton and Jim Mills, have gone on to open their own breweries—Walkabout Brewing and Caldera, respectively. Even mighty Nor'Wester, one of the industry's most significant closings, has been rescued, in a sense; you can still find Nor'Wester on grocery shelves as a line of ales and lagers brewed by Saxer Brewing.

Oregon is also home to the McMenamins empire, one of the essential forces in jumpstarting the current microbrewing renaissance. With more than forty taverns and brewpubs in Oregon and Washington, McMenamins is one of the defining elements of the craft brewing culture in the Pacific Northwest. Not willing to settle for just that the McMenamins brothers are also interested in preserving the culture and history of the places where they brew. The majestic Edgefield manor in Troutdale, an early 1900s train depot in Roseburg, and some of the Prohibition-era speakeasies of Portland have all been restored and reinvigorated under the imaginative care of this Northwest institution.

No matter where you travel in Oregon, from the rugged coastline to the towering peaks of the Cascades, in the smaller towns scattered throughout the state or in Portland, brewing capitol of the continent, breweries with outstanding beer await. Some, such as the distant Terminal Gravity of the eastern Oregon town of Enterprise might be difficult to get to, but all are worth the visit.

Bank Brewing Company

Established 1995

201 Central • Coos Bay, OR 97420
(541) 267-0963

The Bank Brewing Company is a perfect combination of old and new. The 1924 building was once a bank. However, today copper brew kettles stand where the bank manager worked, and the serving tanks are safely protected in the vault. A full restaurant menu highlighting gourmet pizzas and weekend specials, including a "catch of the day," is sure to satisfy the hunger of both regular customers and visitors.

The brewery offers six standard ales and several seasonals. Crowd-favorite Bull Buck Bitter, a wonderfully hoppy amber ale, is a well-crafted version of a traditional English Best Bitter. Tioga Black, brewed in the style of a Bavarian Schwarzbier (literally black beer), is a dark amber-colored beer with a malty, slightly roasted flavor—an outstanding beer rarely brewed in the Pacific Northwest. Bankers Stout, the darkest offering, is a rich, creamy, chocolate stout and will easily satisfy the tastes of stout enthusiasts. Seasonal Hallows Ale, a high alcohol Belgian-style ale, is an amber-colored sipping ale with a fruity finish and just a hint of coriander.

This first brewery in Coos Bay since the close of the Eagle Brewing Company in 1912 is a welcome addition to Oregon's south coast. The town is just minutes from the ocean and is a perfect base for exploring the Oregon Dunes National Recreation Area or the cliffs and beaches around Charleston.

Hours: 11:30 a.m.–10 p.m. Monday–Thursday; 11:30 a.m.–midnight Friday and Saturday
Children: Yes
Food: Excellent pizzas, full menu
Entertainment: Darts, televised sports events, occasional live jazz or blues
Smoking: Yes, in bar area
Payment: Visa, MC
Beer to go: Yes, draft

Directions: From Highway 101 going south, turn right on Central Avenue in downtown Coos Bay. The brewery is visible on the left after one block. From Highway 101 going north, turn left on Commercial, turn left on Highway 101, turn right on Central Avenue, and go one block.

Rogue Ales Bay Front Public House

Established 1989

748 SW Bay Boulevard • Newport, OR 97365
(541) 265-318 • www.rogue.com

The Bay Front Public House was originally Rogue's second pub, opening six months after Ashland's Rogue Brewery & Public House (now closed). Today, the pub is an integral part of the bustling Newport waterfront tourist haven, though it serves more locals than tourists.

Inside, the brewpub is sparsely lit and features wooden paneling and brass rails. Rogue beer memorabilia lines the walls. The main room with its large square bar is the smoking area, with an additional side room for non-smokers. The area of the building which originally housed the brewery now serves as a game room with pool tables, dart lanes and Oregon lottery machines. Rogue has recently added a new room—a museum and card-playing room. Take a look at ten years of Rogue historical artifacts while sitting down to a game of blackjack.

The menu is extensive, with the usual burgers and beer-battered fish and chips, but featured are entrées such as cioppino (seafood stew), baked red snapper, and some appealing pasta dishes. The bar has twenty-two beer handles, pouring the complete line of Rogue Ales, along with a few guest taps. Local favorites include the old standard American Amber Ale, Honey Cream Ale, and the thick, hoppy McRogue Scotch Ale.

After a pint or two, take a bathroom tour. The ceilings of two rooms, labeled only "hops" and "barley" for the discerning beer drinker, are both decorated with fluorescent renditions of the night sky. See if you can spot Venus. If not, you might need another taste of that McRogue.

DIRECTIONS: From Highway 101, turn east toward Newport's Old Town and Bay Front. Go all the way down the hill to Bay Boulevard and turn right. The public house is at the far end of the street on the right.

Hours: 11 a.m.–11 p.m. or later, daily
Children: Yes, with a special play area
Food: Full menu featuring pub fare, pasta, seafood
Entertainment: Winter, Fridays and Saturdays, live trivia show; summer, occasional live music; television, pool, darts, lottery machines, blackjack
Smoking: Yes, in separate areas
Payment: Visa, MC, Discover
Beer to go: Yes, bottles and draft

Brewer's on the Bay/Headquarters for the International Association of Rogues

Established 1992

2320 OSU Drive • Newport, OR 97365
(541) 867-3660 • www.rogue.com

The main Rogue brewery is located in an enormous, old marina building on the water. The fifty-barrel brewhouse and extensive kegging and bottling operations occupy the better part of the building. Brewery tours are given regularly during the day. While you wait, you can sample Rogue brews on tap and enjoy a meal looking out over Newport Bay.

John "More Hops" Maier, brewer, who has been crafting Rogue ales here since day one is now a legend in Northwest microbrewing culture. His ales travel well for great distances, and Rogue president Jack Joyce credits Maier's heavy hand with both hops and malts for this trait, calling Rogue ales virtually bullet-proof, because they travel well. Rogue's ales are now available both on draft and in bottles in forty-two states and six countries

Maier's beers have garnered great recognition. His Amber and Golden have both become standards for their respective styles. He also brews some of Oregon's most exotic brews, including Rogue Smoke, a rauchbier with an intense hop finish; St. Rogue Red, roasty and piney, and Old Crustacean, a powerful barley wine that's malty, bitter, sweet and fruity all in one mouthful.

Brewer's on the Bay, established in 1997, is a two-story pub located inside the brewery. Brewer's has twenty-one different Rogue brews on tap, as well as selected fine spirits. The menu includes salads, soups, pastas and a great selection of seafood.

DIRECTIONS: From Highway 101 northbound, turn east at the stoplight south of the Newport Bridge. At the T, turn north and drive 1/2 mile past the Newport Aquarium to the edge of the bay, and turn west. The brewery is on your right. From Highway 101 southbound, take the first exit after the Newport Bridge. It curves under the bridge headed east. The brewery is on your left.

Hours: Summer, 11 a.m.–8 p.m. Monday–Sunday; winter, 11 a.m.–7 p.m. Monday–Friday
Children: Yes
Food: Pub fare and seafood
Entertainment: No
Smoking: Yes at House of Rogues, no at Tasting Room
Payment: Visa, MC, Discover
Beer to go: Yes, bottles and draft

Siletz Brewing Company

Established 1995

267 Gaither Street • Siletz, OR 97380
(541) 444-7256

Located just a few miles inland from the Oregon Coast, the Siletz Brewing Company is a welcome addition to this quiet community just a few miles off Highway 20 and a short distance from Newport. The ocean is important to this brewery—the founders worked in the regional fishing and harbor industries. The Siletz River, which runs near the brewery, also plays an important role, as the ales are made from the mountain waters that flow into the Siletz.

The interior of the brewpub is sparsely decorated, with a few pictures covering the wood paneling on the walls. Video poker machines occupy one room, and the bar and a few tables take up the rest of the building. Currently, the brewery produces four standard ales. The Siletz SOS Pale Ale, a tasty and smooth malty ale with a crisp finish, is the pub favorite. The dry-hopped amber will please anyone searching for an aromatic, richly hopped ale. A nut brown and a porter round out the Siletz Brewing Company's fine line of ales.

Don't rush away from Siletz too quickly. Take a tour of the community center. Plan a visit in July, when the town hosts one of the biggest pow-wows in the region, then spend time kayaking or fishing on the Siletz. For a scenic drive, follow the river north until it empties into Siletz Bay on the Oregon coast. The longer you stay in the area, the more you appreciate the beauty of the water and the mountains, and the more you enjoy the people who call this place home.

DIRECTIONS: From Highway 101 in Newport, take Highway 20 to Corvallis. At the Dairy Queen, take Highway 229 to Siletz. The brewpub is at the far end of town on the left.

Hours: 11 a.m.–closing, daily
Children: Yes
Food: Full menu including pizza
Entertainment: Pool, darts, video poker, regularly televised sports, live music
Smoking: Yes
Payment: Visa, MC
Beer to go: Yes, draft

The Pelican Pub & Brewery

Established 1996

33180 Cape Kiwanda Drive • Pacific City, OR 97135
(503) 965-7007 • www.pelicanbrewery.com

Until recently, Pacific City was mostly known to surfers, hang gliders, and beach-combers. With the opening of the Pelican Pub & Brewery in 1996, literally a few steps from the beach, people have another great reason to come—the beer.

Located on Cape Kiwanda under the evening shadow of Haystack Rock, the Pelican Pub & Brewery is situated perfectly. An outdoor patio, usually covered by migrating sand dunes in winter, provides an excellent spot to sit on a summer evening. The pub itself is cozy—a long dark wooden bar is usually filled with mug-club regulars. The family-style seating area in the back looks out onto the beach.

Brewer Darren Welch returned to Oregon after a year at the Appleton Brewing Company in Wisconsin to open the brewery at the Pelican. A long-time homebrewer, he took his own American brown ale and turned it into the pub's Doryman's Dark Ale, an award-winning, nicely balanced strong ale with robust character. His Tsunami Stout, another Great American Beer Festival winner, is midnight black in color with a rich dark-roasted flavor.

The other brews at the Pelican include the MacPelican's Scottish Ale, a copper colored ale with a rich, malty aroma, the India Pelican Ale, a smooth and tasty Brown Pelican Porter, and the regionally appropriate Heiferweizen, so named for the abundance of dairy cows in Tillamook County. If Welch wins many more awards for his brews, however, the county icon may soon be a pelican instead of a cow.

Hours: 8 a.m.–10 p.m. winter; 8 a.m.–11 p.m. summer
Children: Yes
Food: Pub fare
Entertainment: Occasional comedy nights
Smoking: Yes, in the bar
Payment: Checks, Visa, MC, AmEx, Discover
Beer to go: Yes, draft and bottles

DIRECTIONS: From Highway 101 take the Brooten Road exit and head west into Pacific City. Cross over the river and turn right onto Cape Kiwanda Drive. The pub is on the beach side of the road a couple of blocks north.

Bill's Tavern & Brewhouse

Established 1997

188 North Hemlock • Cannon Beach, OR 97110
(503) 436-2202

Although the original Bill of Bill's Tavern is long gone, pictures of Bill and the original 1932 tavern can be found throughout the pub. Ken Campbell, the owner of Bill's Tavern for the past twenty years, rebuilt the pub a few years ago and installed a brewery on the second floor, a dream of his for years.

Cannon Beach is a thriving artistic center. Some of the Oregon coast's finest and most eclectic restaurants can be found here. It is a second home for many of Portland's wealthier citizens, and a permanent home for a growing and very active retirement community. Highway 101 misses Cannon Beach by just a hair—a decision that was hotly debated at the time but has served the town well and makes it feel more relaxed than other Oregon Coast towns.

Bill's Tavern is right in the middle of town. The interior is split in half by the bar and serving tanks, with the bar on the right side of the tavern. The gorgeous art deco back bar saved from the renovation of the old Portland Hotel is striking. The walls of the tavern are one continuous oceanside mural painted by a local artist; the blown glass tap handles were made by another local artist.

Hours: 11:30 a.m.–midnight every day
Children: Yes, until 9 p.m.
Food: Pub-style menu, award-winning hamburgers
Entertainment: Occasional live music
Smoking: Yes in the bar
Payment: Checks, Visa, MC
Beer to go: Yes, draft

Jack Harris, the brewer, produces five standard ales and a rotating seasonal. The Duckdive Pale Ale is probably Jack's favorite—a fairly complex ale with a healthy hop aroma and a nice fruity finish. Golden Rye, Bronze Ale—a smooth, malty, slightly sweet ale, Smokey Porter and 2x4 Stout are the brewery's other standards. Definitely try whatever seasonal is on tap, with recent offerings including a spruce-flavored ale in the spring, Old Nut Cracker for winter, and Vitality Ale, brewed with various herbs to keep the cold and flu season at bay.

DIRECTIONS: From Highway 101 take the 2nd Street exit into Cannon Beach (the first Cannon Beach exit from the north, the last from the south). Take 2nd Street to Hemlock Street and turn left. The tavern is on the right.

Pacific Rim Brewery/Wet Dog Café

Established 1997

144 11th Street • Astoria, OR 97301
(503) 325-6975

The Pacific Rim Brewery holds the honor of being located in the oldest American settlement west of the Rockies. Astoria, perched on the northwest corner of Oregon, between the mouth of the Columbia River and the Pacific Ocean, is rich in history. American settlers moved here soon after Lewis and Clark visited the region in 1805.

Climb to the top of the 125-foot-high Astoria Column, built in 1926, for breathtaking views of the Pacific Ocean, Columbia River, Saddle Mountain, and the Clatsop Plain. Museums abound. The Uppertown Firefighters Museum, home to firefighting memorabilia dating from 1877 to 1963, located in the pre-Prohibition North Pacific Brewery building, provides an interesting look at the town's history.

Brewing returned to the region in 1997 when Dirk Beaulieu opened the Pacific Rim Brewery, housed inside the Wet Dog Café on the waterfront in downtown Astoria. Dirk brews six standard ales and a variety of seasonals. Frenchie's Scottish Ale, the brewery's most popular ale, is a deliciously smooth, slightly sweet, dark amber colored ale. Sow Your Wild Oatmeal Stout, dark and rich, is excellent. Ramblin' Rim Rye PA, a slight twist on a traditional IPA, Pacific Pale which is crisp and light, Captain's Porter, and Peacock Spit Golden Ale (you'll have to ask about the name!) are the brewery's other standards.

The Wet Dog Café is also home to a great deal of history. It is housed in a former fruit and produce warehouse first built in 1924. The views from the Wet Dog are second to none—the Columbia River flows just a few feet from the building with the Willapa Hills of southern Washington visible in the distance. The inside of the Café has two rooms—the larger houses the bar, seating area, stage, and dance floor; the other has several pool tables and other games.

Hours: 11 a.m.– closing (usually 1 a.m.)
Children: Yes, until 9 p.m.
Food: Pub grub, daily specials
Entertainment: Live music and dancing weekends, pool and video games
Smoking: Yes
Payment: Checks, Visa, MC
Beer to go: Yes, draft

DIRECTIONS: On the waterfront on 11th and Marine (Highway 30) in downtown Astoria

Southern Oregon Brew Tour

Since 1996, the I-5 corridor in Southern Oregon has experienced a brewing renaissance all its own. Where once five brewpubs operated, now eleven are found in the stretch from Ashland, in the south, to Roseburg, in the north. This bounty, coupled with the amazing beauty of the area and the world renowned Oregon Shakespeare Festival, makes touring the breweries of Southern Oregon an opportunity not to be missed.

The beginning of the tour is dictated by ticket availability for the Oregon Shakespeare Festival in Ashland. The Festival season runs from late February to late October, but in the summer most weekend shows are sold out well in advance. Call (541) 482-4331 or check their website at www.orshakes.org for information. Make your room reservations early as well, especially if you want to stay in one of the fine bed and breakfast inns near downtown Ashland.

The first stop on your brew tour is Standing Stone Brewing Company, just up the street from the theater. The wood-fired pizzas are excellent, and go well with the India pale ale. Ashland is also home to Caldera Brewing, a distribution-only brewery that does not give tours. You can find their ales on tap at the Siskiyou Pub, a block away from Standing Stone, under the bridge. Siskiyou used to be a brewpub, but in the beginning of 1997 a wild Ashland Creek, fed by fierce rains, all but destroyed the brewery. The former Rogue brewery did return later in the year as a pub, and now serves an excellent selection of regional brews.

Heading north on I-5 brings you to Medford, now home to two radically different breweries. Osprey Brewpub is a casual place where folks come to hang out while enjoying a Scottish Ale or Tacoma Pale. The other Medford-area brewery is the Walkabout Brewing Company, owned by Ross Litton. Ross, a transplanted Australian, has a licensed brewery in his home. He can't give tours, but his wonderful brews are regularly on tap at the Siskiyou in Ashland, Howie's on Front Street in Medford, and other locations around Southern Oregon. Look for Worker's Pale and Jabberwocky, a flavorful Strong Ale.

Next stop is Grants Pass. Like Medford, Grants Pass has developed two brewpubs that are almost nothing alike. The Blue Pine, adorned with tie-dyed sheets and Grateful Dead and Jimi Hendrix posters, is very relaxed. Kick back and enjoy a Rip Roarin' Red. Down the road a bit is the Wild River Brewing

Company, a family-oriented pizza restaurant and brewery. Wild River has a second brewery and restaurant in Cave Junction, a little out of the way but worth the stop. Try the Blackberry Porter, made with real berries, for a unique taste sensation.

Last stop is Roseburg, now home to two brewpubs and a distribution-only brewery. Umpqua Brewing Company, in operation since 1991, is a community icon and illustrious host to the Small Brewers Big Beer Festival every

September. Try Umpqua's Roseburg Red or their Downtown Brown. Hawks Brewing Company, owned by Charlie Hawks, brews in Roseburg for distribution only and does not offer tours. You can usually find his Supernatural IPA, made with organic ingredients, on tap at Umpqua and at Roseburg's other brewpub, the Roseburg Station. Roseburg Station, the first McMenamins brewpub in Southern Oregon, is a beautifully restored 1912 train station now serving locally brewed McMenamins ales and upscale pub fare.

End of the line—you might just need to turn around and do it all over again!

Standing Stone Brewing Company

Established 1997

101 Oak Street • Ashland, OR 97520
(541) 482-2448

Ashland is a wonderful place. Nestled under Mt. Ashland, the town is home to Oregon's Shakespeare Festival, drawing some 250,000 theater lovers to this beautiful town each year. Ashland has a remarkable diversity of outstanding restaurants which flourish from early spring to late fall, during the theater season.

Open since August of 1997, the Standing Stone Brewing Company is a welcome addition to that list of eateries. Standing Stone, offering wood-fired pizzas and a small but wide-ranging dinner menu, is located near the theaters, Lithia Park, and Ashland Creek. The building served as a glass and cabinet shop for over forty years and was vacant for several more years before being purchased by Emile Amarotico and his brothers Alex and Mark.

The open warehouse is ideal for a brewery and restaurant. The ten-barrel brewhouse resides in the front of the restaurant and is visible from the street, while the fermenting and conditioning tanks sit above the restaurant on an exposed balcony. Seating which is primarily in the back, provides an excellent view of the wood-fired pizza oven and the open kitchen. During good weather the expansive deck, offers views of the hills surrounding the town.

Alex, the brewer, has created several high quality ales. The India pale ale, their most popular brew, is well balanced, offering a nice hoppy aroma and sufficient bitterness. The nut brown ale is very tasty—a slightly nutty flavor that finishes smooth. The porter is a seasonal brew; if it's available on tap, it makes the whole trip worthwhile.

DIRECTIONS: From the South take exit 14 off I-5. Go West on Hwy 66 towards Ashland and turn right onto Hwy 99, Siskiyou Boulevard. Hwy 99 divides in the downtown area. Go five blocks to Oak Street and turn left. Standing Stone is on the right.

From the North take exit 19 off I-5. Turn right at the end of the off-ramp. At the bottom of the hill turn left onto Hwy 99. Follow this road into downtown Ashland. Hwy 99 divides in the downtown area, just past the Best Western motel. Turn left onto Oak Street, two blocks past the bridge. Standing Stone is on the left near the end of this short block.

Hours: 11:30 a.m.–midnight, daily
Children: Yes
Food: Wood-fired pizzas, upscale pub fare
Entertainment: Live music
Smoking: No
Payment: Visa, MC
Beer to go: Yes, draft

Osprey Brewpub

Established 1996

404 E Main Street • Medford, OR 97501
(541) 734-4808

Something is always happening at the Osprey Brewpub in Medford, Oregon. Live music plays on the weekends, karaoke entertainment happens every Thursday, open-microphone is Mondays and Tuesdays, while Sundays and Wednesdays of each week offer something different. The music runs from blues to jazz, rock to reggae. Downstairs, games include foosball, pool, and darts.

The inside of the pub is a little chaotic in design, but the atmosphere is fun and friendly. A fishing theme predominates, but is not overwhelming. Seating in the back of the pub and outside on the deck is the most relaxed, with the front of the house geared more for music or sports events on the big screen television. The seven-barrel brewery is downstairs, but will eventually move to a building nearby to make room for a full service kitchen.

Osprey offers several ales including Tacoma Pale, a Scottish Ale which is the local favorite, an IPA, and a porter. They have produced a couple of seasonals, but are mostly focused on continuing to refine their standard ales. The nightly crowds of regulars don't seem to mind the process one bit.

Osprey is located in downtown Medford, a block from Bear Creek, an under-appreciated stream that runs through town. The pub, which has made it a point to get involved in local events, sponsors a Rogue River cleanup day and other community efforts. The Osprey Brewpub is growing into a community center of sorts, producing a nightly celebration for the people of Medford.

DIRECTIONS: From the south take exit 27 off I-5. Take a left onto Barnett Road over I-5 to Hwy 99. Turn right on Hwy 99 heading north into downtown Medford. Go approximately two miles and turn right onto Main Street. The pub is on the right hand side of the road, just before the bridge. From the North, take exit 30 off I-5 (the Medford Mall exit). Take a right off the ramp onto Crater Lake Highway. Stay in the right lane—the road will curve to the left. The road becomes Court Street, which in turn becomes Hwy 99. Follow the signs for Hwy 99 into downtown Medford—you'll turn left and right, but keep following the Hwy 99 signs. At Main Street turn left. The pub is on the right hand side of the road just before the bridge.

Hours: 11 a.m.–midnight Monday–Thursday; 11 a.m.–2 a.m. Friday; noon–2 a.m. Saturday; noon–9 p.m. Sunday
Children: No
Food: Limited pizza and sandwich menu
Entertainment: Tons, something different every night
Smoking: No
Payment: Checks, Visa, MC
Beer to go: Yes, draft

Wild River Brewing & Pizza Company

Established 1990

249 North Redwood Highway • Cave Junction, OR 97523
(541) 592-3556 • www.wildriverbrewing.com

Wild River Brewing & Pizza Company had its beginnings as a 1970s pizza parlor in Cave Junction. In 1990, the owners added a brewery to the establishment, making it the oldest brewpub still operating in Southern Oregon. Wild River has since gone on to add a much larger restaurant and brewery in Grants Pass, a restaurant in Brookings on the southern Oregon coast, and most recently has added the Wild River Publick House, a European-style eatery with a full bar, in Grants Pass.

The interior of the Cave Junction restaurant is one large, open room with a mural painted over the entire ceiling. All of the tables, legend has it, were made from a single redwood tree—not hard to believe if you stray south on Highway 199 into the Redwood National Forest in Northern California. The restaurant also has a deck with tables that overlook a creek where you can sit and enjoy the Oregon woods.

The seven-barrel brewery produces the same brews as the larger operation in Grants Pass. Harbor Lights Kölsch, a pale aromatic ale with a dry clean finish, Extra Special Bitter, a copper-colored English-style ale, and Russian Imperial Stout, a rich, dark stout based on an 1880 recipe, are a few of the Wild River brews available throughout the year. The smaller brewery is also used for occasional pilot brews available only at this location.

Cave Junction is the perfect starting point for an exploration of the Oregon Caves National Monument, the Kalmiopsis Wilderness, or the scenic Illinois River. The Wild River Brewing & Pizza Company is the perfect spot to enjoy a brew at the end of a day exploring in the Oregon outdoors.

DIRECTIONS: Wild River is located in the north end of Cave Junction along Highway 199.

Hours: 11 a.m.–10 p.m. every day
Children: Yes
Food: Pizza, sandwiches
Entertainment: No
Smoking: No
Payment: Visa, MC
Beer to go: Yes, bottles and draft

Blue Pine Brewpub

Established 1993

422 SW 5th Street #B • Grants Pass, OR 97526
(541) 476-0760

The Blue Pine Brewpub is easy to miss, because this best-kept secret of Grants Pass is hidden between the historic Schmidt House and a hair salon. A small sign between two buildings is your only clue to finding the pub. The establishment is housed in what was once the Grange Hall; parking and access are easy from the rear.

With its rough-cut, blue pine tables and bar made by the two owners, walls decorated in tie-dyed sheets, Grateful Dead and Jimi Hendrix posters, and a continuous open-microphone music policy, the Blue Pine may astonish unsuspecting visitors into feeling as if they stepped back into the 60s. It has become home to a loyal clientele, who stop by to have a drink, hang out, and relax.

Five regular ales and several seasonals are brewed here. Rip Roarin' Red, the most popular, is a medium-colored ale with a slightly roasted flavor. Pearsoll Peak Pale, a light amber-colored ale, is milder and smoother, with little bitterness. Big Barley Brown, Blue Pine Porter, and Midnite Stout, all progressively darker ales, are the brewery's three other regular offerings. Pumpkin Pie Spice, flavored with cinnamon and other spices, Christmas Red Spice Ale and Autumn Amber are a few of the seasonals you might find during the year.

One of Oregon's smallest breweries, the Blue Pine Brewpub was founded with the goal of brewing beer for, and with, friends. Its neighborly atmosphere, affordable food, and quality beers can easily turn a quick visit into a lazy, relaxing afternoon or the perfect evening.

Hours: 3 p.m.–11 p.m. Tuesday–Saturday
Children: Yes
Food: Sandwiches, salads, soups
Entertainment: Live music, board games, foosball
Smoking: No
Beer to go: Yes, draft
Payment: Checks

DIRECTIONS: Take exit 55 off I-5. Brewery is on 5th Street between I and J streets, between Governor's Mansion Hair Salon and Ace Bookkeepers.

Wild River Brewing & Pizza Company

Established 1994

595 NE "E" Street • Grants Pass, OR 97526
(541) 471-7487 • www.wildriverbrewing.com

In 1994 the Wild River Brewing & Pizza Company opened a 200-seat restaurant and brewery in Grants Pass, establishing this site as the primary brewing location for Wild River. The Cave Junction restaurant brews mostly for local consumption, while the newer and much larger brewery in Grants Pass also meets the additional demands of distribution and bottling.

The Wild River restaurant in Grants Pass is hard to miss. Tall ceilings, two levels of seating—and a speed boat—greet the visitor who enters this beer connoisseur's paradise. The brewery, fully visible from every seat in the restaurant, produces five standard and five seasonal ales. The recipes used to produce the beers are mostly historical, uncovered from brewers' journals dating back to the 1700s and 1800s and recreated with Pacific Northwest ingredients. The success is evident in the medal-winning Nut Brown Ale and Snug Harbor Old Ale. The Wild River Blackberry Porter is based on a 1750 Whitbread London porter, with blackberries added, and is easily one of the finest porters anywhere. Crowd favorite is an authentic German hefeweizen, appealing to first timers as well as to enthusiasts underwhelmed by American recreations of this unique style.

Hours: Monday–Friday 7 a.m.–10:30 p.m.; Saturday and Sunday 9 a.m.–10:30 p.m.
Children: Yes
Food: Complete menu including breakfast
Entertainment: No
Smoking: No
Payment: Visa, MC
Beer to go: Yes, bottles and draft

The Wild River Brewing & Pizza Company also utilizes beer in their cooking. All bread and pizza doughs are made with spent grains produced in the brewing process, and many items in the extensive menu are flavored with Wild River brews. The authenticity and quality of the ales, coupled with the pizzas and calzones cooked in the large wood-fired ovens, make Wild River a stop worth making over and over again.

DIRECTIONS: Take exit 55 off I-5. Go west (toward downtown) one mile. Wild River is at the corner of "E" and Mill Street.

Umpqua Brewing Company

Established 1991

328 SE Jackson Street • Roseburg, OR 97470
(541) 672-0452 • www.teleport.com/~umpqbrew

Roseburg's oldest brewpub is a wonderful mix of Old World style and local charm. A dark wooden bar inside the long brick and wood building frames the collection of beer steins and bottles along the walls, creating the feeling of a small-town English pub.

Umpqua Brewing is also home to the best entertainment in town, with local and regional musicians playing jazz, blues, folk, rock, and even reggae every Friday and Saturday night. Don't be surprised if you happen to hear a reading from one of Roseburg's budding poets.

The brewery produces more than ten different beers at all times, offering something for everyone. Summer Wheat, a light, flavorful ale, is the crowd favorite. Roseburg Red, a medium-colored ale, is full of caramel and roasted flavors, with a wonderful fruity finish. Imperial Stout and No Doubt Stout, both with rich chocolate and roasted flavors, offer slight variations on traditional styles and should please stout enthusiasts. Perry's Old Ale, a rich, malty English-style ale with plenty of hops in the finish, and Double Red barley wine are both "must-try" seasonals.

The brewpub's logos are modeled after petroglyphs found on rocks in the region. The company chose these images because they reflect the history and culture of the Umpqua Valley, and the brewers were committed to producing ales as marvelous and enduring as the pictures. This commitment is evident in the beauty of the building, the variety of entertainment, and the diversity of quality ales produced.

DIRECTIONS: From I-5, take Exit 124. East onto Harvard, cross the Oak Street Bridge to the second light. Turn left on Stephens; go two lights and turn right onto Diamond Lake. Go one block and turn right onto Jackson Street. Umpqua Brewing is $1^1/2$ blocks up Jackson on the right.

Hours: 5 p.m.–closing, Tuesday – Saturday; 5 p.m.–8 p.m. Sunday
Children: Yes, until 9 p.m.
Food: Gourmet pizzas, burgers, nachos
Entertainment: Live music every weekend, poetry readings, games, regularly televised sports
Smoking: No
Payment: Checks
Beer to go: Yes, draft

THE EUGENE BREWPUB SCENE

Eugene is a blessed city. Nowhere else in the Pacific Northwest—or perhaps anywhere outside Germany—can you find four independently owned brewpubs all within a few minutes' walk of each other. Fortunately, due to the combination of a relatively young population, a large University community, strong interest in dining out and the love of great beer, all four breweries thrive.

It's easy to plan a walking tour of Eugene's brewing operations, although something of a challenge to complete! Begin at the High Street Brewery & Café, Eugene's oldest microbrewery. McMenamins opened High Street in 1988 in a funky house at, appropriately enough, 1243 High Street. Working out of a cramped brewery below the café, the High Street brewers produce the standard McMenamins ales, and several wonderful originals.

A few blocks' walk through the downtown area brings you to the West Brothers Brewery at 844 Olive Street, which serves two restaurants located above the brewery, West Brothers Bar-B-Que and Mona Lizza Ristorante.

After a brief rest, walk the two blocks to Eugene's newest brewpub, the Wild Duck, at 169 W 6th Avenue. The establishment offers a restaurant, full bar and concert hall complete with room for dancing. Brewer Glen Falconer's specialty is hops—make sure to try Glen's Best Bitter.

Finally, take a deep breath and walk over to Steelhead at 199 E 5th Avenue, where Teri Fahrendorf is the head brewer of Eugene's second oldest brewery. The Bombay Bomber, a flavorful India pale ale, enjoys near cult status among beer drinkers in this town.

With four brewpubs in a city of just over 120,000 (plus Spencer's, Springfield's first brewpub, just across I-5), it would be easy to suspect fierce competition and healthy amounts of secrecy and suspicion among the brewers. In traditional Eugene style, however, nothing could be further from the truth. Brewers have been known to share their yeast from time to time, or to borrow a particular hop or grain from each other. A recent unique experiment, in which all the brewers took the same brown ale recipe and brewed it with their own yeast, equipment and unique styles, would be unthinkable almost anywhere else.

The Eugene brewing scene offers a wonderful collection of beers and styles served in relaxed, friendly establishments. Each pub and each brewer offers the visitor something refreshingly different. Collectively, they have created a remarkable celebration of beer and brewing.

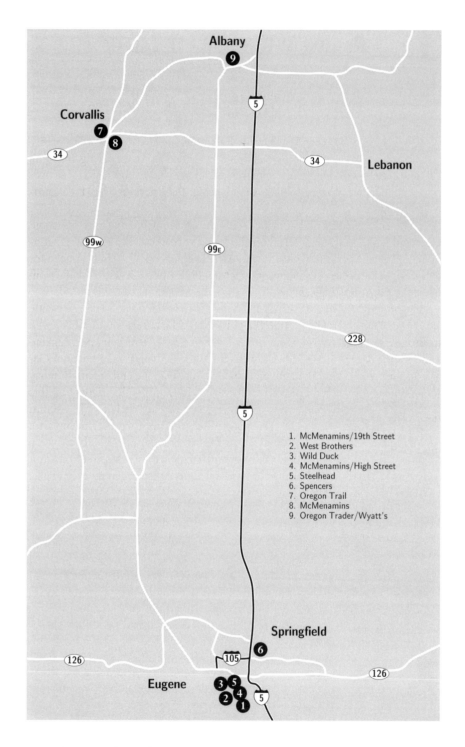

Albany
9

Corvallis
7
8

5

34

34
Lebanon

99w

99E

228

5

1. McMenamins/19th Street
2. West Brothers
3. Wild Duck
4. McMenamins/High Street
5. Steelhead
6. Spencers
7. Oregon Trail
8. McMenamins
9. Oregon Trader/Wyatt's

Springfield
6

126

105

126

Eugene
3 5
2 4
1
5

Steelhead Brewing Company

Established 1991

199 E 5th Avenue • Eugene, OR 97401
(541) 686-2739

T he Steelhead Brewing Company is Eugene's second oldest brewing operation. This busy, exciting pub is located in the middle of a thriving shopping and entertainment district on the edge of downtown Eugene, just a few blocks from the Hult Performance Center, the 5th Street Public Market, and the beautiful Willamette River.

The inside of Steelhead is marvelous—cherry-stained mahogany tables and bar, an old "red box" English telephone booth, antique wood advertisements hanging on red brick walls and decadent wing-backed chairs you'll want to relax in for hours. For those not engrossed in conversation, several large televisions hang from the ceilings broadcasting a game.

The brewery has recently expanded, adding two new brewpubs in Burlingame and Irvine, California. Head Brewer Teri Fahrendorf has been shuttling between the three, getting the new pubs up to speed while working to keep up with demand at the Eugene operation. Steelhead brews three standard ales and a flurry of specials and seasonals. Always on tap are a hefeweizen, a hoppy amber, and Bombay Bomber (a very fruity India pale ale with a strong hop finish). A variety of porters and stouts rotate as the brewery's dark ale, including Java Stout, brewed with roasted coffee beans to impart a strong coffee flavor. Other seasonals include a barley wine and a rye. The tasty Steelhead root beer is also always on tap and well worth a taste.

Hours: 11:30 a.m.–midnight, Sunday–Thursday; 11:30 a.m.–1 a.m. Friday and Saturday
Children: No
Food: Upscale pub menu
Entertainment: Regular televised sports events
Smoking: Yes, in a smoking section
Payment: Checks, Visa, MC
Beer to go: Yes, draft

DIRECTIONS: From I-5 in Eugene, take exit for I-105 to the University of Oregon. From I-105, take Downtown exit. Cross over Ferry Street Bridge and take the second right to 6th Street (99E). Turn right at bottom of ramp on High Street, go one block and turn left onto 5th. Go one block; the brewery is on the right.

West Brothers Brewery

Established 1993

844 Olive Street • Eugene, OR 97401
(541) 345-8489

West Brothers Brewery operates from the basement of two remarkable restaurants situated side-by-side, West Brothers Bar-B-Que and Mona Lizza Ristorante.

The restaurants, both owned by West brothers Mike, Jim, and Phil, offer an incredibly diverse menu. Open door number one and you enter West Brothers, specializing in barbecue and remarkably tasty and unique vegetarian entrées. Photos of barbecues from around the country adorn the walls above tables of hungry customers. Summers, outdoor seating is available under the mural of Eugene's original Eugene City Brewery building, which was built across the street from West Brothers' current location in 1866.

Door number two reveals Mona Lizza, a more upscale, but still casual Italian restaurant offering a wide variety of antipasti, salads, pastas, pizza and other entrées. Mona Lizza is a beautiful place—bare brickwork on the lower half of the walls, ornate mirrors above, and lots of wonderful cherry woodwork throughout.

The brewery produces five standard ales and a rotating seasonal. Honey Orange Wheat, the crowd favorite, is a cloudy, honey-colored ale with a slightly citrus flavor. The India pale ale is a fairly hoppy and somewhat bitter IPA with a mildly fruity finish. The stout, creamy and chocolatey, has a devoted following among Eugene stout drinkers. The amber, a red-colored ale brewed with roasted barley and a smooth balance of malts and hops, is a unique ale definitely worth a try. Seasonals include a porter, barley wine, and brown.

DIRECTIONS: From I-5 in Eugene, take the I-105 exit to the University of Oregon. Take I-105 until it ends at 7th. Turn left on 7th and go to Olive Street. Turn right on Olive. The brewery is on the right side, on Olive between 8th and Broadway.

Hours: 11:30 a.m.–closing daily
Children: Yes
Food: Two separate restaurants with extensive menus
Entertainment: Live music on weekends
Smoking: No
Payment: Checks, Visa, MC, AmEx, Diners Club
Beer to go: Yes, draft

The Wild Duck Brewery

Established 1996

169 W 6th Avenue • Eugene, OR 97401
(541) 485-3825 • www.wildduckbrewery.com

The Wild Duck, Eugene's newest brewpub, offers patrons and visitors a brewpub, restaurant and concert hall all under the same roof. The 500-seat theater, with a completely modern sound system, brings an eclectic mix of jazz, rock, reggae, and more to the Eugene music scene. Combine this with quality ales brewed in-house, and the Wild Duck is sure to please.

The building is enormous, and with the large mural painted on the outside walls, it is impossible to guess that just a few years ago this was a truck repair and rental shop. The bar and restaurant areas are remarkable—a gorgeous bar with two gold-inlaid German beer towers, huge and comical old-fashioned neon signs, and a full view of the all-copper brewhouse. The Wild Duck also has an outside deck on the second floor—with a grill and bar.

Brewer Glen Falconer is passionate about beer. Stints at Rogue and Steelhead, and years of homebrewing, have only increased his love for brewing. The Wild Duck offers five standard ales and a rotation of seasonals. House favorite is the hoppy Duck Wheat Hefeweizen. Ringneck Stout is rich and chocolatey, and should attract many devoted stout fans. Glen's Best Bitter, Falconer's favorite brew, has an intense hop aroma and flavor. The beers of the Wild Duck all reveal Falconer's appreciation for hops, but none more than the seasonal Sasquatch Old Ale, a delightfully malty strong ale with a rich hoppy finish.

DIRECTIONS: From I-5 in Eugene, take the University of Oregon exit to I-105. From I-105, take the downtown exit. Cross over the Ferry Street Bridge and take the downtown exit for 6th Avenue. The brewery is five blocks down 6th, on the right.

Hours: 11:30 a.m.–1 a.m. Monday–Thursday; 11:30 a.m.–2:30 a.m. Friday and Saturday; 11:30 a.m.–midnight Sunday
Children: Yes
Food: Upscale pub food
Entertainment: Live music, concerts
Smoking: Yes, in bar area
Payment: Checks, Visa, MC
Beer to go: Yes, draft

Spencer's Restaurant & Brewhouse

Established 1995

980 Kruse Way • Springfield, OR 97477
(541) 726-1726 • www.spencersbrewhouse.com

It took owner David Andrews more time than he would care to admit to open Springfield's first brewery. But if the restaurant mantra of "location, location, location" is true, Spencer's Restaurant & Brewhouse is doing almost everything right. Located just off I-5 in the growing Gateway area of Springfield, Spencer's attracts tourists, business people, and curious beer enthusiasts from Eugene, Springfield's neighbor across I-5.

The building was constructed specifically for Spencer's, complete with a custom-built 15-barrel brew system, and the rest of the establishment was planned as a relaxed, family-style restaurant. The walls are covered with antique sports and gardening equipment, old produce box labels, and climbing ivy. A rich-grained oak bar is tucked back in the corner next to the fireplace. Beer-battered fish and chips is the specialty of the house, but the menu also offers a varied selection of burgers, sandwiches and entrées.

Spencer's is a restaurant dedicated to serving quality brews. The brewery produces five standards and a number of rotating seasonals. McKenzie Pale Ale, a certified one hundred-percent organic ale, is the first organically produced and bottled ale in the state of Oregon, and is available on tap and bottles. Black Caddis Porter, decidedly thick and chocolately, is Spencer's darkest regular ale. Hofbrau Pilsner, a crisp and refreshing German lager, is one of the first lagers to be brewed in the local area and is delightful. During warm weather, Spencer's patio is the perfect place to sit and enjoy a brew, fresh root beer, or a cocktail from the full service bar.

Hours: 11:30 a.m.–11:30 p.m. daily
Children: Yes
Food: Dinner menu served from 5 p.m.–10 p.m.
Entertainment: TV at the bar and acoustic guitar on Saturdays
Smoking: No
Payment: Checks, Visa, MC, AmEx
Beer to go: Yes, bottles and draft

DIRECTIONS: From I-5, take exit 195 to Gateway/Springfield. Spencers is one block from the Gateway/Beltline intersection, and sits next to the Marriott Courtyard, Comfort Suites, and Holiday Inn Express hotels.

Oregon Trail

Established 1987

341 SW 2nd Street • Corvallis, OR 97333
(541) 758-3527

A visit to the Oregon Trail Brewing Company starts by stepping off 2nd Street in downtown Corvallis and into a beer garden that could have been transported straight from Bavaria. Located inside a three-story building, the beer garden was created with more than a little whimsy. The walls and ceilings are painted with clouds, blue sky, mountains, birds, and scenes of small Bavarian towns. The brewery, Old World Deli, and the homebrew store on the edges of the beer garden blend into this setting, and look a little like Disney World's Main Street, complete with gingerbread-style storefront facades.

Ales are available on tap at the Old World Deli. Designed to take advantage of the building's three stories (the process starts on the top floor, moving downward from kettle to fermenters to conditioners), the brewery has the distinction of being the only gravity-fed brewing system in the Oregon.

Oregon Trail brews six ales, including a very tasty Belgian-style white ale complete with hops, coriander and orange-peel; an award-winning brown ale—a dry, hoppy, slightly roasted brown; the Kölsch-like Trail Ale, as well as a porter, stout and one seasonal. Recent seasonals have included a spiced Christmas Ale, the Morebock Bock and the strong-flavored End of the Trail Ale.

Hours: 8 a.m.–10 p.m. Monday–Saturday; 11 a.m.–5 p.m. Sunday
Children: Yes
Food: Deli-style sandwiches, soups
Entertainment: Live music on weekends
Smoking: No
Payment: Cash only
Beer to go: Yes, bottles and draft

DIRECTIONS: From I-5, take exit 228 to Highway 34. Cross over the Willamette River and at 2nd turn left. The brewery is four blocks down on the left. Call in advance for tours.

Oregon Trader Brewing Company

Established 1993

140 Hill Street NE • Albany, OR 97321
(541) 928-1931

Wyatt's Eatery & Brewhouse

211 1st Avenue NW • Albany, OR 97321
(541) 917-3727

A stop at the Oregon Trader Brewing Company serves two purposes: drinking beer and playing darts with friends. The brewery takes up one third of a converted warehouse. Scattered tables fill the room, and customers like to spend time debating the merits of various malts or hops, and sharing homebrewing tall tales.

Owner Jerry Mathern always wanted to find a way to brew beer for a living. In 1993 he opened the Oregon Trader, a small operation that somehow produces seven standard ales, always on tap, and a rotation of seasonals as well. The beer enthusiast will delight in the high-quality ales and lagers Mathern serves. Choose from a variety of offerings, from the rich, full-bodied chocolate and roasted flavors of the porter to the fairly explosive Green Chili Beer.

The crowd favorites at Oregon Trader are the hefeweizen and Yankee Clipper IPA. Other standard offerings include a nut brown, Scotch ale, oatmeal stout, and an amber lager. Seasonals include Chocolate Stout, Pilsner, and a Doppelbock.

Oregon Trader opened a brewpub in 1997 a few blocks west of the brewery—Wyatt's Eatery and Brewhouse. The pub, located in an historic building in downtown Albany, serves lunch and dinner and offers a full range of Oregon Trader brews.

Albany is a town rich in the recent history of the Willamette Valley, with over 500 historic buildings and covered bridges. The pace of the city is just a bit slower than other large towns in the area. The quality beers and relaxed atmosphere of the Oregon Trader fit this area well.

Hours: Brewery: 3 p.m.–7 p.m. Tuesday–Saturday; Wyatt's: 11:30 a.m.–closing Monday–Saturday
Children: Yes, in Wyatt's
Food: Brewery, none; Wyatt's, pub fare
Entertainment: Darts
Smoking: No
Payment: Checks
Beer to go: Yes, draft

DIRECTIONS: To reach the brewery, take I-5 exit 234A or B to Main Street. Turn right to Water. Turn left on Hill Street NE. To reach Wyatt's, take I-5 exit 234A or B onto Highway 99E. Highway 99E will merge with Highway 20—follow Highway 20 north into downtown. Turn left onto 1st Avenue before you get to the river.

Big Horn Brewery/Ram Restaurant

Established 1995

515 12th Street SE • Salem, OR 97301
(503) 363-1976
320 Oswego Pointe Drive • Lake Oswego, OR 97034
(503) 697-8818 • www.theram.com

The Big Horn Brewery and Ram Restaurant of Salem was the first Ram restaurant/brewery to open in Oregon. The enormous building, with five separate seating areas and an outside patio that overlooks Ditch Creek, has become a remarkably popular sports bar and restaurant since it opened in 1995. The central area features a huge projection screen for viewing sports events and a full bar. The fifteen-barrel brewing system is visible from three of the five rooms.

The Ram Restaurant is one of a growing number of regional chains adding breweries to already successful restaurants. Hiring Tim Chamberlin, a 15-year veteran homebrewer, preserves much of the local character and regional flavor of the Big Horn brews. Proximity to Willamette University and Salem's historic district makes the Big Horn Brewery a natural draw for students and visitors alike.

Currently, Big Horn Brewing produces seven ales. The Big Horn Hefeweizen, a light, slightly hopped wheat, is closer to a true German-style hefeweizen than most. Buttface Amber Ale, a medium-bodied, dark caramel-colored amber, is a well-balanced mix of malt and hops, with a decidedly fruity finish. Red Horn Red, Black Cat Honey Stout, and Blewesberry, a blueberry hefeweizen, are Big Horn's three other standard ales.

A second Big Horn Brewery that opened in Lake Oswego on the banks of the Willamette River, offers the same brews on tap. Check out the "dolphin deck," a floating island on the river used for banquets and additional seating. Tir-Na-Nog, an Irish-themed pub also owned by Ram, opened in Portland at 23rd and West Burnside Street in 1999. (For more about Ram International's Big Horn Breweries, see listings on pages 104 and 134.)

Hours: 11 a.m.–2 a.m. daily
Children: Yes
Food: Mix of pub and Tex-Mex-style foods
Entertainment: Regularly televised sports events, pool, poker machines
Smoking: Yes, in separate areas
Payment: Checks, Visa, MC, AmEx
Beer to go: Yes, draft

DIRECTIONS: Take exit 253 off I-5 in Salem. Head west into Salem on Mission Street. Take a right onto 13th just after crossing over the bridge. The brewpub is on the left at the first light.

Cascade Microbrewery & Public Firehouse

Established 1995

3529 Fairview Industrial Drive SE • Salem, OR 97302
(503) 378-0737

The Cascade Microbrewery, with its antique firehouse gear, two 1915 Model T cars, player grand piano, larger-than-life stuffed-toy Dalmatian dog, twin kling lights, and bright red tables and chairs, is about the last thing a visitor would expect to find in an industrial park minutes from the Salem airport. Opened in 1995 by firefighter and homebrewer Tim Maronay, the brewery has become a quasi-museum of regional fire fighting history, as well as an alehouse serving many of the best Oregon craft brews.

Starting with forty taps pouring beers from mostly small Oregon microbreweries, the Cascade Microbrewery then introduced its own ales to an enthusiastic crowd. Backdraught Ale, the favorite of both brewer and patrons, is a high alcohol, lightly hopped ale with plenty of malt flavors. Backdraught Bitter, a recent addition to Cascade's Firehouse Ales, is a hoppy, medium-amber ale, with a healthy balance of malt and hops. Cascade Wheat, a hefeweizen-style ale, Ember Reizen, a mix of rye, wheat and barley malt, and a series of fruit-flavored wheat ales are Cascade Microbrewery's other standard brews.

Hours: 11 a.m.–10 p.m. Monday–Friday; 11:30 a.m.–midnight Saturday; 11:30 a.m.–8 p.m. Sunday
Children: Yes
Food: Traditional pub fare
Entertainment: Board games, weekend acoustic musicians, televised sports events
Smoking: No
Payment: Checks, Visa, MC
Beer to go: Yes, draft

The diverse offerings typical of an alehouse, combined with the unique flavors and character of its own ales, makes a stop at the Cascade Microbrewery a treat for any beer enthusiast. Ales from many of the best, smallest, and most distant Oregon craft breweries are available here. Rather than distract patrons from Cascade's own fine ales, the selection provides an education along with a celebration of Pacific Northwest brewing.

DIRECTIONS: From I-5, take exit 253 to route 22 West. Turn right on Madrona Avenue. Turn left onto Fairview Industrial Drive and turn right at first parking area. The brewery is visible from Madrona on the left.

Mt. Angel Brewing Company

Established 1995

210 Monroe Street • Mt. Angel, OR 97362
(503) 845-9624

Located in the richly historic town of Mt. Angel, the Mt. Angel Brewing Company is an integral part of the town's past, as well as its future. Envisioned by its owners as a place where members of the local community could meet and celebrate, the company occupies a 100-year-old building which was once a grain and potato storehouse.

The building is well-equipped for the many parties, banquets, meetings, and receptions held there, with over three table-filled rooms and seating or over 300 spread over its two levels. Photographs of the town dating from the early 1900s decorate the wall. While sampling the beer you may hear the peal of bells from the recently restored church tower, which was damaged a short time ago during an earthquake.

Curt Gouverneur is a third-generation brewer, taught by his father and grandmother. He is presently brewing four ales, including the Ale Mari (a German-style hefeweizen), the Halo Pale (a lightly hopped ale with a strong fruity finish), the Angel Ale (an amber), and the Holy Grale (a roasted, fairly light-bodied porter). The names of the beers are quite appropriate for the town: Mt. Angel has strong Catholic roots and has been home to several religious institutions during its history, including both a men's and women's college, a convent, and a monastery. Mt. Angel Brewing Company also produces an outstanding root beer.

The town of Mt. Angel comes alive every year for Octoberfest, an event not to be missed. The Mt. Angel Brewing Company rolls out its seasonal Strawberry Wheat for the celebration each year, a fun and refreshing brew that is an annual hit with the crowds.

DIRECTIONS: Take exit 271 off I-5. Follow signs to Woodburn and Mt. Angel. The brewery is in the middle of town on the main street of Mt. Angel, route 214.

Hours: 11 a.m.–9:30 p.m.
Children: Yes
Food: Extensive menu with German emphasis; all items cooked on wood pellet grills
Entertainment: Acoustic musicians
Smoking: No
Payment: Visa, MC, AmEx, Discover
Beer to go: Yes, draft

Golden Valley Brewery Pub & Restaurant

Established 1993

980 E 4th Street • McMinnville, OR 97128
(503) 472-2739 • www.goldenvalleybrewery.com

In 1993, Peter and Celia Kircher opened the Golden Valley Brewery and Pub, creating a place for family and friends to gather and reviving the tradition of brewing. The working-class town's brewing history dates back to 1878, when Anton Ahrens and W.R. Bachman opened the Ahrens Brewing Company.

The exposed timbers, high ceilings, and copper brewing equipment visible from anywhere in the pub are the traits of the traditional warehouse-style brewpub. The Golden Valley Brewing Company enhances its historic 1921 building with a gorgeous antique bar, complete with intricate stained glass, and plenty of room for weekend blues and rock bands.

Golden Valley produces six standard ales, a root beer, and a variety of seasonal ales and lagers. Red Thistle Ale, their most popular brew, is a wonderful Scottish/Irish red with bold malt flavors. The Golden Valley Amber is a medium bodied, slightly bitter ale, with a malty flavor and soft finish. The Premium Pale, a crisp summer quaffer and the Golden Ale, a fine Pilsner-style ale, are the brewery's lighter offerings. Golden Valley also brews a porter and St. John's Stout, made with smoked peated malt. Seasonals include Tannen Bomb and Geist Bock, a rare pale lager. Both seasonals and the Red Thistle Ale are now available in twelve-ounce bottles at fine beer and wine shops around Oregon.

In a region well-known for its wineries as well as its hops, the Golden Valley Brewing Company has established itself as a vintner of quality, local wines as well, producing a Pinot Noir and Chardonnay from Peter and Celia's vineyard just north of McMinnville. Be sure to get a bottle to take home before you wrap up your visit to Golden Valley.

DIRECTIONS: From Portland, take I-5 exit 294 to 99W to McMinnville. Follow signs to McMinnville (about 35 miles from the Portland exit). Highway 99 splits into Adams going south and Baker going north in McMinnville. Take Adams to 3rd and turn left. Take 3rd through downtown until Johnson (streets are alphabetical). Turn left on Johnson. The brewery is on the left.

Hours: 11:30 a.m.–10 p.m. Sunday–Thursday; 11:30 a.m.–midnight Friday and Saturday
Children: Yes, until 8:30 p.m.
Food: Burgers, pizza, ribs, seafood, salads
Entertainment: Games, live blues and acoustic folk most weekends
Smoking: Yes, in the pub
Payment: Checks, Visa, MC, AmEx
Beer to go: Yes, bottles and draft

PORTLAND: BEERVANA OF THE NORTHWEST

T he *Willamette Week*, Portland's alternative weekly newspaper, refers to Portland reverently as "Beervana." The Oregon Brewers Guild calls this city "Münich on the Willamette." Of the over fifty breweries and brewpubs in Oregon, more than one-third are located in the Portland Metro area. The city is home to some of Oregon's largest and smallest microbreweries. The microbrewery revolution began in Oregon in 1984 with the opening of BridgePort Brewing Company (then Columbia Brewery). The brewery, opened by the Ponzi family of vintners, began with a small "tasting room" modeled after those found in wineries. The open spaces, simple menu and variety of beers and serving styles have made BridgePort a model for warehouse brewpubs.

The revolution might not have come as soon to Portland, however, if it were not for places such as the Horse Brass Pub (www.horsebrass.com), located at 4534 SE Belmont. This pub, serving up the finest British and German beers to a crowd thirsting for full, rich flavor, was an inspiration to many brewers. It still serves as a showplace of the best of both Pacific Northwest and European lagers and ales.

Today, Portland boasts nearly 20 independent breweries. McMenamins alone has 32 pubs in the Portland area, eleven of which brew. Two of Oregon's largest microbreweries, Portland Brewing Company and BridgePort, began in the Portland area. One of Oregon's smallest breweries, with an annual production of around 150 barrels, Philadelphia's Steaks & Hoagies, has been brewing in Portland since the fall of 1994.

There seems to be no end to the growing interest in microbrewed beer. Flavor, quality ingredients, higher alcohol content and local pride are some of the many reasons people are trying and switching to micros. With so much fine beer in the Portland area, however, is the market getting saturated? Consider that microbrews account for only two percent of all beer sales in the United States. In the Portland area, that number is approaching ten percent. Even in "Beervana," there is tremendous room for growth, as more and more beer drinkers discover the wonderful taste of craft brews.

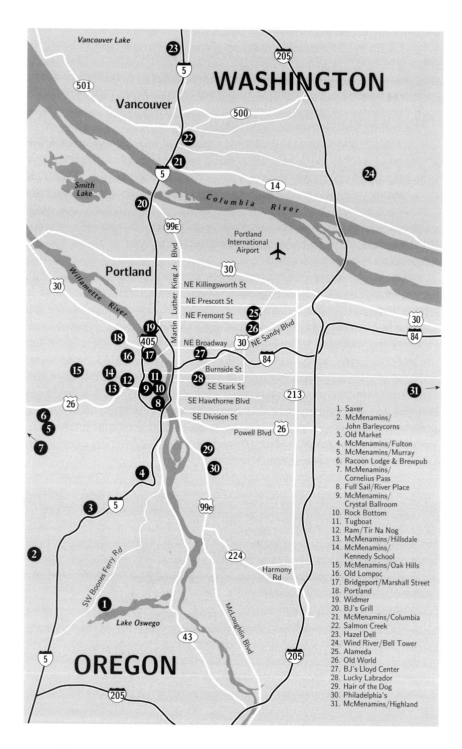

Vancouver Lake

23

5

501

WASHINGTON

Vancouver

500

205

22

21

5

20

Smith
Lake

Columbia   River

14

24

99E

Portland
International
Airport ✈

30

Portland

Martin Luther King Jr Blvd

NE Killingsworth St

Willamette   River

30

NE Prescott St

NE Fremont St

25

NE Sandy Blvd

30

84

19

18

405

NE Broadway

30

26

16

17

27

84

15

14

Burnside St

28

SE Stark St

31

12

11

13

9   10

8

SE Hawthorne Blvd

213

26

SE Division St

Powell Blvd

26

29

30

4

26

3

5

99e

2

224

Harmony
Rd

SW Boones Ferry Rd

1

43

McLoughlin Blvd

205

Lake Oswego

OREGON

5

205

1. Saxer
2. McMenamins/
   John Barleycorns
3. Old Market
4. McMenamins/Fulton
5. McMenamins/Murray
6. Racoon Lodge & Brewpub
7. McMenamins/
   Cornelius Pass
8. Full Sail/River Place
9. McMenamins/
   Crystal Ballroom
10. Rock Bottom
11. Tugboat
12. Ram/Tir Na Nog
13. McMenamins/Hillsdale
14. McMenamins/
    Kennedy School
15. McMenamins/Oak Hills
16. Old Lompoc
17. Bridgeport/Marshall Street
18. Portland
19. Widmer
20. BJ's Grill
21. McMenamins/Columbia
22. Salmon Creek
23. Hazel Dell
24. Wind River/Bell Tower
25. Alameda
26. Old World
27. BJ's Lloyd Center
28. Lucky Labrador
29. Hair of the Dog
30. Philadelphia's
31. McMenamins/Highland

Raccoon Lodge and Brewpub

Established 1998

7424 SW Beaverton–Hillsdale Highway • Portland, OR 97224
(503) 296-0110 • www.raclodge.com

For years Art Larrance, co-founder of the Portland Brewing Company, drove past this site in a Portland/Beaverton suburb before deciding to open a new restaurant and brewery, The Raccoon Lodge and Brewpub, here. The building, which was completed in December of 1998, was built to order. Based on a Northwest hunting lodge theme, the inside of the restaurant is cozy, especially near the large fireplace on a typically rainy winter evening. In addition to the upstairs restaurant, there is a downstairs banquet facility/party room and an outdoor beer garden and barbecue in the back.

The beer garden and grill offer pleasant seating during the summer and fall; beer lines run from the lodge to the outdoor bar. This is also the site for the fairly regular "Raleigh Hills Mini Micro Brewfest," hosted by the Raccoon Lodge and featuring beers from many of the smaller Oregon breweries.

The state-of-art, ten-barrel brewery on the lower level was designed by Ron Gansberg, Raccoon Lodge's brewer. Ron also came from Portland Brewing Company after an eight-year run at BridgePort Brewing Company.

Raccoon Lodge offers several standard ales. Ring Tail Pale Ale is as light as Pale Ale's go—pale gold in color with a light body and a crisp finish. Bandit Bitter, an Extra Special Bitter, is amber in color and offers a little extra hop bitterness and aroma. Badger Bock and Black Snout Stout, the brewery's other original offerings, have been joined by a clean, crisp Hefeweizen.

DIRECTIONS: From I-5 take the Barbur Boulevard exit just south of Portland. From Barbur, get onto the Beaverton–Hillsdale Highway (Highway 10) heading west. Stay on the Beaverton–Hillsdale Highway for approximately three miles. The brewpub is on the left side of the highway, just a few blocks past the junction with Highway 210.

Hours: 11:30 a.m. – 11p.m. Monday – Thursday; 11:30 a.m. – midnight Friday and Saturday; 11:30 a.m. – 9 p.m. Sunday
Children: Yes
Food: Pub style fare, outdoor grill
Entertainment: Occasional music
Smoking: Yes, downstairs and outside
Payment: Cash, Visa, MC
Beer to go: Yes, draft

Saxer Brewing Company

Established 1993

4874 Lakeview Boulevard • Lake Oswego, OR 97035
(503) 699-9524 • www.saxerbeer.com

The Saxer Brewing Company, located in suburban Lake Oswego, is remarkably different from most breweries in the Pacific Northwest. This is strictly a lagering operation—it produces no ales. Saxer beers can be found on grocery shelves in twenty-nine states as well as in Canada and Japan. Saxer took over the brewing and distribution of Nor'Wester Ales after that brewery closed in 1997. In 1999, Saxer became part of Portland Brewing Company, merging brewery administration and distribution. The combined Portland Brewing/Saxer company now ranks as the twelfth largest craft brewery in the U.S.

Housed in a large building just outside of Portland, Saxer is a high-capacity bottling and kegging operation. A renovated tasting room complete with bar is available for private functions, and charitable organizations can use it free of charge. The brewery is directly behind the tasting room, where rows and rows of conditioning tanks handle the time-intensive process of lagering Saxer's six standard beers. Unlike some ales that can be ready for consumption in approximately one week, lagers can take over two months to complete the conditioning process. The result is a smooth, easy-drinking beer with deep, well-rounded flavors.

Saxer's Lemon Lager, winner of many "People's Choice" awards at brew festivals, is a light, refreshing beer flavored with a hint of lemon. The medal-winning Three Finger Jack Hefedunkel is an unfiltered, roasted, dark red beer full of body. Three Finger Jack Amber, Octoberfest category winner, is a clean, well-balanced, malty beer very similar to traditional beers of Octoberfest. If you're seeking out the darkest beers, be sure to sample Three Finger Jack Stout for a bottom-fermented take on the stout style.

Hours: 8 a.m.–5 p.m. Monday–Friday; tours from 3 p.m.–5 p.m. Thursday and Friday
Children: No
Food: No
Entertainment: No
Smoking: No
Payment: Checks
Beer to go: Yes, bottles

DIRECTIONS: Take I-5 to exit 290 (Lake Oswego/ Durham). Go east on Boones Ferry to Jean Road, turn right on Jean to Lakeview Boulevard, and then right on Lakeview to the brewery.

Alameda Brewhouse

Established 1996

4765 NE Fremont Street • Portland, OR 97213
(503) 460-9025

The Alameda Brewhouse, a large converted warehouse building in Portland's relaxed and residential Alameda-Beaumont neighborhood, is a regular spot for locals. Spacious and attractive inside, with artistically designed white oak tables and chairs complementing the long bar, the Brewhouse offers a creative menu with such specialties as Salmon Gyros, Chipotle Barbecue Chicken, and a homemade vegetarian Voodoo Chili.

One of the most interesting beer selections of any brewery in the Pacific Northwest is also available at the Alameda Brewhouse. Brewer Craig Nicholls and assistant Andy Kercheval offer complex, creative brews that demonstrate an attention to detail and to history. Craig describes himself as an "herbal brewer," regularly utilizing herbs and other ingredients in the making of his beers.

Hours: 11 a.m.–10 p.m. Sunday–Thursday; 11 a.m.–closing Friday and Saturday
Children: Yes
Food: Eclectic, upscale pub menu
Entertainment: Occasional music
Smoking: No
Payment: Visa, MC
Beer to go: Yes, draft

Their best known ale, the Burghead Pict Heather Ale, is brewed with organic malts, wild honey and wild Belgian heather flower tips. Heather beer was first brewed by the Picts and later the Scots until a 1707 English law mandated the use of hops instead of heather or other plants in the production of beer. The Alameda Brewhouse is now one of only a few breweries in the world recreating this style of beer.

Craig uses herbs in many of his other brews—from juniper in his tasty Irvington Juniper Porter to several pounds of organic rose petals in his Spring Rose Doppelbock. The wooden barrels sitting between the restaurant tables are normally in use conditioning some other ale, imparting the oaky flavor of the wood to the brew.

Craig is interested in historic and cultural brews as well. In addition to the Heather Ale, Craig is researching ancient Egyptian beers as well as long-cherished and still-brewed Scandinavian ales. Brewery assistant Andy Kercheval is also making a name for himself with a delicious Belgian-style wit named Cheval Blanc, and a remarkably complex barley wine-style ale.

DIRECTIONS: From I-5 take the exit to I-84 East. Take the 33rd Avenue exit off I-84. Off exit turn left onto 33rd (crossing over I-84). Go north on 33rd one mile until you come to Fremont Street. Turn right on Fremont and go to 47th Avenue. The brewhouse is on the left.

BJ's Pizza, Grill and Brewery

Established 1998/1997

Jantzen Beach: 12105 North Center • Portland, OR 97217
(503) 289-5566
Lloyd Center: 825 NE Weidler • Portland, OR 97232
(503)288-0111 • www.bjsbrewhouse.com

BJ's Pizza, Grill and Brewery had its beginnings in 1978 as a Chicago-style pizzeria located in Santa Ana, California. Between 1978 and the early 1990s, BJ's added a few locations in California, but remained a small operation. Since then, however, BJ's has been growing at the rate of four to five locations each year. In 1996, a 30-barrel brewhouse was added to its California operation, and in 1997 two BJ's breweries opened in Portland, Oregon.

BJ's has a number of non-brewing locations around Oregon including Eugene, Salem, and the greater Portland area. All of these serve the BJ's brews produced at the fifteen-barrel brewery in Jantzen Beach just north of Portland. The Lloyd Center BJ's has a tidy 3½ barrel brewery used for pilot and seasonal brews.

Although all BJ's breweries work from the same recipes for the six standard beers, each brewery has individual control over the special and seasonal offerings. Standard brews include BJ's Brewhouse Blonde, brewed in the style of a Kölsch, Piranha Pale Ale, a very hoppy pale, and Tatonka Stout, a high alcohol, richly flavored Imperial Stout. Recent Oregon seasonals have included a refreshingly good Czech Pilsner, the Grizzly Brown Ale, a Smoked Scottish ale and an India pale ale.

The BJ's décor is upscale casual with some clever touches. Distressed window frames serve as partial walls, large posters of their beer logos hang on the walls, and the booths come wrapped in corrugated metal, giving the appearance of either a grain silo or a 1950s sci-fi movie spaceship. The menu emphasizes delicious, deep dish, Chicago-style pizzas but also has a wide array of sandwiches, pastas and salads. As more BJ's enter the market in the Pacific Northwest, it is satisfying to know they will be offering good food and fresh, locally brewed beers.

Hours: 11 a.m.–11 p.m. Sunday–Thursday; 11 a.m.–midnight Friday and Saturday
Children: Yes
Food: Chicago-style pizzas, sandwiches, salads
Entertainment: No
Smoking: No
Payment: Checks, Visa, MC
Beer to go: Yes, draft

DIRECTIONS: From I-5 north of Portland take exit 308 to Jantzen Beach. From the south, take the exit and follow the road back under I-5. Turn left onto N Center Avenue. From the north, take the exit to N Center Avenue and turn left onto N Center Avenue. Call the Lloyd Center BJ's for directions.

BridgePort Brewing Company

Established 1984

1313 NW Marshall Street • Portland, OR 97209
(503) 241-7179 • www.firkin.com

B ridgePort Brewing Company, Oregon's oldest operating microbrewery, introduced craft ales to the Portland area in 1984. Housed in Portland's historic Pearl District, in an impressive 100-year-old rope factory built of brick and timber, the brewery and pub have become a part of the neighborhood. BridgePort also runs an ale house in the historic Hawthorne shopping district in Southeast Portland.

BridgePort has maintained its commitment to producing outstanding English-style ales as it has grown. Its most popular offering, Blue Heron Pale Ale, known as the BridgePort Pale Ale outside of the Northwest, is a medium-bodied amber bitter with a slightly fruity finish. BridgePort Nut Brown Ale, referred to as "The Original," is currently available only in the pub. BridgePort also makes outstanding dark ales—be sure to try the XX Stout and the Fremont Porter, both wonderful renditions of the styles.

Hours: 2 p.m.–11 p.m. Monday–Thursday; 2 p.m.–midnight Friday; noon–midnight Saturday; 1 p.m.–9 p.m. Sunday
Children: Yes
Food: Pizza, focaccia, sausage sandwiches
Entertainment: Darts, live music first Thursday of each month
Smoking: No
Payment: Checks, Visa, MC
Beer to go: Yes, bottles and draft

The brewery's newest offerings are their Firkin Beers. BridgePort offers a full range of cask-conditioned and bottle-conditioned ales, allowing the natural carbonation process and warmer temperatures to bring out the subtle flavors and rich characteristics of their ales.

A tour of the BridgePort facility (weekends between 2 p.m. and 4 p.m.) allows the visitor to explore the dark recesses of this magnificent building. The timbers and floors are still soaked with oils from the original rope factory. Outside seating is available on the dock, with trains passing only a few feet away. The smells and tastes of thick, crunchy pizzas (the crusts are made with unfermented beer wort) are an outstanding accompaniment to the ales.

DIRECTIONS: From I-5 heading north to Portland, take the exit to I-405 and then take the Everett Street exit. Take Everett to Marshall and turn right on Marshall. The brewery is on the corner. From I-5 heading south, take the exit to I-405 and then take the Everett Street exit. Go two lights to Everett and take a left. Go to the first light (14th) and turn left and head down 14th to Marshall.

Full Sail at River Place

Established 1992

0307 SW Montgomery • Portland, OR 97201
(503) 220-1865 • www.fullsailbrewing.com

Full Sail at River Place in downtown Portland is a showcase for the Full Sail Brewing Company's extensive collection of ales and lagers. Though it accounts for only four percent of Full Sail's total brewing production, the River Place Pilsner Room is the source for many seasonals and specialty brews, and serves as the pilot brewery for the newest Full Sail releases.

The River Place Marina is a posh collection of shops, galleries and condos situated between Downtown Portland and the Willamette River. McCormick & Schmick's Harborside restaurant shares space with Full Sail in this building, offering an upscale menu, full bar, several guest taps, and a complete selection of Full Sail ales and lagers, including two cask-conditioned ales.

The restaurant, with its extensive woodwork, columns, and two walls of floor-to-ceiling windows facing the river, encourages visitors to enjoy Full Sail's brews at a leisurely pace. Pilsner is always on tap, and many of Full Sail's seasonals find a home here while waiting for their turn in rotation. The Old Boardhead Barleywine Ale is also available here more regularly than at Full Sail's Hood River facility.

A host of other Pacific Northwest micros are always on tap, mostly from the larger craft brewers. McCormick & Schmick's also features an extensive Northwest wine list and a full bar. Full Sail plans to offer a complete one-day package, including tours of both Full Sail facilities, a tasting and dinner at McCormick & Schmick's, making it the perfect last stop on your tour of Portland breweries.

DIRECTIONS: From I-5 heading north in Portland, take the Front Avenue exit. At the first light turn right, at the blinking red turn left. The brewery is just down the street. From I-5 heading south in Portland, take the Morrison Bridge exit to City Center. Cross over the bridge and take the Front Street exit heading south. Turn left onto Market Street, then left at next light onto Montgomery. The brewery is just ahead, on the left.

Hours: 11:30 a.m.–closing Monday–Saturday; 10 a.m.–closing, Sunday
Children: Yes
Food: Extensive, upscale restaurant menu
Entertainment: Television in the bar
Smoking: Yes, in the bar area
Payment: Checks, Visa, MC, AmEx, Discover
Beer to go: No

Hair of the Dog Brewing Company

Established 1994

4509 SE 23rd • Portland, OR 97202
(503) 232-6585 • www.hairofthedog.com

The Hair of the Dog Brewing Company fills a much-needed niche in American brewing, by producing gourmet brews on a par with some of the best Belgian and German breweries. Using a process unique to the U.S., the company has bottled small batches of wonderfully flavorful, high alcohol ales since 1994.

A tour of the brewery, located in a somewhat dilapidated warehouse in industrial southeast Portland, could be one of the most educational beer-related experiences available in the Pacific Northwest. The three ales, Adambier, Golden Rose and Fred, are produced through an elaborate brewing and conditioning process, and are then refermented in the bottle through the addition of yeast and new beer, in a process known as krausening. The resulting ale can be stored at room temperature and allowed to age for years, with the taste mellowing and improving over time.

Adambier, acclaimed by several prominent industry pundits and publications, is the brewery's flagship ale. A revival of an old German-style, Adambier is a hearty, high alcohol ale with a high hop profile, yet is surprisingly smooth. Best served at room temperature and designed as a "sipping" ale, it is also the progenitor of JD, a "small" ale produced from Adam's original mash and only available on draft. The Dog's other bottled offerings are Golden Rose, inspired by the Belgian tripel style, and Fred, created to honor beer writer and historian Fred Eckhardt. All are available in 12 oz, 1.5 liter, and 3 liter "magnums."

With its commitment to high quality and tradition, Hair of the Dog offers the beer enthusiast an educational experience, royal treatment for the palate and a wicked hang-over (the tongue-in-cheek inspiration for their name) for those foolish enough to think that the "dog" is all bark and no bite.

DIRECTIONS: From I-5 in Portland, take the Ross Island Bridge exit. Follow signs to the Ross Island Bridge and cross over the Willamette River heading west. Take the first right off the bridge to 99E south. Take the Holgate exit and follow Holgate to SE 26th. Turn right on Schiller, turn right on SE 24t, and turn left on Pardee (gravel road). Turn right onto SE 23rd. The brewery is in the corner of the building on the left.

Hours: 9 a.m.–4 p.m.
Monday–Friday
Children: Yes
Food: No
Entertainment: No
Smoking: No
Payment: Checks
Beer to go: Yes, bottles

Lucky Labrador Brewing Company

Established 1994

915 SE Hawthorne Boulevard • Portland, OR 97214
(503) 236-3555 • www.luckylab.com

The Lucky Labrador Brewing Company is housed in a huge, airy warehouse in southeast Portland. Despite the wall-sized Andrew Wyeth reproduction opposite the enormous bar (Labrador appropriately included), this is a sparse and somewhat dark pub. However, on weekends, standing-room only crowds quickly fill up the cavernous space, creating a giant party atmosphere.

The Lucky Labrador, with its wall of canine photos donated by patrons, is more than just a clever name. Since opening in 1994, the brewery has developed several outstanding ales. Hawthorne's Best Bitter, a dry hopped medium amber ale, is the current crowd favorite. Black Lab Stout, with a rich, roasted flavor and ample hops, has a loyal following, and is often served cask-conditioned. Seasonals Scottish Holiday, a heavy, malty dark ale (available winters), and Quality Rye, a wonderful brew using malted rye (available summers), are worth the return trip. The brewery also serves a Kölsch-style golden ale, a porter, an India pale ale and a red ale.

The company specializes in its own version of a bento (chicken or veggie), barbecued on the patio grill. Food is inexpensive and designed to complement the flow of Lucky Lab ales. Though it's one of the least flashy of Portland's many brewpubs, the well-crafted ales will make you glad you stopped by.

Hours: 11 a.m.–midnight Monday–Saturday; noon–10 p.m. Sunday
Children: Yes, until 9 p.m.
Food: Pub grub
Entertainment: Darts and games available, acoustic musicians on weekends
Smoking: Yes, on covered outdoor patio
Payment: Checks, Visa, Discover
Beer to go: Yes, draft

DIRECTIONS: From I-5 Northbound, take the Central Eastside Industrial District exit (a.k.a. Water Avenue). At the stop sign, turn right onto Water Avenue. At the first traffic light, turn left onto Clay Street, stay on Clay for 7 blocks, and then turn left onto 7th Avenue. Go one block and turn right onto Hawthorne Boulevard. The pub is $2^1/2$ blocks up Hawthorne on the left side of the street. The parking lot is behind the building on the corner of 9th and Madison.

McMenamins Brew Tour

f you're a McMenamins fan, a great weekend activity is to visit several McMenamins pubs and breweries in a one- or two-day period. With establishments strewn across the state of Oregon, you're near to a McMenamins location practically anywhere you go, west of the mountains. You can plan an extended expedition through different areas, stopping for pints of Ruby Ale and Gardenburgers all the way, whether you're traveling up the scenic Columbia River Gorge, down the long Willamette Valley, or along the wild Oregon Coast. There are even McMenamins brewpub-hotels offering overnight accommodations.

The company is based in Portland, and that fact plays out on the ground, with a density of McMenamins in the City of Roses that is truly astonishing. From the Barley Mill Pub on Southeast Hawthorne, the company's first establishment, to new locations in downtown Vancouver, Washington, and Forest Grove, Oregon, the McMenamins family of breweries and pubs is waiting for you just around a nearby corner, throughout the greater Portland area.

Any Portland McMenamins tour should include the gargantuan Kennedy School property. Since you might be tempted to not go anywhere else if you started your Portland tour at the Kennedy School, we'll suggest you plan for your exploration to culminate at this restaurant/movie theater/community center complex. McMenamins on Broadway, St. John's Pub, and McMenamins Tavern on NW 23rd offer typical pub experiences of the McMenamins variety.

You'll want to be sure to visit a McMenamins location or two that brews its own beer, so try the Fulton Pub & Brewery on Nebraska, or the Hillsdale Brewery & Pub at 1505 SW Sunset Boulevard. McMenamins also operates a pair of theater pubs in Portland, the Mission Theater & Pub, at 1624 NW Glisan, and the Bagdad Theater & Pub on Southeast Hawthorne. These venues are relaxing places to enjoy a pint and some good pub fare, while watching a second-run Hollywood flick.

In Washington, your McMenamins brew tour choices are more limited. But there's still ample opportunity for a multi-McMenamins mission in the Seattle area. Start on Queen Anne Hill, where the Six Arms brewpub lays claim to title of the Non-Grateful-Dead McMenamins, having opened the day Jerry Garcia died. From here, travel to McMenamins on Capitol Hill's Roy Street, which is brewing lots of fresh beer these days. Your final McMenamins stop in Seattle proper is in Fremont, at Dad Watson's. As with all McMenamins, Dad Watson's is decorated with great eccentricity—take the carved coconut tree standing in the corner, or the painting on the stairwell of a pair of 1960s troll dolls eating apples. Dad Watson's offers more vegetarian fare than most McMenamins, and is named after a Portland Prohibition-era speak-easy proprietor.

Elsewhere in Washington, you can stop into a McMenamins along the I-5 corridor. If you're near the bedroom community of Mill Creek to the north, there's a McMenamins at the shopping center. In southern Washington, Centralia is home of the Olympic Club, and Vancouver has a pair of McMenamins. Enjoy a meal and a round of hand-crafted ales while sitting along the river at McMenamins on the Columbia, in Vancouver. Whatever McMenamins locations you visit, expect good beer and quality pub grub, and plenty of delightful atmosphere.

McMenamins Kennedy School

Established 1997

5736 NE 33rd • Portland, OR 97211
Main Line: (503) 249-3983 or (888) 249-3983 • Courtyard Restaurant:
(503) 288-2192 • Movie Theater Bar: (503) 288-2117 • Movie Line:
(503) 288-2180 • www.mcmenamins.com

What could possibly have followed Edgefield Manor in Troutdale, the Disneyland of Brewpubs (see page 67) It's hard to imagine a brewery/winery renovation project topping Edgefield in terms of vision, actualization, and sheer scale. But Kennedy School is truly on a par with its predecessor.

Self-titled, "A True Community Center," customers come here for McMenamins food, beer and wine, while neighborhood residents play basketball and volleyball in the gym, or tend a garden that's co-sponsored by the Portland Parks Department. The house ale, served only at Kennedy School, is even named Concordia in honor of the neighborhood the school served from 1915 to 1980, when it was a Portland public high school.

For those who remember school as boring, visit the detention room which is now a whisky-and-cigar bar, and the gym, now a psychedelic rock concert venue! The McMenamins also embraced Kennedy School's rich history, decorating the walls with early twentieth-century class photos and murals of former principals.

Exquisite murals adorn the walls everywhere, and a self-guided tour brochure is available at the front desk. Hallways, large common areas, even doors and the smallest of nooks are all carefully painted with imaginative and delightful artwork. Tile murals and bas-reliefs lend an added texture to the amazing pageantry of the place. This tile work culminates in the monumental hearth that blazes in the middle of the school's enclosed courtyard. Sitting on the patio of the Courtyard Restaurant on a cool Northwest evening with this splendid fireplace nearby is one of Kennedy School's many pleasures.

If you're coming to the Portland area, by all means book one of the thirty-five "classroom" guest rooms, each with its own name, unique artwork and murals. You might stay in Rosella's Room, named for the first known African-American student to attend Kennedy, or in the whimsically named Old McDonald's Room, Broom & Basket Room, Tea Party Room, or Thumbelina's Room. Each guest room is furnished with a queen-sized bed and plenty of vintage charm, and includes a private bath, and such niceties as phones and live data ports. And, while you're a guest, make sure to schedule your chance to enjoy the Garden Soaking Pool, a relaxing hot tub in a pretty garden setting that is another tile work of art,

The Kennedy School's movie theater has all the makings for a great evening's entertainment. Here, as with other McMenamins theater-pubs, they show second-run movies in the school's old auditorium, which is now full of antique couches and comfortable chairs, with coffee tables for food and beverages. If you're not in the mood for a movie, check the Gymnasium's calendar to see if there is live music scheduled.

The Courtyard Restaurant, the Cypress Room and the Detention Bar all serve McMenamins-fermented beers and wines. The Cypress Room is a nice place to enjoy tasting the featured McMenamins vintage over dessert, either in the intimate bar area, or on the small patio. Across the hall, the Detention Room features a wood stove, a humidor, and a selection of beers, ports, single-malt Scotches, and other spirits. Note the handsome antique bar, which was crafted in Belgium.

The brewery is located in the original girls' bathroom, and contains a six-barrel brewhouse, adorned with murals of students and teachers. Kennedy School brewers, Bob Vallance and Ryan Mott, brew Concordia Ale (a medium-bodied bitter), Firecracker IPA (a strong full-bodied pale), and other tasty delights. They also whip up seasonal brews sometimes, such as the Half-Pipe Porter or the Shillelagh Stout. Many other McMenamins beers are served on-tap at Kennedy School as well, including their IPA, Hammerhead Ale, and the ever-popular Ruby Ale, flavored with a touch of raspberries. (For a fuller discussion of McMenamins, see page 79.)

Hours: Courtyard Restaurant: 7-10:30 a.m. and 11 a.m.–1 a.m. Monday–Saturday; 7 a.m.– 1 p.m. and 1:30 p.m.–1 a.m. Sunday; Cypress Room: 4 p.m.–1 a.m. Monday–Friday; noon– 1 a.m. Saturday–Sunday; Movie Theater & Theater Bar: 5-11 p.m. daily; Detention Bar: 4 p.m.–1 a.m. Thursday–Saturday
Children: Yes, in most locations
Food: Pub fare, pasta, steaks, and seafood
Entertainment: Movie theater with bar: nightly showings of second-run films; live music on the weekend
Smoking: Yes, in the Cypress Room and Detention Bar
Payment: Checks, Visa, MC, AmEx
Beer to go: Mason jars and kegs sold retail, or fill any jar

DIRECTIONS: From I-5, take the Highway 30 exit and head east on 30, which is Lombard Avenue. Follow Lombard to 33rd and turn right. Kennedy School is 2 blocks down 33rd on your left, between Ainsworth and Killingsworth Streets.

The Old Lompoc Tavern and Brewery

Established 1996

1616 NW 23rd Avenue • Portland, OR 97210
(503) 225-1855

The Old Lompoc Tavern is a neighborhood bar located at the west end of trendy NW 23rd Avenue in Portland. Upscale stores, restaurants and coffee shops mix with stately apartment buildings and homes dating from the early 1900sto create a vibrant and pedestrian-friendly environment.

Opened in 1993, the Old Lompoc has gone through a variety of incarnations over the years. The brewery, began as an idea hatched out on the golf course. Now located in an attached building in the back, it opened in December of 1996. The Old Lompoc currently offers an intentionally cheesy lounge environment, with a painting of the Last Supper which lights up hanging on one wall, couches in the front room, and a delightfully gaudy red and blue paint job on the walls and ceiling. The menu is sparse—a few burgers and sandwiches.

If the inside of the tavern overwhelms you, sneak out the back door to a hidden outdoor beer garden complete with hanging hop and grape vines. There you can enjoy one of the tavern's standard ales such as the IPA, the stout, or the Bald Guy Brown (with a tap handle that sports the profile of the Lompoc's balding brewer, Jerry). Seasonals include a crisp and tasty Rye Ale, 69 (a Munich lager), and a Summer Pale Ale.

Although the Old Lompoc is the only brewpub in the neighborhood, it is joined in the area by two non-brewing McMenamins pubs—the McMenamins Tavern a couple of blocks down 23rd and the Blue Moon Tavern and Grill a little further east on 21st. This collection of pubs make up a fine network of stops to fortify people visiting this part of Portland.

DIRECTIONS: From I-5 take exit 302 to I-405 South (crossing over the Willamette River). Once over the river, take the exit for Highway 30/Columbia River Highway heading west. Get off Highway 30 onto Vaughn Street, and go west on Vaughn to 23rd Avenue. Turn left onto 23rd Avenue; the Old Lompoc is three blocks south on 23rd on the left-hand side of the street.

Hours: 11:30 a.m.–1 a.m., Monday–Friday; 4 p.m.–1 a.m. Saturday and Sunday
Children: No
Food: Limited menu, sandwiches and burgers
Entertainment: Pool tables, video games
Smoking: Yes
Payment: Visa, MC
Beer to go: No

The Old Market Pub & Brewery

Established 1994

6959 SW Multnomah Boulevard • Portland, OR 97223
(503) 244-0450

T he two-mile trip down the narrow and picturesque Multnomah Boulevard to the Old Market Pub & Brewery will make you forget that downtown Portland is just minutes away. However, the bustling Old Market Pub is anything but quiet.

The pub is comprised of a large, open room filled with a long wooden bar, booths and tables in front, and a slightly smaller room that is also used for private parties, which holds a big-screen TV. A third room in back provides ample space for pool tables and shuffleboard. Formerly the Comella and Sons Market (hence the name), the Old Market Pub has incorporated much of the theme and décor of a greengrocer's shop. Giant murals of fruit labels decorate the walls, and what were once hanging scales now make great planters. There are murals throughout the building, including the pool room, where the walls show silhouettes of drinkers, complete with half empty pint glasses.

The brewery produces a range of ales including a light pale ale, the very hoppy Dr. Dan's Backward Bitter, a wheat ale, porter, a rather dry stout, and Mr. Toad's Red Ale—the best of the Old Market's offerings. Seasonals have included a brown ale and a jalapeño-spiced pale ale. A variety of other regional micros are available as well.

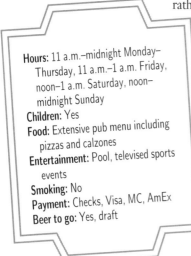

Hours: 11 a.m.–midnight Monday–Thursday, 11 a.m.–1 a.m. Friday, noon–1 a.m. Saturday, noon–midnight Sunday
Children: Yes
Food: Extensive pub menu including pizzas and calzones
Entertainment: Pool, televised sports events
Smoking: No
Payment: Checks, Visa, MC, AmEx
Beer to go: Yes, draft

The menu is almost as expansive as the building. Five calzones, six nacho platters, nine burgers, and ten pizzas are just the beginning of the Old Market offerings. This remarkable pub is definitely a required stop for microbrewing enthusiasts looking for atmosphere as well as quality craft ales.

Directions: From I-5 just south of Portland, take the Multnomah Boulevard exit. The pub is 2 miles on the right at Multnomah and 69th.

Old World Pub & Brewery

Established 1999

1728 NE 40th Avenue • Portland, OR 97212
(503) 335-3384 • www.europa.com/~owpb

The Old World Pub & Brewery is located in Northeast Portland's Hollywood District, which is experiencing revitalization. The venue sits at the confusing intersection of Sandy Boulevard and 40th Avenue. Owner and avid homebrewer Peter Quails concentrates on making traditional British and European-style ales.

Enter brewer Christian Ettinger, formerly of the Eugene City Brewery. Christian is brewing a variety of Old World recipes including a pale ale, a hoppy and slightly fruity India pale ale, a crisp best bitter, and a smooth and satisfying oatmeal stout. The brewery is located below the pub, but the floor has been cut away to display the copper kettles of this seven-barrel brewery. The nine conditioning tanks, more than usual for a brewery of this size, allow the brews to age longer than in many microbreweries, letting their subtle characteristics come through.

Hours: 11 a.m.–1 a.m. Tuesday–Saturday; 11 a.m.–11 p.m. Sunday–Monday
Children: Yes
Food: Upscale pub fare
Entertainment: Occasional music
Smoking: No
Payment: Visa, MC
Beer to go: Yes, draft

The building was originally three different stores—the walls between them were removed for the large dining area. The wood floors are original, as are the exposed beams in the ceilings. The well-worn interior fits in perfectly with the Old World atmosphere that Quails has created. The occasional mural or design on the walls provides additional charm—particularly in the bathrooms!

The Hollywood District has long retained a small neighborhood feel even while Portland has grown up around it. The Old World Pub & Brewery, with its emphasis on old world sentiments and neighborhood values, fits into this area perfectly.

DIRECTIONS: From I-84 West in Portland, take the 42nd Avenue exit. Make a left at the end of the freeway exit ramp and get into the far right hand lane. Turn right onto 42nd Avenue and follow it around a slight jog to Sandy Boulevard. Turn left onto Sandy Boulevard and then right on 40th Avenue. Old World is on the right, $1/2$ block North of Sandy Boulevard, on 40th Ave.

From I-84 East, take the 39th Avenue exit. Make a left at the top of the freeway exit ramp and get next to the far right hand lane. After the first light, get in the far right hand lane. At the next light turn right onto Sandy Boulevard and then take a hard right onto the 40th Avenue exit off Sandy Boulevard, which runs in front of A-Boy, and turn left on 40th Avenue. Once you have crossed Sandy Boulevard, Old World is on the right $1/2$ block north.

Philadelphia's Steaks & Hoagies

Established 1994

6410 SE Milwaukie Avenue • Portland, OR 97202
(503) 239-8544 • www.teleport.com/~phillys

Philadelphia's Steaks & Hoagies, in the Milwaukie area, is a welcome oasis for visitors from the East Coast and transplants to the Pacific Northwest. Owner Steve Moore, originally from the Philly area, has successfully combined the mouth-watering tastes of Philadelphia cheese steaks and hoagies with the creativity and flavors of one of Oregon's smallest microbreweries.

Despite being a suburb community just south of Portland, the Milwaukie area has that small-town feel. Storefronts and buildings have changed little in the past 30 years. Philadelphia's Steaks & Hoagies adds a bit of nostalgia and Philly style and, of course, a variety of cheese steaks and hoagies. A collection of posters, maps, sports memorabilia and a Philadelphia skyline mural painted around the walls of the restaurant complete the theme.

In 1994, Moore added a brewing operation, one of the smallest in Oregon. Despite limited capacity, Philadelphia's produces seven standard ales and five seasonals. Creativity is the watchword at this brewery, and every batch is subject to brewer's fancy. Double Hopped Eagle Ale, an extra hoppy IPA, is the perfect example. The Eagle Ale is darker than most India pale ales due to the addition of some chocolate and Munich malts. Three porter variations—Broad Street Porter, South Street Porter, and Blackberry Porter—all offer something of interest to the dark ale enthusiast. The Ginger Beer, with a wheat base and the added zing of fresh ginger, is a must-try. The brewery also produces a hefeweizen, golden, red, brown, and stout.

DIRECTIONS: Take the Ross Island Bridge exit from I-5 in Portland. Cross over the bridge and take the first right onto 99E. Take 99E south to Milwaukie Avenue. Go right on Milwaukie about 12 blocks. The pub is on the left across the street from a grocery store.

Hours: 9 a.m.–10 p.m. daily
Children: Yes
Food: Philadelphia cheese steaks and hoagies
Entertainment: Television, video poker
Smoking: No
Payment: Checks
Beer to go: Yes, draft

Portland Brewing Company

Established 1993

2730 NW 31st Avenue • Portland, OR 97210
(503) 228-5269 • www.portlandbrew.com

The Portland Brewing Company brewery and pub, built with the financial support of over 5,500 shareholders, is an extraordinary showcase of beers and brewing. Situated in Portland's industrial Northwest district, the massive, multi-story building will catch a first-time visitor completely by surprise. The front room is completely taken up by two 140-barrel copper brewing kettles, brought to Portland from the centuries-old Sixenbrau Brewery in Bavaria.

Decorated in a fairly consistent Bavarian style, the pub includes large murals, stunning multi-handled beer towers, and a collection of antique beer steins beside the fireplace. The tastes and smells of a German-influenced kitchen permeate the air. The beers, in contrast to the décor, favor styles from the British Isles and America. Pub favorite is the Oregon Honey Beer, a pale, light-bodied ale with only a hint of honey flavor and a dry finish. MacTarnahan's Ale, a copper-colored, Scottish-style ale, has a rich caramel flavor and smooth finish. Wheat Berry Brew, a wheat ale with the added flavor of Oregon marionberries, is a summer favorite. Portland Brewing Company's latest bottled offering, the Haystack Black, is a reddish-brown ale with a satisfying blend of roasted and chocolate malts.

The brewery has grown from an annual production of around 5,000 barrels in 1991 to over 40,000 barrels. Tours of this state-of-the-art, 100,000-barrel capacity brewing operation are conducted Saturdays, every hour from 1 p.m. to 5 p.m. Visitors can also collect a wealth of printed information about the brewery, buy a shirt or cap, and learn about becoming a shareholder in this fast-growing, quality brewery.

DIRECTIONS: From I-5 North, take Exit 3 to Highway 30. Take a left on Nicolai and turn right on 26th.which becomes Industrial Street. The brewery is on the corner of Industrial and 31st.

Hours: 11 a.m.–10 p.m. Monday–Thursday, 11 a.m. midnight Friday and Saturday; noon–7:30 p.m. Sunday
Children: Yes
Food: Full pub-style menu with German overtones
Entertainment: Live music on weekends
Smoking: No
Payment: Checks, Visa, MC
Beer to go: Yes, bottles

Rock Bottom Brewery

Established 1994

210 SW Morrison Street • Portland, OR 97204
(503) 796-2739 • www.rockbottom.com

The downtown Portland Rock Bottom Brewery was this brewery chain's first foray into the Pacific Northwest. The company started in Boulder, Colorado, in 1991, and now includes breweries in such cities as Los Angeles, Chicago, and Denver, as well as Seattle and Bellevue, Washington (see page 133).

Characterizing itself as a "restaurant that brews beer," Rock Bottom takes advantage of its downtown location, serving as a lunch-time spot for businesses. It also makes a great place to stop before or after a basketball game or a theater or music event, and is a destination for restaurant and microbrewery enthusiasts.

The brewery boasts five standard beers and a variety of seasonals. A bit tamer than most Pacific Northwest ales, Rock Bottom downplays the strong hop flavors popular in this region. The White Pelican Pale Ale, one of its most popular drinks, is the hoppiest of the Rock Bottom offerings, with a light honey color and a fairly bitter finish. Falcon Red Ale, a medium-bodied, malty red, is a smooth, darker ale, while the Black Seal Stout, served cellar-temperature with very little carbonation, will appeal to those who find most stouts too roasted or heavy.

The Rock Bottom Restaurant is an expansive, bustling, crowded place. The second floor is devoted almost entirely to pool tables and the brewery, with the fermenters and conditioning tanks visible from the bar area. Though it has the feel of a big city restaurant, it also offers the qualities and temptations of an in-house microbrewery.

Hours: 11 a.m.–1 a.m. Monday–Saturday; 11 a.m.–midnight Sunday
Children: Yes
Food: Upscale pub fare
Entertainment: Pool, televised sports, weekend musicians
Smoking: Yes, in bar area
Payment: Checks, Visa, MC, AmEx, Diners Club
Beer to go: Yes, bottles

DIRECTIONS: From I-5 in Portland, take the Morrison Bridge exit heading to downtown Portland. Go forward off the bridge to 3rd and turn left. Turn left onto Morrison. The brewery is on the right side at 2nd and Morrison.

Tugboat Brewing Company

Established 1993

711 SW Ankeny Street • Portland, OR 97204
(503) 226-2508

Unassuming as brewpubs go—tucked down an alley off Broadway in downtown Portland—the Tugboat is frequented by faithful regulars, the city's bicycle messenger fleet, and the slightly baffled visitor in search of Portland's most eclectic brewing operation.

Somewhere between the dark mustard-colored paint, and the pickle barrels holding a vast array of beers, is the true nature of the company—he owners and employees of the Tugboat are out to have fun.

To date, the brewery has turned out more than fifty styles of beers. While it is unlikely the same brews are on tap at every visit, Russian Imperial Stout, English Brown, India Pale Ale, and an alt are some of the most regular offerings. Root beer, sarsaparilla and other sodas are also brewed in-house.

Hours: Noon–midnight Monday–Friday; 3 p.m.–1 a.m. Saturday; 3 p.m.–11 p.m. Sunday
Children: Yes
Food: Small vegetarian menu
Entertainment: Lots of live music
Smoking: Yes
Payment: Cash only
Beer to go: No

A limited, and affordable, menu of burritos, nachos and garden burgers caters to the tastes of Tugboat's regular customers. The art work decorating the walls is for sale, and old copies of National Geographic or yesterday's paper are likely to be scattered on several tables, creating a comfortable, lived-in atmosphere. The brewpub is at its best weekend evenings, when live blues or folk music often blends into free-for-all jams, and anyone with a bit of talent (or possibly without) can add his or her own sounds to the on-going music. The Tugboat brews under a similar philosophy—experimentation, group input and a bit of recklessness are just as important as the yeast, malt, and hops.

DIRECTIONS: From I-5 in Portland, take exit 301 to the Burnside Bridge to downtown Portland. Cross the river and take Burnside to Broadway. Turn left on Broadway. The Tugboat is located just down Ankeny, the first street (almost an alley) on the right.

Widmer Brewing & Gasthaus

Established 1984

955 N Russell Street • Portland, OR 97227
(503) 281-3333 • www.widmer.com

Widmer brothers Kurt and Rob, with their pioneering German-inspired brewing, have had a tremendous impact on the growing popularity of microbrews over the past decade. The Widmer Brewing Company is known throughout the Pacific Northwest and beyond for its amazingly popular hefeweizen. This number-one draft micro in the Pacific Northwest accounts for over ninety percent of the brewery's total production.

The new brewery and bottling operation and the Widmer Gasthaus (literally, "guest house") in northeast Portland serve as the nucleus for the company's empire. The Gasthaus, a beautifully restored historic brick and wooden building, offers most of the brews on tap, complemented by a German-influenced menu with a Northwest flair. Visible behind glass windows is the original Gasthaus brewery.

The new, greatly expanded brewery is just across the street and also holds Widmer's new bottling line. Beer passes beneath the street from each brewery—to the Gasthaus for kegging, across the street for bottling. Widmer also operates a small brewery out of the Jody Maroni's Sausage Kingdom, located next door to the Portland Rose Garden. The brewery currently produces a line of seven original European and American style beers year-round. These offerings include their America's Original Hefeweizen, Hop Jack Pale Ale, Big Ben Porter and Ray's Amber Lager. Widmer offers a variety of seasonal favorites such as the Widmer Oktoberfest and the Sommerbräu.

Hours: 11 a.m.–11 p.m. Monday–Thursday and Sunday; 11 a.m.–1 a.m. Friday and Saturday. Tours: 3 p.m. Friday; 1 p.m. and 2 p.m. Saturday
Children: Yes
Food: Extensive German-styled menu
Entertainment: No
Smoking: No
Payment: Checks, Visa, MC
Beer to go: Yes, bottles

DIRECTIONS: From I-5 northbound in Portland, take Weidler exit and turn left on Broadway. Turn right on to Interstate, then right on Russell. From I-5 southbound, take the Coliseum exit and turn right on Broadway. Turn right on Interstate, and right on Russell.

McMenamins Edgefield Brewery

Established 1990

2126 SW Halsey Street; Troutdale, OR 97060
(800) 669-8610; www.mcmenamins.com

If there is a heaven for microbrew lovers, this is it. Edgefield operates a bed and breakfast, a winery, brewery, pub, movie theater, upscale restaurant, and much, much more, all from a picturesque, fully restored, 1911 County Poor Farm. Don't believe any of the exaggerated tales people will tell you about the place. An actual visit is even better.

The best way to enjoy Edgefield is to stay overnight. There are over 100 bed and breakfast rooms available every night of the year. The hundreds of hand-painted murals and portraits covering the hallways and bedroom walls depict the various stages of the place's history, including its original role as an operating poor farm and its later incarnation as a nursing home.

The most stunning mural of all may very well be found in the gorgeous second floor Grand Ballroom—the perfect place to hold a banquet or wedding celebration. Spanning the entire length of one wall, the mural creatively captures some of the agricultural history of the region. Every image throughout Edgefield is unique—don't rush to see them all, and be sure to look everywhere as some are tucked in unlikely corners.

McMenamins wines and ales are available in the first floor Black Rabbit Restaurant and Bar. For mouth-watering meals served in an elegant setting, dinner at the Black Rabbit is a must. The menu empha-

Hours: Something is always happening at Edgefield from 7 a.m. to 1 a.m. daily

Children: Yes

Food: Upscale menu in restaurant; burgers and fries at the pub

Entertainment: Movie theater, live music, seasonal events

Smoking: Yes, in the Icehouse, Little Red Shed, and the Distillery Bar

Payment: Checks, Visa, MC, AmEx, Discover, Diners Club

Beer to go: Yes, draft

sizes Northwest cuisine, and is top notch. The Black Rabbit also schedules several Brewer's Dinners each year, matching each course of the meal with a particular ale. Breakfast at the Black Rabbit is included in the price of the room, but don't forget to make reservations by the night before. The Crunchy French Toast with Ruby Ale Compote is out of this world.

Late night opportunities abound at Edgefield. The Little Red Shed, the smallest pub on the property, and the Icehouse, behind the restaurant, both typically are last to close at night. If you're looking for more casual eats, head over to the Power Station Pub and Theater. The Pub serves burgers, salads and the famous McMenamins French fries. It also houses a movie theater. Bring a pint of Hammerhead or Ruby into the theater, sit back and relax.

Edgefield also operates an 18-hole golf course. Along with trying to hit under par, the most important goal is to make it to the 18th green and the nearby Distillery Bar, where Edgefield-made whiskey, as well as a range of other spirits, await.

If wine is more to your liking, stop down to the Edgefield Wine Cellar and Tasting Room, open from noon to 8 p.m. every day, later on weekends and in the summer. The Edgefield Winery opened in 1990 and now produces a full range of styles including chardonnay, pinot gris, pinot noir and even a hard cider.

With all there is to see and do, you might forget that it was the beer that originally brought you here. Established in 1991, this 20-barrel system serves as the main brewery for McMenamins, and produces Terminator Stout, Black Rabbit Porter, Bagdad Golden and other standard McMenamins ales for several of the company's Oregon pubs. The beers are available throughout the Edgefield compound, so you'll have plenty of opportunities for sampling.

Before leaving this remarkable place, tour the Edgefield Gardens, the vineyard and the Corcoran Glassworks. Then head up the Columbia Gorge to the spectacular waterfalls, or back into Portland to visit some of the other McMenamins pubs and breweries.

DIRECTIONS: From I-84 east from Portland, take exit 16A. Follow 238TH and drive south to the first light and turn left on Halsey. Go $1/2$ mile; Edgefield is on the right.

Big Horse Brewing Company

Established 1995

115 State Street • Hood River, OR 97031
(541) 386-4411

The Big Horse Brewing Company is the latest in a series of great ideas from owner and brewer Randy Orzeck. In 1987, Orzeck opened Horsefeathers, a restaurant and bar, and later launched a successful pasta business, which now distributes to Portland and other Oregon markets. Deciding to start a brewery seemed liked the next logical venture.

In 1995, Horsefeathers changed its name to the Big Horse Brewing Company, and the brewery was launched. The company currently produces six standards and three seasonals, much to the delight of Hood River natives and Columbia Gorge tourists and windsurfers. Pub favorites Night Mare Russian Imperial Stout, a well-balanced, full-bodied stout, and the dry-hopped Pale Rider IPA, provide something for both the recent convert and the seasoned craft brew enthusiast. The seasonal Scotch Ale, a smooth, high-alcohol, darker ale, the Chompin Bitters, and the Branded Black Porter are also well worth a try.

The three-story pub is built right into the hillside that climbs toward snow-capped Mount Hood. The brewery is located on the ground floor, and is visible from the street. On the second and third floors, wooden decks extend the pub and restaurant out-doors. A variety of games, televised sports events, darts, two full-sized billiards tables and summertime horseshoes are available for those not otherwise enjoying the beautiful setting. Visitors can sample Big Horse ales while admiring the Columbia River and surrounding cliffs, mountains and waterfalls.

DIRECTIONS: From I-84, take exit 63 for Hood River City Center. Take 2nd Avenue right until it deadends at State Street. The brewery is impossible to miss.

Hours: 4 p.m.–9 p.m. Monday–Thursday; 11:30 a.m.–11 p.m. Friday and Saturday; 11:30 a.m.–9 p.m. Sunday
Children: Yes
Food: Lunch and dinner menu, including gourmet burgers, pastas, clam chowder
Entertainment: Pool, darts, horseshoes, board games, televised sports, live music
Smoking: No
Payment: Checks, Visa, MC
Beer to go: Yes, draft

Full Sail Brewing Company-Hood River

Established 1987

506 Columbia Street • Hood River, OR 97031
(503) 386-2281 • www.fullsailbrewing.com

Full Sail Brewing Company, the largest craft bottler in Oregon, began in a small building overlooking the Columbia River in downtown Hood River. Recent expansion has enlarged the building tremendously, and boosted Full Sail's annual capacity to around 100,000 barrels a year. Still a small operation by commercial beer standards, the brewery has become a giant among craft breweries.

While many of Full Sail's beers are bottled and available throughout the Pacific Northwest and beyond, a visit to the Hood River brewing facility is well worth the trip. Staring down into a two-story kettle, watching the machinery crank out thousands of bottles of beer, and walking beneath the giant fermenters are just some of the grand-scale features of the tours conducted hourly, every day (Thursday through Sunday in winter).

Don't miss a trip to the pub, where you can sample many of the ales. It's housed in the original portion of the building and usually has eight of the fourteen beers on tap. The Full Sail Nut brown, India Pale, Top Sail Porter, or Full Sail Extra Special Bitter (the newest bottled Full Sail ale) are a few of the ales offered. The company also brews several lagers, including the Full Sail Pilsner, Maibock, Mercator Dopplebock and Octoberfest, a malty Bavarian-style lager.

The pub, which is a simple room with a few tables, is usually filled year-round with Hood River natives and people visiting the magnificent Columbia Gorge region. Summers, folks sit on the outdoor patio overlooking the Columbia River and watch the windsurfers. In winter, the rustic wood-burning stove keeps out the chill of winter rain.

Hours: Summer, noon–8 p.m. daily; winter, noon–8 p.m. Thursday–Sunday
Children: Yes, until 7 p.m.
Food: Bar snacks, nachos
Entertainment: Board games
Smoking: No
Payment: Checks
Beer to go: Yes, bottles and draft

DIRECTIONS: From I-84, take exit 63 to Hood River City Center. Turn right from the exit heading into town. Turn right on Cascade Street and take another right on 5th, which deadends into Columbia at the Full Sail Brewing Company building.

Elliot Glacier Public House

Established 1997

4945 Baseline Road • Parkdale, OR 97041
(541) 352-1022

Without a doubt the most impressive thing about the Elliot Glacier Public House is the view. Sitting outside at a picnic bench, you can't help but stare at Mount Hood, awestruck by its enormity and beauty. It is truly mesmerizing. Luckily, the beer and food at Elliot Glacier could hold their own whether the mountain was there or not. So most folks combine the mountain gazing with an Elliot Glacier brew and a dish off the creative menu. The brewery produces several standard ales and an array of seasonals. Parkdale Pale Ale is a moderately hopped ale, while Red Hill Scottish Ale is a well-balanced, amber colored ale that offers a sweet, malty flavor. Seasonals have included a Belgian-style ale, a summertime crystal wheat, and an imperial stout.

The menu offers tantalizing, unique meals. Entrées of salsa-simmered pork with cilantro cream sauce or chili Colorado burrito taste as good as they sound. Start out with the cheddar and Swiss cheese fondue, made with a touch of Baseline Porter, and served with bread and apples.

The Elliot Glacier Public House resides in the historic Valley Theater, origi-nally built in 1936. The town has several other attractive old buildings, such as the Old Parkdale Inn. The town is the destination terminus of the Mount Hood Rail-road, and over 50,000 visitors still take the train every year. The train stops a block from Elliot Glacier Public House, making it an excellent place to begin or end your visit to this spectacular re-gion of the Pacific Northwest.

DIRECTIONS: From I-84 in Hood River take exit 64 to Highway 35. Go north 17 miles and turn West onto Baseline Road, following the signs to Parkdale. The pub is at the corner of Baseline Road and 3rd Street in Parkdale.

Hours: Summer, 11 a.m.–9 p.m. daily; winter, call for hours
Children: Yes
Food: Pub menu
Entertainment: Occasional live music
Smoking: No
Payment: Cash and checks
Beer to go: Yes, draft

Mt. Hood Brewing Company

Established 1992

87304 Government Camp Loop • Government Camp, OR 97028
(503) 622-0724

Tucked under Oregon's highest peak, on the edge of the town of Government Camp, is the Mt. Hood Brewing Company, the ideal watering hole for visitors drawn to the beauty and adventure of Mt. Hood.

While appropriately named for its mountain location, the brewery actually takes its name from the original Mt. Hood Brewing Company, which operated from 1905 to 1913 in Portland. The current brewery produces six standards and two seasonals, offered both at the Mt. Hood Brew Pub and many Portland and Willamette Valley restaurants and taverns. The popular Ice Axe India Pale Ale is wonderfully smooth, rich and hoppy. Pinnacle Extra Special Bitter, always cask-conditioned, will also appeal to hop enthusiasts. Hogsback Oatmeal Stout is strong and thick, with a dominant roasted flavor. Seasonals, including Old Battleaxe Barleywine, and Pittock Wee Heavy, a winter-released Scotch ale, are well suited to warming up chilled visitors.

Decorated in a rustic fly fishing and skiing motif, and with the brewhouse visible from the restaurant, the Mt. Hood Brewing Company building has a ski lodge atmosphere well-suited to its location. Whether you're here for fishing, hiking, climbing or skiing, a trip to the Mt. Hood Brewing Company is the perfect end to a long, satisfying day.

Hours: Noon–10 p.m. daily
Children: Yes
Food: Pizza, sandwiches, entrées, salads
Entertainment: Board games
Smoking: No
Payment: Checks, Visa, MC, AmEx
Beer to go: Yes, draft

DIRECTIONS: From I-5 North to Portland, take exit 288 to I-205. Take the Gresham exit to Highway 26 east, then take the first Government Camp exit (45 miles from Gresham). The brewery is visible from the exit on the left side of Highway 26.

Seventh Street Brew House/
Cascade Lakes Brewing Company

Established 1995

855 SW 7th Street • Redmond, OR 97756
(541) 923-1795

There's just one brewpub in the small town of Redmond, Oregon, but it's definitely worth the stop. The Seventh Street Brew House is the tasting grounds for the Cascade Lakes Brewing Company, Redmond's first and only brewery.

The Brew House has managed to fit a brewery for cask-conditioned ales, a bar, an eating area, and an entertainment room. into less than 1,300 square feet. In the warmer months, tables, chairs and live music are pushed out to an expansive deck, doubling the space. It's possible even to get a little exercise by joining in a friendly game of volleyball; the pub comes with its own court.

Between the entertainment and the extensive list of tasty beers, it's easy to spend an entire afternoon at this pub. Locals rave about the Red Rooster Ale, but based on distribution outside of Redmond, Monkey Face Porter is also in demand. Other offerings include a Blackberry Kölsch, Grizzly Mountain Stout and the latest, Angus MacDougal's Scotts Ale, named after the brewer's great, great, great grandfather. In the summer, the brewery also produces Bandits Best Bitter, named after the local semi-pro baseball team. (Consider catching a game while you're in town.)

Hours: 11 a.m.–10 p.m. Monday–Thursday; 11 a.m. –11 p.m. Friday and Saturday; 11 a.m.–9 p.m. Sunday
Children: Yes
Food: Simple pub fare
Entertainment: Pub has live music throughout the year
Smoking: Yes, on the deck
Payment: Checks, Visa, MC
Beer to go: Yes, draft

DIRECTIONS: To find the pub, take Highway 126 (Highland) to 7th Street. Turn right on 7th Street. The pub is across the street from the fairgrounds.

Bend Brewing Company

Established 1995

1019 NW Brooks Street • Bend, OR 97701
(541) 383-1599 • www.sharplink.com/bbb

Old town Bend is like entering a Hollywood Western set—rustic, quaint and somewhat unreal. But inside Bend's newest brewpub, the cowboys give way to tired skiers, golfers, or families just back from a long day of rafting.

Bend Brewing is more upscale than its friendly competitor, Deschutes Brewing Company, just up the road, but the atmosphere is still relaxed and comfortable. Large windows offer a pleasant view of the park and the Deschutes River. Antique tables and chairs, which possibly once graced an old English pub, are scattered about the main dining and bar area. During warmer months, outdoor seating is available.

Brewmaster Chris Skovborg brews several standards, including Outback Old Ale, Elk Lake IPA, Metolius Golden, and High Desert Hefeweizen, as well as the summertime seasonal favorite Paulina Plunge Pale Ale. All of the brews take their names from the regional geography.

Bend Brewing prides itself not only on its fine hand-crafted beers, but also on its broad menu of deliciously prepared foods, including pizza, fish, pasta dishes, burritos, and burgers. The daily specials are also tantalizing to the palate.

Hours: 11:30 a.m.–11 p.m. Monday–Thursday; 11:30–midnight Friday and Saturday; 11:30–10 p.m. Sunday
Children: Yes
Food: Full menu
Entertainment: Regular televised sports events
Smoking: No
Payment: Checks, Visa, MC
Beer to go: Yes, draft

DIRECTIONS: Head west on Greenwood from U.S. 97. Take a left on Brooks Street.

Deschutes Brewery & Public House

Established 1988

1044 NW Bond Street • Bend, OR 97701
(541) 382-9242 • www.deschutesbrewery.com

One of the most successful microbreweries in the state is the Deschutes Brewery, located in Bend, a town famous for its outstanding recreational opportunities. This brewery has thrived since it first opened in 1988. It's a comfortable and contagiously friendly place. You'll soon find yourself swapping ski stories with the bartender while anxiously waiting for your hand-pumped beer.

Deschutes is best known for its Black Butte Porter, the best-selling porter in Oregon. It is also one of the few microbreweries in the region to use whole hops in the brewing process. The head brewer claims this brings out a better-bodied beer and, from the way it's selling, it appears many others agree!

Mainstays include Cascade Ale (sweet with a fabulous burst of flavors), Mirror Pond Pale Ale, Obsidian Stout, a Guinness-style stout with a thick cream top, and local favorite Bachelor Bitte. Don't miss the Jubelale, made especially for the holiday season, and on tap throughout the winter.

Deschutes' great beer is accompanied by an expansive menu offering pub-style food, soups, salads, and sandwiches, along with pie for dessert. Kids can do their own sampling of homemade root beer or ginger ale.

Hours: 11 a.m.–11:30 p.m. Monday–Thursday; 11 a.m.–12:30 a.m. Friday and Saturday; 11 a.m.–10 p.m. Sunday
Children: Yes
Food: Standard pub fare
Entertainment: Basket o' Tips, televised sports events
Smoking: No
Payment: Checks, Visa, MC
Beer to go: Yes, bottles and draft

The Mt. Bachelor ski resort is just a short ride from town, the raging Deschutes River offers rafters and kayakers a thrilling course, and Smith Rock State Park offers some of the best rock climbing in the world. What could be better than a stop at Deschutes Brewery to finish off a day at one of these spectacular destinations?

DIRECTIONS: From Highway 97, go west on Franklin to Bond. Right onto Bond. The brewery is $2^1/2$ blocks on the right.

Mia & Pia's Pizzeria & Brewhouse

Established 1996

3545 Summers Lane • Klamath Falls, OR 97603
(541) 884-4880

Klamath Falls is located in the middle of some spectacular country. Nearby destinations include Crater Lake, the Hart Mountain National Antelope Refuge, and towering Mt. Shasta to the south. The town sits on the southern shore of Upper Klamath Lake, the largest body of fresh water in the northwest. This area is home to the largest wintering concentration of bald eagles in the lower forty-eight states—sometimes up to 1,000 birds.

Klamath Falls was originally built on lumber and agriculture, but has diversified as it has grown. Rod Kucera and his family, the owners of Mia & Pia's, have been in this area for several generations as dairy farmers. In the late 1980s they got into the restaurant business by opening Mia & Pia's. In 1996, Rod Kucera added the Brewhouse, converting the old Kucera family dairy farm—and equipment—into the brewery.

Rod brews in small batches, experimenting with various styles. There are usually at least eight or nine beers on tap, including a seasonal or two. Crowd favorites include the tasty Applegate Trail Pale Ale and a seasonal dopplebock. Rod's Rodeo Red, in honor of Rod's professional rodeo career, is also definitely worth a try. All of the beers go well with the extensive pizza menu.

The restaurant is large and the décor is simple. Video games and pinball machines line one wall and tables are scattered in the main room and near the bar. Look up to see the old milking equipment which has been converted into ingenious light fixtures! If the weather is nice, take advantage of the attractive outdoor patio, complete with gardens and fountains.

Hours: 11 a.m.–11 p.m. Sunday—Thursday; 11 a.m.–midnight Friday—Saturday
Children: Yes
Food: Pizza and sandwiches
Entertainment: Occasional live music, televised sports
Smoking: Yes in bar area
Payment: Checks, Visa, MC
Beer to go: Yes, draft

DIRECTIONS: From the west, the most enjoyable route is along Highway 66. Take 66 through the town of Keno and under Route 97. Route 66 becomes the South Side Expressway/Highway 140. Take 140 over the river and past the airport and turn left on Summers Lane. Mia & Pia's is about $1^1/_2$ miles down on the right. If you come from the north, take Highway 97 to the South Side Expressway/Highway 140 exit and head east, following the directions above.

Terminal Gravity Brewing Company

Established 1997

803 School Street • Enterprise, OR 97828
(541) 426-0158

erminal Gravity Brewing Company holds the distinction of being the most eastern brewery in the state. Operating since August, 1997, in this remote corner of the state better known for its wilderness, Terminal Gravity is quickly earning a name for itself. In 1998, Terminal Gravity's India Pale Ale was named Oregon's "Beer of the Year" by Portland newspaper, *The Oregonian.*

Brewer and co-owner Steve Carper got his start at BridgePort Brewing Company in Portland. Since then, he has worked as plant engineer at Portland Brewing Company and designed systems for other breweries, including Pike Brewing in Seattle. His experience designing brew systems has paid off with the creation of his own brewery and beers in Enterprise. In addition to the well-known IPA, Terminal Gravity offers an Extra Special Golden Ale and the Bar X Stout. Seasonals include a brown, a bock, and a wintertime Festive Ale.

The building, constructed in the mid-'80s, is fashioned after the architecture of the 1920s and has a look and feel that gives the illusion that the building is old. Seating inside the building is limited—a few tables around the bar and couches upstairs are available. But folks will only be inside if they have to, because the real action is outside on the two-acre property. A large porch, several picnic tables sitting next to the creek, a horseshoe pit, and bonfire area beckon.

In addition to outdoor recreation, this part of Oregon is home to several art galleries and foundries. The artists of this area are well known for their work with bronze. The town of Joseph, a few miles south of Enterprise, annually hosts the Bronze, Blues and Brews Festival in August, which is well worth the trip.

Before heading off into the wilds of the Wallowa Mountains or Hells Canyon, be sure to stop off at Terminal Gravity for a pint. It's a long way back to town.

Hours: 3:30 p.m.–11 p.m.
Wednesday–Sunday
Children: Yes
Food: Pub fare
Entertainment: Horseshoes, darts
Smoking: No
Payment: Checks
Beer to go: Yes, draft

DIRECTIONS: From I-84 take exit 261 onto Highway 82. Take Highway 82 about 65 miles to Enterprise. The pub is about $1^1/2$ blocks off Highway 82 once you get into Enterprise.

Barley Brown's Brewpub

Established 1998

2190 Main Street • Baker City, OR 97814
(541) 523-4266

Baker City is located on the historic Oregon Trail that brought over 250,000 immigrants to the Pacific Northwest. In the 1870s, Baker City was at the heart of Oregon gold rush country. By the beginning of the 1900s, Baker City sported several hotels, an opera house, a trolley service, and two local breweries.

Barley Brown's Brewpub, operating out of an old brick building in the historic downtown, captures some of the city's history within its walls. The solid oak bar stools were originally jury chairs used in the 1890s at the local court house. The dining room sports an impressive stamped tin ceiling.

Tyler Brown and his family have operated a variety of restaurants from this location since the mid-1970s. In 1998 he decided to incorporate his interest in homebrewing into the restaurant and added a four-barrel Elliott Bay brewing system to the center of the building. Visible through large windows from the dining area, this small brewery now turns out five standard ales and a couple of seasonals, to the delight of locals and visitors alike. The ESB is nicely balanced between malt and hop, while the strong ale is rich and full-flavored, with a distinct fruitiness. Naturally, he also brews a brown ale. Seasonals have included an espresso stout and a hoppy India pale ale.

This being cattle country, the menu favors beef—New York steaks, fresh hand-patted burgers, and more. You'll also find a few unexpected dishes for this part of Oregon including favorites such as fajitas, grilled salmon, and crab cakes. Brown hopes to expand hours to offer lunch in the near future, but for now it is dinner only. Judging by the popularity of the place and the quality of the brews, the expansion in hours will probably come about sooner rather than later.

Hours: 4 p.m.–10 p.m. Monday–Thursday; 4 p.m.–midnight Friday and Saturday
Children: Yes
Food: Pub fare with a few surprises
Entertainment: Darts, board games, televised sports, monthly live music
Smoking: Yes, in bar area
Payment: Checks, Visa, MC
Beer to go: No

DIRECTIONS: From I-84 take exit 304. Go west on Campbell Street into Baker City. Take a left onto Main Street (first light). Go three blocks; the pub is on the left at the corner of Main Street and Church Street

McMenamins Pubs & Breweries, "A Neighborhood Place for Family & Friends"

In the Pacific Northwest, McMenamins breweries and pubs are practically as familiar and enjoyable as the magnificent forests for which the region is famous. In the early 1980s, Portland brothers Mike and Brian McMenamin saw the potential for opening a brewpub in the already draft-crazed beer market of Oregon. Little did they dream that without so much as writing a business plan, they would one day be operating a privately held, multi-million dollar company of approximately fifty brewpubs, theater pubs and taverns.

After a few semi-successful forays into the restaurant business, the McMenamins lobbied the Oregon legislature to change the laws that prohibited brewing and retail beer sales on the same premises. With lobbying leadership from the Ponzis, founders of the BridgePort Brewing Company, the laws were finally changed and the McMenamin brothers opened the Barley Mill Pub on SE Hawthorne in Portland. The Hillsdale Brewery and Pub, also in Portland, which followed in 1984, began in-house brewing the following year.

McMenamins grew from these humble beginnings to the empire it is today by providing a clean, cozy, and definitely funky atmosphere. They also consistently offer a menu of quality pub fare, a commitment to employees and patrons (their slogan is "A Neighborhood Place for Family & Friends"), and really good beer. Each brewpub has its own special features—from sit-down restaurants in strip malls, to remodeled houses, to taverns with pool tables—but all are recognizably McMenamins, owing largely to the psychedelic paintings on the walls, brewing equipment, and unique restrooms.

Several artists who are staff employees of the company have created a tremendous array of murals, coasters, and signs for the various pubs, as well as wall art with recurring themes. This splashy artwork is as much a part of the McMenamins culture as the historic buildings and the fresh beers.

In the mid-1980s, the company began to grow, adding such establishments as the Greenway Pub and the Blue Moon Tavern & Grill in Portland, the Riverwood Pub in Beaverton, and the Lighthouse Brewpub in Lincoln City on the coast. In 1987, McMenamins opened several new pubs including their first combination brewpub/movie theater, the Mission Theater & Pub in Portland. As establishments opened, the company developed a loose system of matching brewpubs with sister, non-brewing McMenamins taverns, each brewpub supplying beer to a different tavern.

In 1990, the McMenamins began developing what would soon become a tourist destination in the microbrewing field and a veritable Disneyland for beer drinkers: Edgefield Manor in Troutdale, just up the Columbia River Gorge from Portland (see page 67). This tremendous complex is a showcase for the famous McMenamins artwork; fourteen artists spent an entire year painting every nook and cranny of the over-100-room lodge. Edgefield continues to grow in scope, with many fun additions over the years. These include the likes of a golf course, and the Little Red Shed cigar and brandy-warming hut.

Another rapid growth year came in 1995 when McMenamins entered the Washington State marketplace and opened four brewpubs in just over six months. The Olympic Club, billed as a "gentlemen's resort" when it opened in Centralia, Washington in 1908, became a McMenamins brewpub in 1997. The furthest north the McMenamins empire has spread is Mill Creek, northeast of Lynnwood, Washington. To the south, the company now has locations all the way to Roseburg, Oregon.

The McMenamin brothers have made a point of restoring old, historic buildings and putting them to good use. The Crystal Ballroom in Portland, a 1914 building known as a center of late-1960s psychedelic culture in Portland, reopened in 1997 as a McMenamins pub and concert hall. It once again offers live music every week and features a remarkable wooden dance floor that sways and bounces right along with the dancers. The Kennedy School, a former elementary school in Northeast Portland, is now a bed and breakfast pub. It also houses a local community center, swimming pool, and garden. A 1912 train station in Roseburg has also become a recent outpost of the McMenamins kingdom.

The Oregon Hotel, built in 1905 in downtown McMinnville, now ranks among the McMenamins holdings, giving you a total of three McMenamins lodging venues to choose from, along with Edgefield and the Kennedy School. These ranks will continue to grow, first with the addition of the Oxford Hotel in downtown Centralia, which will open above the Olympic Club, a restored pre-prohibition saloon and pool-hall.

Other McMenamins projects in the works include additional pubs, brewpubs and theater-pubs throughout Oregon and Washington. Look for a renovated Masonic Temple to open under the McMenamins banner in Forest Grove, Oregon (southwest of Portland). The company continues scouting for an ideal location for a theater-pub in the Seattle area, as well. Where the McMenamin brothers will take us next, no one can say for certain. But it's sure to be fun . . . for the whole family.

McMenamins Beers

With over twenty separate breweries that regularly produce beer, and a handful of others that occasionally brew, McMenamins makes a lot of beer. In addition to the standard ales brewed at the primary facility at Edgefield, each brewer routinely comes up with his or her own unique recipes. Many of the locations also brew some standard McMenamins beers in-house, or offer slight variations of regular recipes.

The Oregon standards are Ruby Ale, which is a light ale brewed with a touch of raspberries, Terminator Stout, Black Rabbit Porter, Hammerhead, India Pale Ale, Cascade Head, and Crystal, which was named for the Crystal Ballroom long before McMenamins acquired it. The Washington standards are Ruby, Terminator, Crystal, Troll Porter, Temperance, and Empire India Pale Ale. As for seasonals, winter brings Kris Kringle and Scotch ale; spring offers Raspberry Stout, Nebraska Bitter, and bock; and summer favorites are Purple Haze, Strawberry Fields, and Stella Blue—all brewed with berries.

McMenamins Establishments

BREWERY-PUBS:
OREGON

McMenamins/Murray
6179 SW Murray Boulevard
Beaverton, OR 97005
(503) 644-4562

High Street Brewery & Café
1243 High Street
Eugene, OR 97402
(541) 345-4905

Highland Pub & Brewery
4225 SE 182nd
Gresham, OR 97030
(503) 665-3015

Cornelius Pass Roadhouse Brewery
4045 NW Cornelius Pass Road
Hillsboro, OR 97124
(503) 640-6174

Lighthouse Brewpub
4157 N Hwy 101, Suite 117
Lincoln City, OR 97367
(541) 994-7238

Concordia Brewery at Kennedy School
(See page 57)
5736 NE 33rd
Portland, OR 97211
(503) 249-3983

Crystal Brewery
1332 West Burnside
Portland, OR 97205
(503) 225-0047

Fulton Pub & Brewery
0618 SW Nebraska
Portland, OR 97201
(503) 246-9530

Hillsdale Brewery & Pub
    1505 SW Sunset Boulevard
    Portland, OR 97201
    (503) 246-3938

Oak Hills Brewpub
    14740 NW Cornell Road, Suite 80
    Portland, OR 97229
    (503) 645-0286

Roseburg Station
    700 SE Sheridan
    Roseburg, OR 97470
    (541) 672-1934

Thompson Brewery & Pub
    3575 Liberty Road South
    Salem, OR 97302
    (541) 363-7286

John Barleycorns
    14610 SW Sequoia Parkway
    Tigard, OR 97223
    (503) 684-2688

Edgefield Lodge/Brewery (See page 67)
    Powerstation Pub & Theater
    2126 SW Halsey Street
    Troutdale, OR 97060
    (503) 669-8610 or (800) 669-8610

McMenamins Brewery/West Linn
    2090 SW 8th Avenue
    West Linn, OR 97201
    (503) 656-2970

BREWERY-PUBS: WASHINGTON

Olympic Club
    112 North Tower Avenue
    Centralia, WA 98531
    306/736-5164

McMenamins/Mill Creek
    13300 Bothell-Everett Highway,
    Suite 304
    Mill Creek, WA 98012
    (206) 316-0520

Dad Watsons
    3601 Fremont Avenue North
    Seattle, WA 98103
    (206) 632-6505

McMenamins/Roy Street
    200 Roy Street, Suite 105
    Seattle, WA 98109
    (206) 285-4722

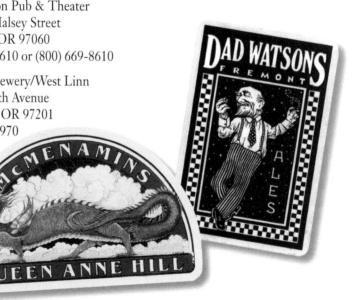

Six Arms
    300 E Pike Street
    Seattle, WA 98122
    (206) 223-1698

McMenamins on the Columbia
    1801 SE Columbia River Drive
    Vancouver, WA 98661
    (360) 699-1521

NONBREWING-PUBS

McMenamins/Cedar Hills
    2927 SW Cedar Hills Boulevard
    Beaverton, OR 97005
    (503) 641-0151

Riverwood Pub
    8136 SW Hall Boulevard
    Beaverton, OR 97008
    (503) 643-7189

McMenamins/Sunnyside
    9751 SE Sunnyside Road #K
    Clackamas, OR 97015
    (503) 653-8011

McMenamins/Corvallis
    420 NW 3rd
    Corvallis, OR 97330
    (541) 758-6044

East 19th Street Café
    1485 E 19th Street
    Eugene, OR 97403
    (541) 342-4025

Rock Creek Tavern
    10000 Old Cornelius Pass Road
    Hillsboro, OR 97124
    (503) 645-3822

Hotel Oregon
    130 NE Evans Street
    McMinnville, OR 97128
    (888) 472-8427

McMenamins/Oregon City
    102 9th Street
    Oregon City, OR 97045
    (503) 655-8032

Bagdad Theater & Pub
    3702 SE Hawthorne Street
    Portland, OR 97214
    (503) 236-9234

Barley Mill Pub
    1629 SE Hawthorne Street
    Portland, OR 97214
    (503) 231-1492

Blue Moon Tavern & Grill
    432 NW 21st
    Portland, OR 97209
    (503) 223-3184

Greater Trumps
    1520 SE 37th
    Portland, OR 97214
    (503) 235-4530

Greenway Pub
    12272 SW Scholls Ferry Road
    Tigard, OR 97223
    (503) 590-1865

Market Street Pub
1511 SW 10th
Portland, OR 97201
(503) 497-0160

McMenamins/Mall 205
9710 SE Washington Street, Suite A
Portland, OR 97216
(503) 254-5411

McMenamins on Broadway
1504 NE Broadway, Suite 900
Portland, OR 97232
(503) 288-9498

McMenamins St. Johns Pub
8203 N Ivanhoe
Portland, OR 97203
(503) 283-8520

McMenamins Tavern
1716 NW 23rd
Portland, OR 97210
(503) 227-0929

Mission Theater & Pub
1624 NW Glisan
Portland, OR 97209
(503) 223-4527

Raleigh Hills Pub
4495 SW Scholls Ferry Road
Portland, OR 97005
(503) 292-1723

The Ram's Head
2282 NW Hoyt
Portland, OR 97210
(503) 221-0098

Ringlers Annex/Crystal Ballroom
1223 SW Stark
Portland, OR 97205
(503) 525-0520

The White Eagle
836 N Russell Avenue
Portland, OR 97227
(503) 282-6810

McMenamins Boons Treasury
888 Liberty Street, NE
Salem OR 97301
(503) 399-9062

McMenamins/Sherwood
15976 SW Tualatin-Sherwood
Road
Sherwood, OR 97140
(503) 625-3547

HOTEL-BREWPUBS

Hotel Oregon
130 NE Evans Street
McMinnville, OR 97128
(888) 472-8427

Kennedy School (see full listing, page 57)
5736 NE 33rd
Portland, OR 97211
(503) 249-3983 or (888) 249-3983

Edgefield Lodge (see full listing, page 67)
2126 SW Halsey Street
Troutdale, OR 97060
(503) 669-8610 or (800) 669-8610

WASHINGTON

The twenty-first century finds Washington blessed with a nice balance of brewpubs and other craft breweries. This was much less the case a decade ago, when Washington was a state of several microbreweries supplying souped-up craft beer taverns known as alehouses (see The Seattle Alehouse Scene, p. xx) but relatively few brewpubs—for the West Coast, that is. Washington's dozen true brewpubs in 1992 still added up to five or ten more than there were in most states at the time, neck and neck with California, Colorado, Massachusetts, New York, Ohio, Pennsylvania, and Wisconsin which then were the leaders.

Savvy tavern owners in Washington seized the day at the birth of the craft brewing revolution and, in effect, preempted a takeover of the taverns by brewpubs until the late 1990s. Tavern owners expanded and revamped the saloons they already owned to create tasting destinations for regionally brewed draft beer with

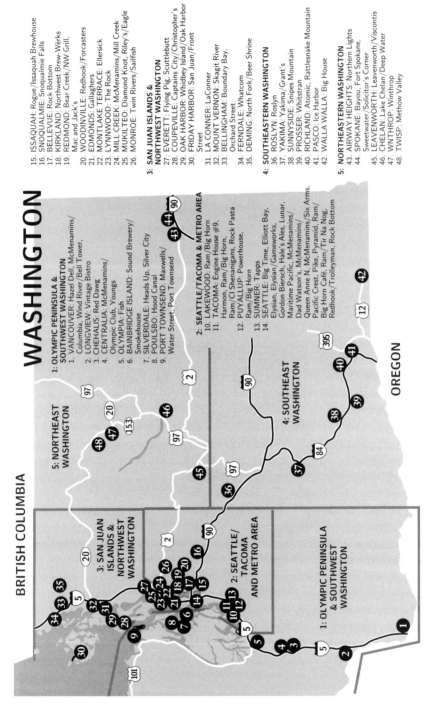

WASHINGTON

BRITISH COLUMBIA

OREGON

1: OLYMPIC PENINSULA & SOUTHWEST WASHINGTON
1. VANCOUVER: Hazel Dell, McMenamins/Columbia, Wind River/Bell Tower, Mac and Jack's
2. LONGVIEW: Vintage Bistro
3. CHEHALIS: Red Dawg
4. CENTRALIA: McMenamins/Olympic Club, Youngs
5. OLYMPIA: Fish
6. BAINBRIDGE ISLAND: Sound Brewery/Smokehouse
7. SILVERDALE: Heads Up, Silver City
8. POULSBO: Hood Canal
9. PORT TOWNSEND: Maxwells/Water Street, Port Townsend

2: SEATTLE/TACOMA & METRO AREA
10. LAKEWOOD: Ram/Big Horn
11. TACOMA: Engine House #9, Harmon, Ram/Big Horn, Ram/CI Shenanigans, Rock Pasta
12. PUYALLUP: Powerhouse, Ram/Big Horn
13. SUMNER: Tapps
14. SEATTLE: Big Time, Elliott Bay, Elysian/Gameworks, Gordon Biersch, Hale's Ales, Lunar, Maritime Pacific, McMenamins/Dad Watson's, McMenamins/Queen Anne N, McMenamins/Six Arms, Pacific Crest, Pike, Pyramid, Ram/Big Horn Café, Ram/Tir Na Nog, Redhook/Trolleyman, Rock Bottom

3: SAN JUAN ISLANDS & NORTHWEST WASHINGTON

4: SOUTHEAST WASHINGTON

5: NORTHEAST WASHINGTON

15. ISSAQUAH: Rogue/Issaquah Brewhouse
16. SNOQUALMIE: Snoqualmie Falls
17. BELLEVUE: Rock Bottom
18. KIRKLAND: Northwest Brew-Werks
19. REDMOND: Bear Creek/NW Grill, Mac and Jack's
20. WOODINVILLE: Redhook/Forcasters
21. EDMONDS: Gallaghers
22. MONTLAKE TERRACE: Ellersick
23. LYNNWOOD: The Rock
24. MILL CREEK: McMenamins/Mill Creek
25. MUKILTEO: Diamond Knot, Riley's/Eagle
26. MONROE: Twin Rivers/Sailfish

3: SAN JUAN ISLANDS & NORTHWEST WASHINGTON
27. EVERETT: Flying Pig, Scuttlebutt
28. COUPEVILLE: Captains City/Christopher's
29. OAK HARBOR: Whidbey Island/Oak Harbor
30. FRIDAY HARBOR: San Juan/Front Street
31. LA CONNER: LaConner
32. MOUNT VERNON: Skagit River
33. BELLINGHAM: Boundary Bay, Orchard Street
34. FERNDALE: Whatcom
35. DEMING: North Fork/Beer Shrine

4: SOUTHEASTERN WASHINGTON
36. ROSLYN: Roslyn
37. YAKIMA: Yakima/Grant's
38. SUNNYSIDE: Snipes Mountain
39. PROSSER: Whitstran
40. RICHLAND: Atomic, Rattlesnake Mountain
41. PASCO: Ice Harbor
42. WALLA WALLA: Big House

5: NORTHEASTERN WASHINGTON
43. AIRWAY HEIGHTS: Northern Lights
44. SPOKANE: Bayou, Fort Spokane, Sweetwater/Solicitor's Corner
45. LEAVENWORTH: Leavenworth/Viscontis
46. CHELAN: Lake Chelan/Deep Water
47. WNTHROP: Winthrop
48. TWISP: Methow Valley

twenty and thirty tap-handles, giving beer enthusiasts unprecedented opportunities for sampling fresh local beers (several now boast over fifty). This is not to say that Washington craft brewers have not had to lobby for change. Were it not for the vision and persistence demonstrated by the pioneering instigators of the Washington craft beer scene (Paul Shipman and Gordon Bowker of Redhook, Bert Grant, and Mike Hale were the leaders of the first wave),we would not enjoy the real ales that now exist in Washington.

Seattle itself has much to offer: great coffee of course, a thriving downtown, great museums, a couple of new stadiums, and a great many quality hometown beers (see Seattle/Tacoma and Metro Area, p. 104). There are some good Seattle breweries not featured in this book, since they offer no tasting area at their facilities. Keep your eyes open in Seattle alehouses for brews such as Moon Ales.

But the nearby cities that stretch up the shores of Puget Sound are rich with microbreweries these days as well. Half a dozen brewpubs can be found in greater Tacoma, and a couple each in Everett, Mukilteo, Tukwilla, and Puyallup. Eastern Washington has twenty or so microbreweries and brewpubs at the end of the 1990s, roughly a fifth of the state's total. Both Spokane and the Tri-Cities (Richland, Pasco, and Kennewick) are oases offering numerous good local brews to quench a hot ranch-lands thirst. The honors for being Washington's most remote brewing outposts these days go to Walla Walla, in the southeastern corner of the state, and in the northwestern corner either Friday Harbor, on San Juan Island, or Port Angeles, on the Olympic Peninsula. For brewery expedition ideas in Washington state, see the Fourth Corner Brew Tour (p. 150), the Greater Puget Sound Shores and Islands Brew Tour (p. 95) and the Yakima Valley Brew Tour (p. 159).

The exciting variety of cottage breweries, brewpubs, and large craft breweries interact in an ever-changing marketplace of increasingly savvy consumers with discriminating palates. Brewers push the limits of consumer consciousness with beer styles unheard of in these parts since the early twentieth century: Kölsch, saison, and abbey ale interpretations grace the tap handles and the grocery store shelves. Consumers help shape beer styles, voting with their pocketbooks. As the brewers continue to devise exciting quality beers, beer enthusiasts continue to be excited about the latest microbrewed sensation. So if you're in Washington for a visit, just as with Rome, remember to do as the locals do and head out for a couple of rounds and some good pub grub at one of the neighborhood brewpubs or alehouses. In Washington, there's bound to be one right nearby.

Region 1: The Olympic Peninsula & Southwest Washington

Bell Tower Brewhouse/ Wind River Brewing Company

Established 1998

707 SE 164th Avenue • Vancouver, WA 98684
(360) 944-7800 • www.thebelltower.com

As you drive out past the last cluster of businesses and shops in this fast-developing section of Vancouver, Bell Tower appears suddenly, looking a lot like a large country church. The shape of the building, including the prominent bell tower, is taken from the original church that once occupied this spot. The size and grandeur of the Brewhouse, however, draws a new crowd of faithful to its halls.

The downstairs "Pitcher's Sports Bar" offers a full bar, several televisions for watching a game, and a small outside patio hidden from the parking lot above. Antique sports memorabilia and a large stained-glass Bell Tower logo adorn the bar. The main level restaurant and outside seating will appeal to families stopping in for dinner and lunch, while the upstairs offers couches and pool tables for those looking for a relaxed, more intimate setting.

The common thread connecting all of these locations is the beer. Brewer Eric Munger produces six standard brews and a rotating seasonal beer from his ten-barrel system. Be sure to try the Wind River ESB, a tasty, English-style extra special bitter with a crisp, hop finish, and the Bell Ringer Rye Pale Ale, a hoppy India pale ale brewed with the addition of malted rye. Seasonals tend more towards lagers and include a springtime doppelbock, a Pilsner, and an Octoberfest lager.

Converts to the Bell Tower also come for the food, and just about everyone swears by the halibut and chips. Lightly dipped in a beer batter, it is a great complement to the Bell Tower brews.

Hours: 11 a.m.–10 p.m. Monday–Thursday; 11 a.m.–midnight Friday and Saturday; 12 p.m.–10 p.m. Sunday
Children: Yes
Food: Pub fare
Entertainment: Occasional music, pool tables
Smoking: No
Payment: Visa, MC, AmEx
Beer to go: Yes, draft

Directions: From I-205 take the Mill Plain exit, 28. Go east on Mill Plain for several miles. At 164th Ave. take a left. The brewhouse is on the right.

Hazel Dell Brewpub

Established 1993

8513 NE Highway 99 • Vancouver, WA 98665
(360) 576-0996

The Hazel Dell Brewpub is an unassuming place. Tucked between business offices and a mobile home sales lot on Highway 99, it's easy to miss if you're not looking closely. But once inside, with the noise and traffic of the highway left behind, you can get down to the wonderful work at hand—sampling various Hazel Dell ales.

After entering the pub, the first thing you'll notice is the brewery, housed to the left of the bar. The elaborate larger-than-life hop vines painted in crawling and twisting designs on the heating and cooling ducts, ceiling and walls behind the bar will surely grab your attention next. The abundance of hops in Pacific Northwest beers, and the many hop farms that dot the landscape throughout the region are two of the primary reasons for the success of Pacific Northwest microbrewing.

Brewer Phil Stein produces several standard ales and four seasonals. Red Zone, a pale ale, is a highly hopped and fairly bitter brew, deep red in color. The beer's name refers to the area around Mt. St. Helens that was off limits after its 1980 eruption. Captain Vancouver's Irish Stout, a creamy and dense brew with coffee and chocolate flavors, is the brewery's darkest offering. Stein also produces the "Steinweizen," his own spin on a hefeweizen. Hazel Dell's seasonal brews include an Oktoberfest, a winter ale called Weihnacbier, a spring porter and, for summer, Stoneberry, a golden ale flavored with marionberries.

DIRECTIONS: From I-5 south, take the 78th Street exit. At the bottom of the exit, get in the left lane and go left at the light onto Highway 99. The brewery is five blocks up, on the right.

Hours: 11:30 a.m.–11 p.m. Monday–Thursday; Friday and Saturday 11:30 a.m.–midnight; Sunday 2 p.m.–10 p.m.
Children: Yes
Food: Standard pub fare
Entertainment: Regularly televised sports events
Smoking: Yes
Payment: Visa, MC
Beer to go: Yes

Salmon Creek Brewery & Pub

Established 1998

108 W Evergreen Boulevard • Vancouver, WA 98660
(360) 993-1827

At a few taverns and restaurants in Vancouver, Washington, you may find an ale on tap (most likely a Scottish ale) made by the understated Salmon Creek Brewery. But their brewpub itself is a nice place—good for a relaxing get-together downtown. It's housed in an inviting one-story brick building with a beautiful ivy-covered entrance that leads into a courtyard with outdoor seating.

Following a stint as a distribution-only craft brewery in Woodland, Larry Pratt and Dennis Stebbins moved their operation into downtown Vancouver, changed the name to Salmon Creek, and are now publicans through-and-through. These self-trained brewers got into the business out of a love for craft beer; they brew their unfiltered ales in a converted three barrel-capacity still.

The interior of the pub proper features an antique pressed-tin ceiling and a copper bar—and no TV screen. If it's Friday you can feast from a free nacho bar. The Salmon Creek Brewery hasn't settled on a standard beer lineup—and may never. You're apt to encounter their aforementioned Scottish ale, a golden ale, a best bitter made with three hop varieties, a nut brown that is smooth, with hints of smoke, and a stout. For seasonals, Larry and Dennis have offered an IPA that is fairly light-bodied for the style, and ruby-colored Thunderbolt Porter with malty caramel tastes. They also brew a contract brown ale for R.P. McMurphy Restaurant and Pub in Vancouver.

Hours: 11 a.m.–10 p.m. Monday–Thursday; 11 a.m.–midnight Friday; 1 p.m. to midnight Saturday
Children: Yes, until 9 p.m.
Food: Pub fare
Entertainment: Occasional live acoustic music
Smoking: No
Payment: Visa, MC, AmEx, Discover
Beer to go: Yes, draft

To accompany your beer, there's fish and chips, deli sandwiches, and burgers—including a sirloin burger and a salmon burger. Choose from three seating areas: the courtyard patio, an upscale-but-intimate pub on one side of the patio, and a retro diner-like café space on the other side.

DIRECTIONS: From I-5 Northbound, take Exit 1-B City Center. At the second traffic light turn left on Evergreen. The brewpub is $2^1/2$ blocks down Evergreen on your right. From I-5 Southbound, take Exit 1-B Mill Plain and keep right. At the end of the exit ramp turn right on Mill Plain, and at the second light turn left onto Broadway. At the second light on Broadway turn right on Evergreen and continue for $1^1/2$ blocks.

The Vintage Bistro

Established 1996

1329 Commerce Avenue • Longview, WA 98632
(360) 425-8848

The Vintage Bistro's niche in the center of Longview's revitalized downtown is that of antique-mall-gone-uptown. The brick pedestrian areas and neat shop fronts make this a pleasant small-town "city center." And, near the very center you'll find a café with a country theme (black-and-white Holstein cow spots adorn most surfaces) that has a well-kept antique store above it and a small fine dining room in the rear. This dining room is the Vintage Bistro.

If you've never been to Longview, the Vintage Bistro's New York pepper steak might be reason enough to stop through. You'll find mostly locals in the restaurant, along with an occasional fellow beer traveler who has ducked off I-5 or maybe a few birders who are headed down the Columbia River to the wildlife refuges along the delta. The massive deli sandwiches create a busy lunch-scene buzz, and the fish 'n chips are very popular too. Later, couples dining is the norm, with pairs and groups enjoying entrées such as slow-roasted prime rib, Chicken Cordon Bleu and Prawns Provençal.

This is a family operation, headed up by Gary and Bonnie Elsey, and the family ownership comes through in touches such as the antique vases, candelabra and knick-knacks around the room's perimeter, as well as the homemade breads and desserts baked by Bonnie, and the craft beers made by Gary. Black tablecloths and ornate mirrors add a touch of class.

The tiny (two-barrel) brewing system by Renaissance Systems of Portland sits prominently in the center of the dining room next to the tiny bar. This is about as close-up to an all-malt brewhouse as you can get in a restaurant. Elsey's three-beer lineup follows the antique shop theme with their names: Antique Amber, Shopkeeper Stout and Bistro Red (a zippy, citrusy, copper-colored ale).

DIRECTIONS: From I-5 take Exit 36 Kelso-Longview/Highway 432. Take 432 West about $2^1/_2$ miles into Longview as it becomes Tenant Way. Turn right on Commerce Avenue. Follow Commerce about 20 blocks into the heart of downtown. The brewpub is on Commerce, on your left.

Hours: 10 a.m.–9 p.m. Monday–Saturday
Children: Yes
Food: Deli sandwiches, burgers, steaks, and seafood
Entertainment: Antique store adjoining
Smoking: No
Payment: Visa, MC, AmEx
Beer to go: Yes, draft

Red Dawg Brewpub

Established 1996

492 N Market Boulevard • Chehalis, WA 98532
(360)740-8072 • www.reddawgpub.com

The Red Dawg Brewpub is the second evolution in brewing for Dave and Sue Moorehead. They began in 1991 as the Onalaska Brewing Company, producing bottles and kegs from a backyard brewery located at their rural home. In December of 1996, however, they moved the brewery to Chehalis and opened the Red Dawg, a relaxed "mom and pop" brewpub tucked into an old storefront in the center of town.

Dave handles the brewing and the front of the store, while Sue creates delicious desserts, her soon-to-be-famous beer bread, and a selection of satisfying sandwiches. Her Chocolate Stout Cake, served with an espresso chocolate sauce, is worth the trip all of its own.

The pub is decidedly casual, with books and magazines available up front, a small stage for weekend and Wednesday night music events, and a red 1947 Harley Davidson motorcycle propped in front of the brewhouse. Make sure to peruse the collection of 1900s photos from the area's once thriving hop farms.

Dave brews several standards and an occasional seasonal. Chehalis Gold, formerly known as Onalaska Ale, is a light, slightly fruity ale. Red Dawg Ale (not to be confused with Red Dog Ale, made by Miller) is a darker, richer ale with a definite hoppy finish. Howlin' Stout, Meriwether's Best Brown, and an India pale ale are also usually on tap.

DIRECTIONS: From I-5, take exit 79. Turn east onto Chamber Way (left from North I-5, right from South I-5). At the T-intersection turn right onto National and stay in the left lane. After passing the museum, turn left onto Boistfort. Go one block to the signal. The pub is on the corner.

Hours: 11 a.m.~9 p.m. Tuesday~Thursday; 11 a.m.~11 p.m. Friday and Saturday
Children: Yes
Food: Pub menu
Entertainment: Occasional music
Smoking: No
Payment: Checks, Visa, MC
Beer to go: Yes, in growlers

Youngs Brewing Company

Established 1994

5945 Prather Road SW; Centralia, WA 98531
(360) 736-7760 • www.dicksbeer.com

Youngs Brewing Company is the story of homebrewing getting out of hand and going crazily, desperately, right. Dick Young, owner and head brewer, added the brewery to his Northwest Sausage and Deli business in 1994. Visitors can sample any of the various outstanding, hand-crafted ales as well as purchase the handmade sausages and smoked meats produced at the deli.

Dick was long famed in the local area for his homebrewing. The cry, "Dick's beer is here!" would often greet Young when he entered a party with his cooler full of brew. The brewery now produces several standard ales in six-packs and 22-ounce bottles, and the names are still familiar to the faithful: Dick's Wheaton, Dick's Cream Stout, and the wonderfully dark and malty Dick Danger Ale. Dick's Harvest Ale, an Octoberfest-style ale, is also a must-try. Summer seasonal Raspberry Wheat is also worthy of a taste when available.

With growing distribution to Olympia, Tacoma and other Puget Sound cities, Young eventually hopes to boost production to near 1,000 barrels. For the moment, though, "Dick's Beer" is one of the best kept secrets of the Pacific Northwest craft brewing renaissance.

Hours: 9:30 a.m.–5 p.m. Monday–Friday; 10 a.m.–3 p.m. Saturday
Children: Yes
Food: Deli sandwiches
Entertainment: No
Smoking: No
Payment: Checks, Visa, MC
Beer to go: Yes

DIRECTIONS: From I-5, take the Harrison Street exit (exit 82). Go west on Harrison (left off I-5 South, right off I-5 North), go through all the lights and drive another three miles. The brewery is on the left side of the street across from Crescent Grocers.

Fish Brewing Company/
Peppers Mexican Restaurant

Established 1993

515 Jefferson Street SE • Olympia, WA 98501
(360) 943-6480

L ocated in downtown Olympia, The Fish Brewing Company is appropriately decorated with a variety of charming fish art—some owned by the pub, but most for sale. A giant carved fish mounted on the north wall watches over the room. The brewery is visible through full-length windows, with shining fermenters and conditioners in plain view.

The aromas of Mexican cuisine from the adjoining Peppers Restaurant, and the rumble of an occasional train passing over the street in front of the pub, add to the mellow feel of the Fish Brewing Company. You can order off the full menu of the restaurant next door while at the pub. This brewery is also deeply involved in distribution, and Fish Tale Ales are available throughout Washington, in Portland, Oregon, and in taverns in San Francisco's East Bay area.

The Fish Brewing Company offers a rotation of six to eight regular and several seasonal ales, which always include at least one cask-conditioned ale. Pub favorite is the Fish Eye India Pale Ale, a light, golden India pale ale that is dry-hopped in the keg to add even more hops to the finish. A strong second is the Fish's Best Bitter, a traditional-style English bitter with a lower alcohol content than other Fish Tale Ales. Also popular is the "kindly brewed:" Fishtale Amber, made with organically grown barley and hops.

Specialty and seasonal ales include the Leviathan Barley Wine and Poseidon's Old Scotch Ale, an ale brewed with peated malt, which is used to make Scotch whiskey. The Fish Brewing Company also offers an Octoberfish, Winterfish Ale and Catfish Brown, available during summer.

Hours: 11 a.m.–midnight Monday–Saturday
Children: No
Food: Full menu at adjoining Mexican restaurant
Entertainment: Acoustic music on Saturday night
Smoking: No
Payment: Checks
Beer to go: Yes

DIRECTIONS: From I-5, take exit 105. Follow signs for Port of Olympia onto Plum Street. Take Plum Street north about one mile. Take a left onto 5th. The brewery is on the southwest corner of 5th and Jefferson.

GREATER PUGET SOUND BREW TOUR

Puget Sound and the waters farther to the north—including the many bays that edge the northern Washington inland waterway on the way to Canada: Skagit, Samish, Chuckanut, Bellingham, Birch, and Boundary—are lined with a lace-like pattern of quality brewpubs and small craft breweries. By starting at the north end of these waters, you can do a great two or three-day exploration, with real beer close at hand all the way. On the U.S. side of the international border, the tour starts in the settlements of Blaine and Birch Bay, where establishments pour Whatcom Brewery's ESB and IPA, and the Workshop Pub in Birch Bay pours a Whatcom-made house pale. Or, if you're approaching by boat, start your tour at Friday Harbor's San Juan Brewing Company's Front Street Ale House for a great variety of house brews on tap.

Heading south along the water, past Bellingham, Chuckanut Mountain, Fidalgo Island, and the Skagit Flats (see Washington's Fourth Corner Brew Tour, page 150), you come to beautiful Whidbey Island. Nestled on the leeward side of the island, about ten miles south of breathtaking Deception Pass, is the town of Oak Harbor, home to a naval air station and a fun brewpub, the Oak Harbor Pub and Brewery. Whidbey Island Brewing Company's homebase has a restaurant and patio for families, as well as a beer bar, a snug, and a game room area.

Travel another dozen miles to Coupeville, a little town facing the Washington mainland, that is home to Captains City Brewing Company. Continue on to the very charming town of Langley to spend the night at a bed and breakfast, or end your journey by taking the ferry from Clinton to Mukilteo on the mainland. At the ferry landing in Mukilteo, you can pop into the Diamond Knot Brewing Company & Alehouse, or nip up the hill a few blocks for a calzone and a pint at Eagle Brewing Company and Riley's Pizza.

For an extended tour, cross from Whidbey Island to the Olympic Peninsula via the Keystone–Port Townsend ferry run. Port Townsend makes a great first stop on the peninsula, with the Water Street Hotel and Maxwell's Pub as a homebase, and the great beers of the Port Townsend Brewing Company on tap around town.

Cross Hood Canal onto the Kitsap Peninsula to turn the journey southward. It isn't long before you'll come to Poulsbo, home of the Hood Canal Brewery. Keep your eyes open for their kegs on tap and their bottles for sale throughout these parts as you continue down the peninsula to Silverdale, and some great pub fare and craft beers at Silver City Brewing Company. Just a few blocks away is the Heads Up Brewing Company, too. If you're up for a sidetrip, drive across the Agate Passage bridge onto Bainbridge Island and check out the undersea décor and specialty smoked cuisine at the Sound Brewery & Smokehouse. A ferry from Bainbridge takes you to downtown Seattle.

From the Kitsap Peninsula, take a jaunt south, which brings you to the southern tip of Puget Sound. Here, on one of the remote fingers of the Puget Sound's saltwater, Washington's state capital is home to the Fish Brewing Company, an excellent craft brewery with a taproom serving its line of Fishtail Ales. For more craft beer adventures from here, head north to Woodland, Tacoma, and Puyallup, where you'll find a few Ram Restaurant & Big Horn Brewery locations (including the original), as well as several other high quality brewpubs, such as the Harmon Pub & Brewery in Tacoma and the Powerhouse Restaurant & Brewery in Puyallup.

Throughout whatever portion of this brew tour you choose to do, you'll find gorgeous natural areas. All along the shores of Puget Sound there are excellent birdwatching opportunities, from Nisqually in the south, to the Skagit River with its bald eagle season, and the Skagit Flats' snow goose season. This region is renowned for its sea kayaking as well, and there are some outstanding lowland hikes up and down the coastline. No matter what your mode of travel, be on the lookout for orcas and dolphins in the water. Whether you see a pod or not, with all the out-of-doors adventure to be found in the area, you'll still have the makings of your very own whale's tale for the evening's rounds of ale.

Silver City Brewing Company

Established 1996

2799 NW Myhre Road • Silverdale, WA 98383
(360) 698-5879

Silverdale is the shopping destination for much of the Kitsap Peninsula, and Silver City Brewing Company is conveniently located right by the mall. Playing to the shopping crowd, this brewpub is a family-oriented restaurant. And a big one at that—with two seating areas downstairs and a loft above, as well as a forty-seat patio that is open in the summer.

Owners Scott and Steve Houmes have taken a regular strip-mall restaurant space and turned it into a bright, fun brewpub experience, with a diverse menu and an equally diverse beer lineup. High ceilings draw your eyes up to the balcony seating, next to the grain loft for the gravity-fed grist mill and hopper.

Brewer Don Spencer, formerly of Thomas Kemper Brewery, juggles five different yeast strains to produce the brewpub's distinctive beers. Silver City's standards start with the full-flavored Big Daddy's ESB, and move up in gravity through Clear Creek Pale Ale and rich and peaty MacFarlane's Scotch Ale, to the black and smooth Panther Lake Porter. Then, there are the standard authentic Bavarian hefeweizen and Gold Mountain Pilsner. Seasonal beers have included Copper Mountain Maibock, a winter bock, an IPA and a dunkelweizen. Every Wednesday the bar staff taps a cask-conditioned ale, but you'd better be there early to get a taste.

The restaurant serves a collection of appetizers, burgers, seafood dishes, and pizzas. Under "Pub Favorites" you'll find items such as Silver City Gumbo, or for just a snack, try the Gorgonzola Pub Fries.

DIRECTIONS: From the Bainbridge Island ferry dock head north on Highway 305 for about 15 miles to the junction with Highway 3. Take Highway 3 south about 10 miles to the Silverdale exit. At the end of the exit ramp, turn left onto Kitsap Mall Boulevard. Go to the second light and turn left on Randall Street. The Kitsap mall is on your right, and the brewpub is at the northeast end of the mall. From Highway 303, take the Silverdale Way exit and turn south. Take Silverdale to Myhre Road and turn right. The brewpub is on your left.

Hours: 11 a.m.–10 p.m. Monday–Thursday; 11 a.m.–11 p.m. (11:30 in summer) Friday and Saturday; 11 a.m.–9 p.m. Sunday
Children: Yes, except in the bar
Food: Upscale pub fare
Entertainment: TV sports, quarterly brewmasters dinners
Smoking: No
Payment: Checks, Visa, MC, AmEx
Beer to go: Yes, draft

Heads Up Brewing Company

Established 1998

9960 Silverdale Way NW • Silverdale, WA 98383
(360) 337-2739 • www.youbrew.com

The Heads Up Brewing Company combines the full service on-premise-brewing experience for the interested hobbyist, with the production of their own house brews for the marketplace. If you've ever wanted to try making your own beer but didn't want to invest in a lot of equipment, you can give it whirl on one of Heads Up's half-dozen 30-gallon kettles. You can also try your hand at making sodas, wines and hard ciders using the dozens of recipes available.

Owner Ted Farmer also brews beers on contract for several local taverns. The Heads Up facility includes a tasting room where you can for sampling beers that you can look for elsewhere, or consider brewing for yourself. The establishment offers a seating area with tables, chairs, and a service counter. Computers at Heads Up can be used for internet access, as well as for designing homebrew labels and flyers. Children are welcome, and there are TVs and darts for entertainment.

The most popular house brews are the Pub Bitter, the Cream of Porter, and the Nordic Brown. Many others are brewed on the three-barrel system (The Brew Store, Ontario) and rotated into the lineup. A blonde ale is available in the summer months and the crowd-pleasing Imperial Stout is brewed when the weather turns chilly. You'll always find the Heads Up Root Beer on tap. If you're more interested in hard ciders and wines, you'll be pleased to have those to sample as well—all under one roof.

Hours: 1–10 p.m. Tuesday–Friday; Noon–8 p.m. Saturday; 2–7 p.m. Sunday; by appointment only Monday
Children: Yes
Food: No
Entertainment: Steel-tip and electronic darts, TV sports, internet access
Smoking: No
Payment: Checks, Visa, MC
Beer to go: Yes, draft

DIRECTIONS: From the Bainbridge Island ferry dock head north on Hwy 305 for about 15 miles to the junction with Hwy 3. Take Hwy 3 south about 10 miles to the Silverdale exit. At the end of the exit ramp, turn left onto Kitsap Mall Boulevard. At the second light turn left on Randall Street. Take Randall to Silverdale Way. The brewpub is on Silverdale Way. From Highway 303, take the Silverdale Way exit and turn south. Take Silverdale to the Kitsap Mall.

Hood Canal Brewery

Established 1996

25877 Tytler Road NE • Poulsbo, WA 98370
(360) 697-1673

There's a small ranch just outside Poulsbo, near the Hood Canal Bridge. The land here is rolling, with stands of forest interspersed with farms, orchards and livestock. Saltwater is close by—about a mile as the seagull flies. On the property next to this mini-ranch is a house with a couple of nondescript out-buildings, in one of which is a small brewhouse.

An instructor by profession, owner and brewer Don Wyatt worked briefly for the Thomas Kemper Brewery in Poulsbo prior to its closing in 1997. Wyatt now runs his own brewing operation, using a seven-barrel system by Elliott Bay Metal Fabricating. His beers are widely available on draft and in bottles in Kitsap, Mason and Jefferson Counties, and in select locations throughout the Puget Sound area.

Hood Canal's three standard ales are all robust Northwest interpretations of English-style ales. Dosewallips Special Pale Ale, named for a river on the Olympic Peninsula, is a balanced Pale Ale, golden in color. South Point Porter, named for the point of land where the Hood Canal Bridge stands today, but was once a ferry crossing, sports a rich, chocolatey head. Agate Pass Amber, a rich malty brew with a handsome copper color and a full, flowery hop aroma, is named for the waterway that separates Bainbridge Island from the Olympic Peninsula. Past seasonals have included Big Beef Oatmeal Stout, and Dabob Pale (as in Dabob Bay)—a lighter, crisper version of the house pale ale—and Wyatt doesn't skimp on the hops.

Groups are welcome for a tasting; just give a call to see if Don's available, and he'll give you directions to find your way on up the hill. Check out his hop vines as you enter the property.

Hours: Tours by appointment
Children: Yes
Food: No
Entertainment: No
Smoking: No
Payment: Checks
Beer to go: No

DIRECTIONS: Call for directions

Port Townsend Brewing Company

Established 1997

330 10th Street, Suite C • Port Townsend, WA 98368
(360) 385-9967

Port Townsend is set on a point of land overlooking both the Puget Sound and the Strait of Juan de Fuca. The old-town area, situated on the water's edge, is rightly renowned for its great charm. Shops, restaurants, historic hotels, and cafés occupy buildings dating from the late nineteenth and early twentieth centuries.

The modern-day Port Townsend Brewing Company is a brewery taproom that draws a great mix of clientele, from locals, to tourists, to anglers and other mariners in port. Very small and full of character, it's tucked into the back of a warehouse. It fills with quite a few happy patrons in the evenings, who enjoy cask-conditioned real ales flowing from beer engines and cold taps alike, and sit out on the tiny patio.

Usually, food is not served, but you can try to schedule your visit to coincide with one of their special occasions. In summer, Friday evenings are sometimes oyster and stout fests.

Brewer Guy Sands is a self-trained brewer with a self-sufficient outlook on brewhouse design. He's pieced together some Ripley Stainless brewing equipment and a locally fabricated, seven-barrel gas-fired kettle, along with some dairy tanks and grundies. Try Port Townsend Brewing Company's tangy Bitter End IPA, made with five types of hops. Sands also makes a light-bodied brown porter that's chocolatey with hints of smoke, as well as a rich, dry stout served on nitro. Past seasonal brews have included Boatyard Bitter and a English-style old ale made with Belgian rock candy. If you get hooked on their fine brews, you can find Port Townsend Brewing Company tap handles around the Puget Sound area.

Hours: 3–7 p.m. Monday; 2–7 p.m. Tuesday–Thursday; 2–9 p.m. Friday; 12–7 p.m. Saturday–Sunday
Children: Yes
Food: No
Entertainment: No
Smoking: No
Payment: Checks
Beer to go: Yes, draft

DIRECTIONS: From the ferry dock, turn south (left) onto Highway 20, which becomes Sims Way. Follow this road about 1 mile to Haines Street—watch for the shopping center on the west side of 20/Sims. (From the south, follow Highway 20 north to Port Townsend and watch for the shopping center.) Turn east on Haines Street into the marine-front industrial park. The brewery and taproom are in the south end of the first blue warehouse building on your right (Building No. 2).

Water Street Hotel/Maxwell's Brewery & Pub

Established 1998

Maxwell's: 126 Quincy Street • Port Townsend, WA 98368
(360) 379-6438
Water Street Hotel: 635 Water Street
(360) 385-5467 or (800) 735-9810
www.virtualwebdesign.com/hotel/home.htm

The Waterstreet Hotel's location in the middle of Port Townsend's historic downtown makes it a worthy destination for a unique getaway. Port Town send is somewhat off the beaten track, and has thereby retained much of its old-time charms. If you're looking for a place to forget about the twenty-first century by dawdling in a coffee shop furnished in exquisite Victorian style, or strolling along timbered boardwalks just above the choppy surf, this may be a good choice for you.

The Waterstreet Hotel and Maxwell's Brewery & Pub are housed in the historic N.D. Hill Building. Built in 1889 and renovated in 1990, this building houses both the brewpub and the hotel, two separate businesses that offer a symbiotic homebase for the traveler. This brick building serves as an anchor to the historic Quincy Street Dock, and is within easy walking distance of the entire downtown area, and even the ferry dock.

The hotel's second- and third-story rooms are quaint and sparsely furnished, with high ceilings; some rooms offer views of the Cascades or the Olympics. The furnishings include some antiques, with pedestal sinks in the bathrooms. A few suites boast kitchenettes or private decks complete with porch swings overlooking Port Townsend Bay. The ground floor includes a Native American art gallery and a classic saloon called the Town Tavern, in addition to Maxwell's pub.

The brewpub is a handsome brick space

Hours: Summer, 11:30 a.m.– 11 p.m. daily; winter, call for hours
Children: Yes, except bar area
Food: Pub fare, steaks and seafood
Entertainment: Steel-tip darts, occasional live music on weekends
Smoking: No
Payment: Checks, Visa, MC, AmEx
Beer to go: Yes, draft

with a high ceiling and original carved wood trim and wainscotting. Antique tables and chairs, along with a few huge potted plants, complete the period feel of the place. Upon entering, the only tip-off that you're in a brewpub rather than a restaurant is a small copper brew tank perched decoratively above the dining room.

Ferry boats will come and go as you take an afternoon meal on the waterside deck, or toss some darts in the loft area above the bar after dark. The lunch menu offers burgers and sandwiches, while the dinner fare is a collection of salads, pastas, steaks, and seafood. Ask about the nightly seafood specials and the homemade desserts.

Maxwell's is a family-run operation. Owner/brewer Chris Sudlow is in business with his mother, the chef, and his siblings, who work in the bar and dining room. Sudlow is a self-trained brewer, whose construction background came in handy for things such as building a cold room in the basement with serving tanks feeding up to cold-taps at the bar. He also pieced together his brewing system from some Ripley Stainless equipment and fermenters fabricated in Mexico. You can view the open-air brewhouse directly behind the bar by stopping into the nook-like microbar area to check the score of the game on the TV or to order a cocktail.

Sudlow usually keeps a half-dozen standard brews on tap at Maxwell's, including a blonde bitter, a pale ale, a nut brown ale, a porter, and a dark copper-colored beer called Red Roaster. (Try the nut brown.) His first couple of seasonals were a Pilsner and an oatmeal stout. You can stop into the Town Tavern during your stay as well. This traditional joint is a good place to have a drink and a smoke, play some darts, and maybe catch some live rock 'n roll or bluegrass on the weekend.

DIRECTIONS: From the ferry dock, turn north (right) onto Highway 20, which becomes Water Street as it enters downtown. From the South, follow Highway 20 until it becomes Water Street. The hotel/brewpub is on the corner of Water and Quincy Streets, on the east side of Water Street. The hotel entrance is on Water Street and the brewpub entrance is on Quincy Street.

Sound Brewery & Smokehouse

Established 1999

403 Madison Avenue, Suite 100 • Bainbridge, WA 98110
(206) 842-9478

B ainbridge Island is arguably one of the most attractive places to live in the world, with immediate proximity to downtown Seattle via public ferry, but with the culture and landscape of the idyllic Kitsap Peninsula. There is easy access to the peninsula as well, via a bridge that spans the water from Bainbridge to the Port Madison Indian Reservation near the town of Poulsbo.

The Sound Brewery and Smokehouse on Bainbridge Island is a Northwest brewpub through-and-through, with unique décor, done up to feel as if you're underwater. The walls are a deep royal blue, with a collection of fish art, most notably the iron salmon sculptures mounted on the dining room walls. A salmon is also the centerpiece for the bar's cold-tower, and the bar itself is artfully sculpted to resemble a rocky coastline.

The small dining room features tiered seating levels that maximize privacy, and outside, a covered patio overlooks an open air plaza and fountain. The menu's "small plates" include Dungeness crab and corn fritters, and organic spinach salad with a bleu cheese vinaigrette. The "large plates" include chipotle-braised ribs, roasted half-chicken, or grilled salmon on Tuscan toast. After dinner, you can catch a movie at the theater right in the same complex as the brewpub.

Publicans Jon and Pam Henderson come from a background in the restaurant business and as homebrewers. Pam is in charge of the 7½ barrel brewhouse by Ripley Stainless. She makes four standard ales: a golden, an amber, a stout, and the Bainbridge Island Pale Ale, a very pale brew with assertive hop flavor and a creamy head. Her first pair of seasonals include an American-style wheat, with a rounded malty character, and an English-style nut brown.

DIRECTIONS: From the Highway 305 bridge, continue onto Bainbridge Island to the third traffic light. Turn right onto High School Road, then turn left on Madison. The brewpub is two blocks down Madison on your right. From the ferry dock, follow the signs to City Center and turn left on Winslow Way. Follow Winslow through the main core of the town and turn right on Madison. The brewpub is a block up Madison on your left.

Hours: 11:30 a.m.–midnight
Children: Yes, except in the bar
Food: Upscale pub fare, smoked meats and seafood
Entertainment: Pool table, live blues/rock/jazz on weekends
Smoking: No
Payment: Visa, MC
Beer to go: Yes, draft

Region 2: Seattle/Tacoma & Metro Area

Ram International's Restaurants, Pubs, and Big Horn Breweries in Washington

Established 1995

Lakewood Ram & Big Horn Brewery
Established 1995
10019 59th Avenue SW
Lakewood, WA 98499-2757
(253) 584-3191; www.theram.com,
www.bighorn.com

Puyallup Ram & Big Horn Brewery
Established 1997
103 35th Avenue SE
Puyallup, WA 98374-1231
(253) 841-3317

Tacoma Ram & Big Horn Brewery
Established 1997
3001 N Ruston Way
Tacoma, WA 98402-5306
(253) 756-7886

CI Shenanigans Seafood & Chop
House
Established 1997
3017 N Ruston Way
Tacoma, WA 98402-5306
(253) 752-8811

Seattle Ram Café
Established 1998
4730 University Village Place NE
Seattle, WA 98105-5011
(206) 525-3565

Tir Na Nog
Established 1998
801 1st Avenue
Seattle, WA 98104-1404
(206) 264-2700

Spokane Ram & Big Horn Brewery
Established 1996
908 N Howard Street
Spokane, WA 99201-2261
(509) 326-3745

CI Shenanigans, Spokane
Established 1996
332 N Spokane Falls Court
Spokane, WA 99201-0238
(509) 455-5072

The Ram's brewpub-restaurants, now numbering five in Washington state, are fun places with lots of bright décor and comfortable dining areas. The massive menus feature long lists of appetizers, salads, burgers, and sandwiches. Most Ram locations offer a half-dozen chicken entrées, two or three pastas, and several seafood options. Often, there's a hint of a Southern theme to the menu selections, with items such as Cajun crawfish pasta, jambalaya, and Southern fried shrimp.

In addition to the large restaurant dining room, a Ram Big Horn has a pub space, also usually large. Some, such as the Lakewood property, have pool tables; other Rams offer electronic trivia or video golf games. Folks often gather for televised sports events at Ram pubs. Some locations have house teams, with contests and regular game-day events. Most locations have mug clubs for regulars, and offer a couple of traditional, English-style cask-conditioned ales, hand pulled. Ask if it's a "Firkin Friday"—a regular event where they tap a small cask right on the bar in the late afternoon. Some locations, notably the Tacoma Ram, offer big annual events, such as the 4th of July party on the waterfront in Tacoma, held in conjunction with the Washington Brewers Guild and the City of Tacoma, or their Halloween Party.

Hours: Restaurant, approximately 11 a.m.–11 p.m.; bar or pub, 11 a.m.– 2 a.m. Call individual locations for specifics.

Children: Yes, at portions of all locations

Food: Extensive menus of upscale pub fare

Entertainment: TV sports

Smoking: Yes in the pubs, no in the restaurants

Payment: Debit, Visa, MC, AmEx, Discover, Diners Club

Beer to go: Yes, draft

Based at the corporate head office at the Lakewood Ram, company brewmaster David Hollow oversees various brewers around the country. The head brewer for the Washington locations is Tom Hoare, who produces the Big Horn Brewery standardized recipes. The standard Big Horn beer lineup includes Big Red Ale (with a full malt palate), Washington Blonde (one of their most popular), Buttface Amber (with caramel malt flavors and a crisp finish), Big Horn Hefeweizen (a hybrid German and Northwest style), and Total Disorder Porter (a smooth, chocolatey brew with a creamy head that leaves nice Brussels lace on your glass). You'll always find the Big Horn Fruit Pale on tap as well. This light-bodied ale features different fruits, ranging from blackberries to apricots to peaches, in different batches.

The CI Shenanigans restaurants are more upscale than the Ram Big Horn pubs, though they still feature Northwest casual fine-dining, and offer sumptuous menus. The Tacoma location, right on Puget Sound, has a dock where you're welcome to put in your boat and have lunch on a patio overlooking the water. The CI Shenanigans locations do not make their own beer, but serve several Ram beers on tap, so you'll find fresh beer of a variety of types, brewed right next door at the Ram Big Horn.

DIRECTIONS: Visit their website, or call the location for directions

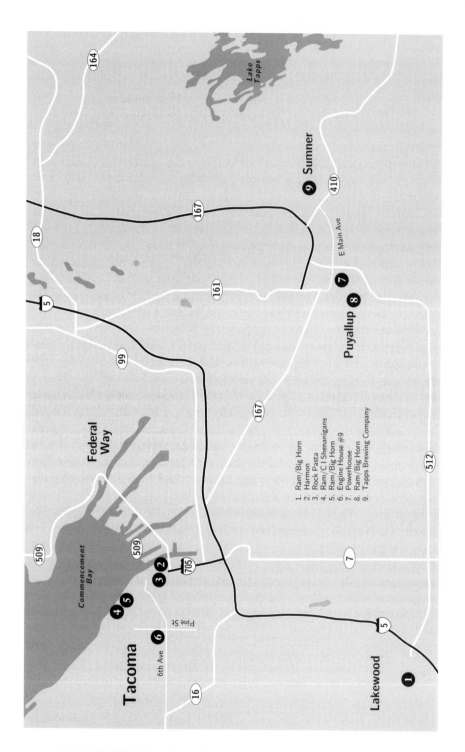

Lake Tapps

164

18

5

99

Federal Way

509

Commencement Bay

509

509

705

Pine St

6th Ave

Tacoma

16

167

161

167

7

512

5

Lakewood

E Main Ave

Sumner

Puyallup

410

167

1. Ram/Big Horn
2. Harmon
3. Rock Pasta
4. Ram/C I Shenanigans
5. Ram/Big Horn
6. Engine House #9
7. Powerhouse
8. Ram/Big Horn
9. Tapps Brewing Company

❶ ❷ ❸ ❹ ❺ ❻ ❼ ❽ ❾

Harmon Pub & Brewery

Established 1997

1938 Pacific Avenue • Tacoma, WA 98402
(253) 383-2739 • www.harmonbrew.com

The Harmon Pub & Brewery is located in the historic Harmon Building in downtown Tacoma. This big, handsome brewpub, marked with a silo in front of the building's façade, is becoming an anchor establishment for the new Tacoma Museum District.

The theme at the brewpub creates the feeling of a basecamp; their slogan is "Rivers, Mountains, Microbrew." Hikers, kayakers, skiers and climbers can meet over a pint to plan trips or sign up for excursions sponsored by Harmon in conjunction with Tahoma Outdoor Pursuits. A "trailhead" informational kiosk with internet access and books on outdoor and brewpub topics is an inspired addition.

A long bar stretches away from the entrance, with the brewhouse (Liquid Assets, fifteen-barrel system) visible behind it. A relaxed area with comfortable chairs conducive to relaxing conversation, is bordered by the open kitchen on one side and a stage for live music on the other. The House Musician is an acclaimed local blues figure, and Tuesdays are dance nights. The menu is Northwest-pubby— the calamari steaks with garlic Caesar fries are excellent!

The brewery is the sister operation of Marin Brewing Company in Larkspur, California. Brewer Mike Davis is making tasty brews—and a wide variety of them. There are four standard ales: Pinnacle Pale Ale, Wollochet Bay Wheat, Brown's Point Bitter, and the Puget Sound Porter—a great entry in the porter style, with a creamy mouthfeel, hints of licorice, and a roasty finish. You might also find an occasional lager, such as Paradise Pilsner or Fox Island Lager, or any of a wide range of other beers, such as Carbon River Common Beer, White River Rye, or McNeil Island Mild.

DIRECTIONS: From I-5 take the Tacoma City Center exit 133, Highway 705 North. Stay right to take the first exit, 21st Street/Highway 509 North. At the top of the ramp turn left over the highway. Take an immediate right onto Pacific Avenue; the brewpub is on your left. Free parking is available on weekends across Pacific Avenue in the Washington State History Museum lot.

Hours: 11 a.m.–10 p.m. Sunday, Monday, and Wednesday; 11 a.m.–2 a.m. Tuesday; 11 a.m.–midnight Thursday–Saturday
Children: Yes, except in the bar
Food: Full menu of pub fare, pizzas, seafood
Entertainment: Live music Thursday–Saturday; adventure sports info center
Smoking: No
Payment: All types
Beer to go: Yes, draft

Rock Pasta Brick Oven Pizza & Brewery

Established 1997

1920 Jefferson Street • Tacoma, WA 98402
(253) 627-7625 • www.wsim.com/rock_pasta

The Rock Wood-Fired Pizza & Brewery

4010 196th Street SW • Lynnwood, WA 98036
(425) 697-6007 • www.wsim.com/rock_pasta

The Rock Pasta Brick Oven Pizza restaurant has occupied this handsome nineteenth century brick, wedge-shaped island of Tacoma streetscape—aptly called "the Wedge"—since 1995. The Tacoma Rock Pasta got into the brewing business in 1997, along with a sister establishment in Seattle. The brewpub is located convenient to downtown and the new Museum District.

The unique angles of the brick brewpub building lend a European feeling, replete with details such as broad arches and old-fashioned lampposts. A door that is downright medieval in its heft and wrought metalwork opens into a hidden, private dining room. The main dining room features vivid murals and tall windows set in high walls, with ivy spilling downward.

The nationally recognized, wood-fired pizzas feature an extensive list of toppings, from sliced almonds, to eggplant, to teriyaki. A variety of pastas, appetizers, salads, and alder-smoked calzones round out the menu.

The small brewhouse here (Elliott Bay, four-barrel) supplies the beer for this establishment, while the Lynnwood location brews and serves a higher volume. Greg Doss brews a lineup of four standards: Sledge Hammer IPA, Wild Thing Honey Wheat, Rock Steady Red, and Jumpin' Jack Black Porter. A variety of seasonals show up, including the toasty-roasty St. Stephen's 90-Shilling Scotch Ale, James Brown Ale, a dunkelweizen, and a pair of stouts.

Hours: 11:30 a.m.–10:30 p.m. Sunday–Thursday; 11:30 a.m.–1 a.m. Friday and Saturday
Children: Yes, except in the bar
Food: Pizzas, calzones, pastas, salads
Entertainment: Video games
Smoking: Small, separated smoking section
Payment: Visa, MC, Check, Debit
Beer to go: No

DIRECTIONS: From I-5 take the Tacoma City Center exit 133, Highway 7 North. Stay right to take the first exit, 21st Street/Highway 509 North. At the top of the ramp turn left over the highway. Go uphill 2 lights and turn right on Jefferson. The brewpub is one block down, on the left. Call the Lynnwood location for hours and driving directions.

Engine House No. 9 Restaurant & Brewery

Established 1995

611 N Pine Street • Tacoma, WA 98406
(206) 272-3435

Engine House No. 9, built in 1907, is the oldest standing fire station in Tacoma. Besides firehouse paraphernalia, the establishment now offers a distinct British pub ambiance, complete with darts, low ceilings and a step-up-to-order food counter. The bar, a superb example of woodcrafting, was made in New Brunswick, Canada, and was originally part of the Old Saint Louis Tavern in Tacoma. It is situated in the rear of the pub. The Engine House offers spirituous liquors, and a 47-Beers-to-Taste Beer Club. Graduates who have tried them all earn a plaque, which is displayed on a wall of the pub.

The Engine House's brewery is located in a separate building. Between the dining room and brewery sits a true beer garden, with tables scattered among trees and flowering shrubs. The food is quite tasty and the portions generous, and the beer is served in twenty-ounce imperial pint glasses.

The Engine House and its sister establishment, The Powerhouse, in Puyallup (see page 110), are fortunate to have brewer Rhett Burris at the helm. Between the pair of seven-barrel breweries, Burris exercises his brewing creativity crafting a wide selection of fine beers. He makes different house brews at both the Engine House and the Powerhouse. But don't worry—as a visitor to either place, you can enjoy the best of both worlds with beers from the other establishment on tap along with the local brews.

Standard brews include Tacoma Brew (based on a recipe from Pacific Malting Company's pre-Prohibition brewery in Tacoma); the aptly named Fire Engine Red, a light and refreshing Belgian-style wit, the Four Alarm Oatmeal Stout, a Scottish ale, an extra special bitter, and an India pale ale. Look for the latest offering in their line of "Amocat Seasonal Ales."

DIRECTIONS: From I-5, take the Bremerton/ Gig Harbor exit onto Highway 16 West. Quickly cross into the right lane to catch the Sprague Street exit. Follow Sprague to 6th. Turn left on 6th, then right on Pine. The brewery is one block down Pine on the right.

Hours: 11 a.m.– midnight Sunday–Thursday; 11 a.m.–2 a.m. Friday and Saturday
Children: Yes
Food: Pub fare, pizzas and pastas
Entertainment: Darts
Smoking: No
Payment: Visa, MC
Beer to go: Yes, draft

Powerhouse Restaurant & Brewery

Established 1995

454 E Main Street • Puyallup, WA 98372
(206) 845-1370

The Powerhouse Restaurant & Brewery is the sister establishment to the Engine House No. 9 brewpub in Tacoma (see page 109). Both brewpubs are housed in early 1900s brick buildings restored by the owner/architect, Dusty Trail, and both are registered as historic. This building originally housed an electricity utility booster station, which explains the name and the recurring electrical theme in the décor.

The restaurant is a popular local eatery, with a menu that offers delicious options. Try one of the pizzas, or an entrée such as smoked salmon, capers, and red onions in a dill sauce. The main dining room has a high ceiling, with an enormous philodendron hanging from the massive original wooden beams that span the center of the building. Old electrical industry paraphernalia adorn the walls. Stretching up one corner of the main dining room is a long electrical voltage carrier known as a Jacob's Ladder, which sends an arcing current dancing up the wall any time a train passes by outside.

Hours: 11 a.m.–11 p.m. daily
Children: Yes
Food: Pub fare, pizzas and salads
Entertainment: TVs, Jacob's Ladder (see listing)
Smoking: No
Payment: Checks, Visa, MC
Beer to go: Yes

A small, square bar occupies the area immediately inside the front door, with the seven-barrel brewhouse visible behind a glass wall. This multi-level stainless brewery is set up in traditional gravity-fed vertical fashion, and is a striking sight from the dining area. The cozy mezzanine upstairs holds a lounge, with a fully stocked bar and a view of the dining area below.

Rhett Burris' standard beers include a dunkelweizen and a hefeweizen, a pale ale and an India pale ale, the Four Alarm Stout, and the Powerhouse Porter. Another regular offering is the delightful medium-bodied Amperage Amber, with plenty of smooth malt flavors and a fairly hefty body. In the cold season, they offer a winter warmer, and year-round you can find beers on tap here from the Engine House No. 9, too.

DIRECTIONS: From I-5, take 161 East or 167 East to Puyallup. On 161, follow it as it becomes Meridian about seven miles inside Puyallup. Turn left on Main. The brewery is 4 blocks down on your left. On 167, follow it to 512 West. Then take the Pioneer Square exit. Turn left on Pioneer, then right on 5th. The brewery is in the three-story brick building.

THE SEATTLE ALEHOUSE SCENE

The growing demand for quality Northwest ales has, in turn, created a demand for multi-tap pubs in many cities throughout the region. Whether an establishment is a tavern, a pub, or a restaurant, if it offers many different craft-brewed beers on tap, it is known as an alehouse. Early in the Pacific Northwest microbrewing renaissance, Portland Established itself as a city of many brewpubs and fewer microbreweries, while Seattle went the other direction. Prior to about 1996, Seattle boasted hardly any brewpubs, but several microbreweries and an assortment of neighborhood pubs that collectively refined the alehouse formula.

Though certainly not unique to Seattle, the alehouse phenomenon became the city's forte in the new craft beer age of the 1990s. The alehouse setting is an ideal way for the casual beer enthusiast to sample beers from a variety of breweries in one sitting.

Many alehouses also hire craft breweries to make house beers for them under contract, a lucrative and steady business happily obliged by brewing outfits. The lively alehouse scene in Seattle is particularly given to relationships such as these. Two of Mac & Jack's popular ales, African Amber and Serengeti Wheat, were originally house brews at the Woodland Park Pub. Newer breweries continue to foster these relationships; for example, Captains City Brewing Company, makes four different variations of a red ale for four different contract house brews.

Legend has it that the multi-tap alehouse phenomenon began in 1984, when Cooper's Northwest Alehouse on Lake City Way emerged from what was formerly a modest, traditional tavern. Close on its heels was the Virginia Inn Tavern perched above Pike Place Market. These ventures proved to be successful, and before long other entrepreneurs decided to "tap into" the alehouse concept.

Several enjoyable tour possibilities are available among the many clusters of alehouses within the city. The collection of alehouses along 45th and University Avenue in the University District is an excellent example. Within a few blocks are such diverse public houses as The Blue Moon, The College Inn, The Unicorn, and The Rainbow Inn. The next step for the local enthusiast is a larger tour encompassing several of these clusters over multiple sessions. Located at the famous Pike Place Market are both Kell's Irish Pub and The Virginia Inn (featured in the film "Singles"), making the market a great starting point for an alehouse tour.

A few blocks up 1st Avenue in Belltown is the Belltown Pub, known for its Brewmaster's Dinners, which match imaginative multiple courses with handcrafted beers. Heading back down 1st Avenue is Pioneer Square's loosely affiliated group of pubs, including The Bohemian, J&M Café and the Pacific Alehouse. The Pioneer Square area is particularly good for pub crawls on weekend nights, when a single cover charge is good for entrance into all neighborhood pubs! However, this bargain often draws crowds of college students, resulting in long lines and plenty of waiting.

The following list of alehouses in the Seattle area, while definitely not exhaustive, will get you started. The alehouses are divided by geographic regions and the neighborhoods covered in that region, and are listed alphabetically. Ask your favorite bartender for ideas about neighboring alehouses and breweries as well, and create your own mini-tour. All these establishments have at least ten craft beers on tap. For a sample list of alehouses throughout the Pacific Northwest, see page 242.

NORTHEAST SEATTLE
(BALLARD, FREMONT, GREEN LAKE, PHINNEY RIDGE, QUEEN ANNE HILL)

74TH STREET ALEHOUSE; 7401 Greenwood Avenue N; (206) 784-2955
English-style pub with fifteen-plus craft beers on tap, cask-conditioned ales, upscale pub fare. One of Seattle's oldest alehouses, it is sister to Hilltop Alehouse.

BAD ALBERT'S TAP AND GRILL; 5100 Ballard Avenue NW; (206) 782-9623
Upscale pub with ten-plus craft beers on tap, good pub fare including breakfast. Live blues/rock/jazz on Thursday and Saturday; establishment was named for the owner's cat.

BALLARD GRILL & ALEHOUSE; 4300 Leary Way NW; (206) 782-9024
Spacious, blue collar sport bar with fifteen-plus craft beers on tap. Pool tables, darts, basic pub fare.

BALLARD FIREHOUSE FOOD & BEVERAGE CO.; 5429 Russell Avenue NW; (206) 784-3516
Pub and live music venue with forty-plus craft beers on tap. Live blues/rock/ swing seven days.

THE BUCKAROO; 4201 Fremont Avenue N; (206) 643-3161
Rustic tavern with frequent Harley scene and fifteen-plus craft beers on tap. Pub fare, pool, pinball and video games.

CONOR BYRNES PUB; 5140 Ballard Avenue NW; (206) 784-3640
Irish pub with fifteen-plus craft beers on tap, steel-tip darts; known to pour one

of America's best Guiness pints. Basic bar snacks, but The Other Coast Café delivers sandwiches.

DUBLINER; 3405 N Fremont Avenue; (206) 548-1508
Rustic Irish pub specializing in imports, ten-plus craft beers on tap, Irish pub fare.

DUKE'S GREENLAKE CHOWDER HOUSE; 7850 Greenlake Drive N; (206) 522-4908
Restaurant with fifteen-plus craft beers on tap; specializes in seafood.

FLOYD'S PLACE BEER & BBQ; 521 1st Avenue N; (206) 284-3542
Sports bar with picnic tables next to Seattle Center/Key Arena. Twenty-plus craft beers on tap, cask conditioned ales, live music on Fridays, pool and darts, game-boards. Pub menu featuring applewood-smoked BBQ.

GEORGE AND THE DRAGON PUB; 206 N 36th; (206) 545-6864
British pub with ten-plus craft beers on tap, pool, steel-tip darts. British pub fare, and a wide selection of imports.

GREEN LAKE ALEHOUSE; 7305 Aurora Avenue N; (206) 781-8337
Smoke-free establishment on Highway 99 with ten-plus craft beers on tap, shuffleboard.

HILLTOP ALEHOUSE; 2129 Queen Anne Avenue N; (206) 285-3877
English-style pub with fifteen-plus craft beers on tap, cask-conditioned ales. Upscale pub fare; sister to 74th Street Alehouse.

HOYT'S PUB; 1527 Queen Anne Avenue N; (206) 284-2656
Sports-oriented pub with fifteen-plus craft beers on tap, pool and darts; nicely renovated after a recent fire. "Finest Creole and Cajun cuisine in the Northwest."

LA BOHEME TAVERN; 6119 Phinney Avenue N; (206) 783-3002
In business since 1934, with twelve-plus craft beers on tap. Pub fare, pool and darts, game boards, eclectic crowd.

LATONA PUB; 6423 Latona Avenue NE; (206) 525-2238
Great neighborhood pub in Green Lake with twelve-plus craft beers on tap and no mega-brews on tap (one of Seattle's best bottled micro selections). Pub grub fare, live music on weekends; original of Bob Brenlin's group of establishments.

NICKERSON STREET SALOON; 318 Nickerson Street; (206) 284-8819
Neighborhood pub across the Fremont Bridge with patio seating and twelve-plus craft beers on tap. Pool and darts, patio, upscale pub fare.

OLD PECULIAR; 1722 NW Market Street; (206) 782-8886
Irish pub with fifteen-plus craft beers on tap, steel-tipped darts games and live music Saturdays. Specializes in imports and offers a stocked bookshelf.

PARK PUB (formerly Woodland Park Pub); 6114 Phinney Avenue N; (206) 784-3455
Full menu pub with fifteen-plus craft beers on tap (no megabrews). Pool and darts, upscale pub fare; "seek the unique ales."

RAY'S BOATHOUSE; 6049 Seaview Avenue NW; (206) 782-0094
Upscale restaurant overlooking Puget Sound, with twenty-plus craft beers on tap, upscale Northwest cuisine. Hosts annual summer beer festival.

READING GAOL; 418 NW 65th; (206) 783-3002
Neighborhood pub with fifteen-plus craft beers on tap.

RED DOOR ALEHOUSE; 3401 N Fremont Avenue; (206) 547-7521
Pub with twenty-plus craft beers on tap. Full menu, electronic darts.

SIX DEGREES; 7900 East Greenlake Drive N; (206) 523-1600
Bistro-style pub overlooking Greenlake with twelve-plus craft beers on tap, cask-conditioned ales, and full menu.

THE SLOOP; 2830 NW Market Street; (206) 782-3330
Tavern with ten-plus craft beers on tap. First tavern in Seattle to pour Redhook's Ballard Bitter.

SULLY'S SNOW GOOSE; 6119 Phinney Avenue N; (206) 783-3002
Bar with twenty-plus craft beers on tap, game boards.

TRIANGLE TAVERN; 3507 Fremont Place N; (206) 632-0880
Chicago-style pub with fifteen-plus craft beers on tap, full bar, and full menu.

T.S. MCHUGH'S; 21 Mercer Street; (206) 282-1910
Upscale Irish pub with twenty-plus craft beers on tap, Irish and Northwest fare. Live Irish and Celtic music on weekends.

NORTHEAST SEATTLE
(GREENWOOD, LAKE CITY, MADISON PARK, MAPLE LEAF, MONTLAKE, RAVENNA, ROOSEVELT, UNIVERSITY DISTRICT, WALLINGFORD)

ATTIC ALEHOUSE & EATERY; 4226 E Madison Street; (206) 323-3131
Full-menu pub with fifteen-plus craft beers on tap, live music on weekends, pool and steel-tip darts. Breakfast on Sundays.

BLUE MOON TAVERN; 712 NE 45th St; (206) 545-9775
Historic ex-Beat Generation tavern with twelve-plus craft beers on tap, pool and darts, pinball. Past hangout of Pulitzer Prize-winning poets, now the home of some of Seattle's best restroom graffiti.

BLUE STAR; 4512 Stone Way N; (206) 548-0345
All-American diner with fifteen-plus craft beers on tap. Eggs Cetera's kitchen focuses on breakfasts.

BRICKS BROADVIEW GRILL; 10555 Greenwood Avenue N; (206) 367-8481
Restaurant with ten-plus craft beers on tap, patio deck, upscale pub fare.

COLLEGE INN PUB; 4006 University Way NE; (206) 634-2307
Basement English-style bar with ten-plus craft beers on tap, steel-tip darts, pinball. Basic pub fare.

COOPER'S ALEHOUSE; 8065 Lake City Way NE; (206) 522-2923
Founding member of the Seattle alehouse scene, with pool and steel-tip darts, twenty-five-plus craft beers on tap, cask-conditioned ales, and pub grub. Host of the Northwest Ale Festival.

CROSSWALK TAVERN; 8556 Greenwood Avenue N; (206) 789-9691
Sports bar with fifteen-plus craft beers on tap, electronic darts, pinball, video games, pull tabs. Italian cuisine.

DANTÉ'S; 5300 Roosevelt Way NE; (206) 525-1300
Full menu pub with ten craft/import beers on tap. All-American fare, game boards and pool tables.

DUCHESS TAVERN; 2827 NE 55th Street; (206) 527-8606
Bar and grill with twelve-plus craft beers on tap, pool tables and darts, pull-tabs, pub fare and pizza. Home of the Beer Hunter Club.

FIDDLER'S INN; 9219 35th Avenue NE; (206) 525-0826
Cozy neighborhood pub with ten-plus all-craft beers on tap, pub fare, beer garden, live music on weekends. Sister establishment to the Latona and Hopvine.

GLOBE TAVERN; 9736 Greenwood Avenue N; (206) 783-6727
Tavern with fifteen-plus craft beers on tap and remote-control trivia game, steel-tip darts, beer garden. English pub fare.

GRADY'S; 2307 24th Avenue E; (206) 726-5968
Restaurant/pub with ten-plus craft beers on tap, pool and darts. Upscale pub grub with lots of veggie choices.

LESCHI LAKE CAFÉ; 102 Lakeside Avenue S; (206) 328-2233
Restaurant with full bar overlooking Lake Washington with twelve-plus craft beers on tap. Large beer garden, known for seafood.

MAD DOG ALEHOUSE; 10200 Greenwood Avenue N; (206) 782-9056
Tavern with ten-plus craft beers on tap, pool tables and pull-tabs.

Maple Leaf Grill; 8909 Roosevelt Way NE; (206) 523-8449
Restaurant with ten-plus craft beers on tap.

Monkey Pub; 5305 Roosevelt Way NE; (206) 523-6457
Small pub with ten-plus craft beers on tap, pool and darts, pinball.

Murphy's Pub; 1928 N 45th Street; (206) 634-2110
Handsome Irish pub and college hang-out with fifteen-plus craft beers on tap, cask-conditioned ales, steel-tip darts. Good pub fare.

Pacific Inn Pub; 3501 Stone Way N; (206) 547-2967
Neighborhood tavern with ten craft beers on tap, pub fare with lots of seafood. Owner, Robert Julien, was the singing bartender at the original Jake O'Shaugnessey's.

Rainbow Inn (formerly the Kerryman); 722 NE 45th Street; (206) 545-2960
Live-music venue with ten-plus craft beers on tap.

Rory's; 2245 Eastlake Avenue; (206) 329-9071
Tavern with fifteen-plus craft beers on tap and pool tables/pinball. Upscale bar menu.

Santa Fe Café; 2255 NE 165th Street; (206) 524-7736. Second location: 5910 Phinney Avenue N; (206) 738-9755
Restaurant with ten-plus craft beers on tap, Southwest cuisine.

Teddy's Tavern; 1012 NE 65th Street; (206) 526-9174
Sports-oriented tavern with occasional Harley scene and ten craft beers on tap, patio, pool and darts, ping pong.

Wedgwood Alehouse & Café; 8515 35th Avenue NE; (206) 527-2676
Tavern with fifteen-plus craft beers on tap and live music. Good pub fare, small beer garden.

CENTRAL SEATTLE
(BELLTOWN, CAPITOL HILL, DOWNTOWN, FIRST HILL, PIONEER SQUARE, PIKE PLACE MARKET)

Athenian Inn; 1517 Pike Place; (206) 624-7166
Pike Place Market's quintessential bar and grill overlooking Elliott Bay, with ten-plus craft beers on tap. Menu specializes in seafood.

Belltown Pub; 2322 1st Avenue; (206) 728-4311
Full-menu upscale pub with fifteen-plus craft beers on tap.

Bohemian Café; 111 Yesler Way; (206) 447-1514
Restaurant and bar with ten-plus craft beers on tap, live music; college hangout.

Brooklyn Seafood, Steak & Oyster House; 1212 2nd Avenue; (206) 224-7000
Restaurant and bar with twelve-plus craft beers on tap, beer sampler set-ups. Hosts Northwest Oyster and Microbrewery Festival in the fall.

CASA U-BETCHA; 2212 1st Avenue; (206) 441-1989
Mexican restaurant with ten-plus craft beers on tap.

COMET TAVERN; 922 E Pike Street; (206) 323-9853
Funky, rough-edged pub with ten-plus craft beers on tap. Just down the street from the Elysian Brewing Company's Public House.

CROCODILE CAFÉ; 2200 2nd Avenue; (206) 441-5611
Restaurant and bar with ten-plus craft beers on tap, live music and other performers. Occasional celebrity sightings.

DOC MAYNARD'S; 600 1st Avenue; (206) 682-4649
Restaurant and nightclub with ten-plus craft beers on tap, live music. Headquarters of the Seattle Underground Tour to view the pre-1889-fire underpinnings of Seattle.

DELUXE BAR & GRILL; 625 Broadway E; (206) 324-9697
Full menu pub with twelve-plus craft beers on tap and live music.

FLOYD'S PLACE BEER & BBQ; 521 1st Avenue N; (206) 284-3542
Sports bar with ten-plus next to Seattle Center/Key Arena. Pool and darts, TV sports.

F.X. MCRORY'S; 419 Occidental Avenue S; (206) 623-4800
Restaurant/sports alehouse known for its proximity to the Stadium District, and house oyster and microbrew pairings. Twenty-five-plus craft beers on tap (a dozen Christmas beers in the winter); "World's largest Bourbon selection." Anchor of a chain that includes J. O'Shaunaughassy's, Leschi, and T.S. McHugh's.

HOP SCOTCH; 322 15th Avenue E; (206) 322-4191
Scottish bar with upscale pub menu, fifteen-plus craft beers on tap. Excellent selection of 80-plus whiskeys.

HOPVINE; 507 15th Avenue E; (206) 328-3120
Full menu, upscale pub with twelve craft beer line. Live music venue. A Bob Brenlin establishment, along with Latona and Fiddler's.

J&M CAFÉ; 201 1st Street S; (206) 624-1670
Historic pub and college hang-out with stone table tops and ten-plus craft beers on tap, pub fare. One of Seattle's oldest bars.

JAZZ ALLEY; 2033 6th Avenue; (206) 441-9729
Restaurant and jazz club with ten-plus craft beers on tap. Live music most nights.

JERSEY'S ALL AMERICAN SPORTS BAR; 7th Avenue and Virginia Street; (206) 343-9377
Large sports bar with fifteen-plus craft beers on tap, lots of pool tables, electronic darts and other games. Pub fare.

KELL'S IRISH PUB; 1916 Post Alley; (206) 728-1916
Full-menu, upscale pub; sister establishment of pub by the same name in downtown Portland.

KINKORA; 518 E Pine Street; (206) 325-0436
Irish pub with ten-plus craft beers on tap and steel-tip darts.

McCORMICK & SCHMICK'S; 1103 1st Avenue; (206) 623-5500
Restaurant and saloon with ten-plus craft beers on tap. Menu specializes in seafood.

MERCHANTS CAFÉ; 109 Yesler Way; (206) 624-1515
Restaurant/alehouse with marble table tops and ornate bar that was shipped by sea from the Eastern U.S. Ten-plus craft beers on tap.

PIONEER SQUARE SALOON; 73 Yesler Way; (206) 628-6444
Historic bar with ten-plus craft beers on tap, pool and electronic darts. Bar snacks.

RC'S BILLIARDS, BREW AND EATERY (formerly Shakey's); 10 Broad Street; (206) 256-0100
Pub with fifteen-plus craft beers on tap. Pub fare with pizzas, pool, live music, beer garden.

ROANOKE PARK PLACE TAVERN; 2409 10th Avenue E; (206) 324-5882
Comfortable, neighborhood pub with ten-plus craft beers on tap, electronic darts, pub grub. Eclectic crowd, with regular Husky TV game events.

ROMPER ROOM; 106 1st Avenue N; (206) 284-5003
Dance club and bar with ten-plus craft beers on tap. Hardened Artery is the name of the restaurant; self-proclaimed "Alice in Wonderland meets the Little Mermaid."

VIRGINIA INN TAVERN; 1937 1st Street; (206) 728-1937
Light menu bar with twelve-plus craft beers on tap and sidewalk seating; one of Seattle's original alehouses; featured in the film "Singles."

VON'S; 619 Pine; (206) 621-8667
Upscale pub with full American menu and fifteen-plus craft beers on tap; known for their martinis and Manhattans.

MERCER ISLAND

ISLANDER PUB AND GRILL; 7440 SE 27th; (206) 232-0174
Full-menu pub with fifteen-plus craft beers and thirty-plus total on tap. Darts, pool and game boards.

Roanoke Tavern; 1825 72nd Avenue SE; (206) 232-0800
Neighborhood pub with ten-plus craft beers on tap, pool and pinball. In a house that was a speakeasy during Prohibition.

West Seattle

Alki Tavern; 1321 Harbor Avenue SW; (206) 932-9970
Sports bar with occasional Harley scene and fifteen-plus craft beers on tap; pool tables and video games. Full menu next door at Thai on Alki.

Admiral Pub; 2306 California Avenue SW; (206) 933-9500
Neighborhood pub with ten-plus craft beers on tap.

RockSport; 4209 SW Alaska Street; (206) 935-5838
Sports bar with big screen TV and twelve-plus craft beers on tap. Good pub fare, pool, darts and games.

Seattle Bottled-Beer Retail Shops

Big Star; 1117 N Northgate Way; Seattle, WA (206) 729-0797

Bottleworks; 1710 N 45th Street #3; Seattle, WA (206) 633-2437

Queen Anne Thriftway; 1908 Queen Anne N; Seattle, WA (206) 284-2530

Stumbling Monk; 1635 E Olive Way; Seattle, WA (206) 860-0916

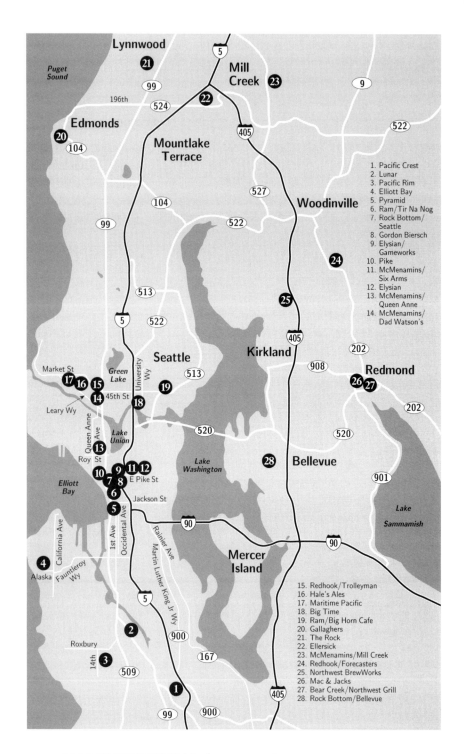

Puget
Sound

Lynnwood

Mill
Creek

Edmonds

Mountlake
Terrace

Woodinville

1. Pacific Crest
2. Lunar
3. Pacific Rim
4. Elliott Bay
5. Pyramid
6. Ram/Tir Na Nog
7. Rock Bottom/
   Seattle
8. Gordon Biersch
9. Elysian/
   Gameworks
10. Pike
11. McMenamins/
    Six Arms
12. Elysian
13. McMenamins/
    Queen Anne
14. McMenamins/
    Dad Watson's

Seattle

Kirkland

Redmond

Market St

Green
Lake

45th St

Leary Wy

Queen Anne Ave

Lake
Union

Roy St

Lake
Washington

Bellevue

Elliott
Bay

E Pike St

Lake
Sammamish

Jackson St

Mercer
Island

California Ave

Alaska

Fauntleroy Wy

1st Ave

Occidental Ave

Martin Luther King Jr Wy

Rainier Ave

15. Redhook/Trolleyman
16. Hale's Ales
17. Maritime Pacific
18. Big Time
19. Ram/Big Horn Cafe
20. Gallaghers
21. The Rock
22. Ellersick
23. McMenamins/Mill Creek
24. Redhook/Forecasters
25. Northwest BrewWorks
26. Mac & Jacks
27. Bear Creek/Northwest Grill
28. Rock Bottom/Bellevue

Roxbury

14th

Big Time Brewery & Alehouse

Established 1988

4133 University Way NE • Seattle, WA 98105
(206) 545-4509 • www.bigtimebrewery.com

Big Time, located on the main drag in Seattle's hip University District, is Seattle's oldest brewpub. Housed in an old building with a handsome wooden bar dating back a century, the brewpub is decorated in traditional pub style, with beer artifacts adorning the walls. The fourteen-barrel brewhouse is visible through wall-sized windows behind the bar. Given its age, the Big Time has served as an inspiration for many of Washington's newer brewpubs.

On any given day, you'll find a mix of University folks relaxing after work, students reading, and locals chatting. The pub's most unique offering is the shuffleboard set in the back room. Be sure to sign up on the chalkboard to get a turn. The deli sandwiches, prepared behind a traditional deli-style counter, are hard to beat. Layered with cold cuts or veggies stacked on a variety of good breads, these sandwiches are the perfect complement to a fresh pint or two. You can also choose from a selection of pizzas, baked potatoes, and other options.

The bar generally features ten or twelve high quality house beers on tap. These always include Prime Time Pale Ale, Atlas Amber Ale, Coal Creek Porter, and the unfiltered and very flavorful Bhagwhan's Best. Other options are drawn from brewer Kevin Forhan's pool of about thirty seasonals, such as Dublin Stout, Yulefest, Octoberfest, a Scottish ale, a brown ale, an unfiltered rye, a barley wine, an oatmeal stout, a Pilsner and a couple of other lagers. Their most popular brew is Bhagwhan's Best India Pale Ale, but be sure to try their Northwest-style amber, nicely balanced with good malt character and plenty of hop flavor.

DIRECTIONS: From I-5, take the 45th Street exit and turn east on 45th. Turn right on University Avenue, drive three blocks, and the brewpub is on your right.

Hours: 11:30 a.m.–12:30 a.m. Sunday–Thursday; 11:30 a.m.–1:30 a.m. Friday and Saturday
Children: No
Food: Pub fare, deli sandwiches, pizza
Entertainment: Shuffleboard
Smoking: Yes, in separate rooms
Payment: Visa, MC
Beer to go: Yes, draft

Elliott Bay Brewery & Pub

Established 1997

4270 California Avenue • Seattle, WA 98116
(206) 932-8695 • www.elliottbaybrewing.com

California Avenue between Alaska and Hudson Streets is a bustling small commercial center for the West Seattle neighborhood called Junction. At the Alaska Street end of this short district is an exquisitely restored brick building. Formerly the home of West Seattle Brewing Company (now Pacific Rim Brewing Co.), this homebrew house is currently the Elliott Bay Brewery & Pub.

You'll usually find it hopping—live blues or jazz playing while servers bring burgers and salads to lots of neighborhood folks, along with beers made and served only in-house. Brewer Doug Hindman, author of *Field Guide to Seattle Area Brewpubs and Tasting Rooms by Bike and Bus*, keeps three standard ales on tap There's usually a seasonal brew as well, and the pub also has a few guest taps. Elliott Bay IPA, Alembic Pale Ale, and No Doubt Stout are Hindman's regular offerings, while seasonals have included the likes of Rockin' Organic Rye and El Niño Fall Fest.

Wednesday is open mike night, so if you have talent, make a performance out of a visit. Monday night is Grateful Dead night, and on the weekends live mellow blues or cool jazz ripples out into the dining room and up to the game room.

All of the service areas line one side of the long, brick-walled space, and are open to the dining room: the pub in front, the seven-barrel brewhouse in the middle, and the kitchen in the rear. The menu is straightforward pub grub, but the burgers are big and you can choose a beef, veggie, or chicken burger. The salads are above-average with lots of veggies—this is one place to definitely get the salad instead of the fries. After dinner and a round of beer, a stretch of the legs could take you to Schmitz Viewpoint Park, a dozen blocks to the west, overlooking Puget Sound.

DIRECTIONS: From I-5 take Exit 163 West Seattle Freeway and head west. Go over the bridge to the top of the hill. At the fourth traffic light, turn right onto Alaska Street. Follow Alaska through two stop lights to California and turn left. The brewpub is half a block up on your left.

Hours: 11:30 a.m.–11 p.m. Monday–Thursday; 11:30 a.m.–1 a.m. Friday and Saturday; Noon–10 p.m. Sunday
Children: Yes, except during live music
Food: Pub fare
Entertainment: Pool tables (free on Tuesdays); live music most Wednesdays–Saturdays, Grateful Dead Mondays
Smoking: Yes, in upstairs mezzanine
Payment: Checks, Visa, MC
Beer to go: Yes, draft

Elysian Brewing Company & Public House

Established 1996

1221 E Pike Street • Seattle, WA 98122
(206) 860-1920 • www.elysianbrewing.com

Located on Capitol Hill, this spacious brewpub has an urban feel of the Seattle variety—hip, but understated. The Elysian's Public House is a straight shot up the hill from downtown.

Amidst the studied mish-mash of décor, the bar area is the decorating *pièce de résistance* here. An entirely copper-plated structure, the bar features an inlaid slice of old-growth wood formed naturally in the shape of the capital section of an ornate ancient Greek column. This piece of wood, a gift to owner and brewer Dick Cantwell, was the inspiration for the Elysian's Greek mythology theme, and its name. Above the bar a nifty tap system dispenses beer directly from tanks in the brewhouse via overhead pipes.

Hours: 11:30 a.m.–1 a.m. Monday–Friday; noon–1 a.m. Saturday–Sunday
Children: Yes, except bar area and Saturday after 8 p.m.
Food: Pub fare, pastas
Entertainment: Live music
Smoking: Designated area
Payment: Visa, MC
Beer to go: Yes, draft

The beers that flow from above (raising your consciousness toward Elysian heights), a combination of ales and lagers, have garnered Cantwell national recognition. Zephyrus Pilsner offers an authentic Pilsner flavor; an array of interesting bocks, such as the dark, malty Pandora's Bock, await the intrepid adventurer. The standard ales include Golden Fleece Ale, Perseus Porter, Dragon's Tooth Stout (a hefty Imperial), The Wise ESB, and the Immortal IPA. Seasonals might include a punch-packing Valkyrie Strong Ale, a best bitter, or a Belgian-style tripple. The Elysian also offers homemade sodas.

The full menu spans the realms of pub fare and eclectic soups, salads and entrées, with a wide selection for the vegetarians in your party. Try starting with a zesty cilantro vinaigrette salad and warm pita chips with hummus.

DIRECTIONS: From I-5 Northbound, take the Madison Street exit and turn right on Madison. Continue on Madison, cross Broadway, and turn left on 13th. The brewpub is on the corner of 13th and Pike. From I-5 Southbound, take the James Street exit and turn left on James. Go under the freeway and take the first left when you come out onto city streets. Turn right on Madison, cross Broadway to 13th. Turn left on 13th and find the brewpub on the corner of 13th and Pike.

Elysian Brewing Company/GameWorks

Established 1997

1511 7th Avenue • Seattle, WA 98101
(206) 283-4263 • www.gameworks.com

GameWorks establishments are *arcades extraordinaires* brought to you by the fun-loving guys at Hollywood's DreamWorks studio. The Elysian Brewing Company of Capitol Hill holds the contract for brewing in-house at the Seattle location of the GameWorks chain. This enormous place offers most forms of indoor leisure entertainment, from the latest in interactive video games to carnival midway-type basketball hoops to an internet café.

To partake of the various gaming options here, purchase a plastic debit card of game credits. Then wend your way through the race-car simulators to the martial-arts video games—or stake out the good old-fashioned pool tables. Consider a visit to the retro-room upstairs, where you'll find a fun assortment of first generation video games—remember Pac-Man, Centipede, and Space Invaders? They're all here.

When it's time for a breather from all the excitement, stop into a "Rejuvenation Station" for a bite and a drink. There are appetizers such as shrimp potstickers and jalapeño poppers, and meals ranging from pepperoni pizza to a turkey focaccia sandwich. And, while much of the beer served here is brought from the Elysian Brewing Company's Public House (a short journey for the fresh brew), a small brewing system in the lower level of GameWorks qualifies this as a brewpub.

The Elysian kiosk offers their full line of malted beverages in schooners, pints and pitchers. If you've been working up a sweat at the shooting range, refresh yourself with a Zephyrus Pilsner or a Golden Fleece Ale. Been battling electronic monsters? Perhaps you'll want a Perseus Porter or a Dragon's Tooth Stout. Or, maybe a glass of The Wise ESB or the Immortal IPA is just what you'll need to wash down a burger and fries before you go vanquish another virtual ninja.

Hours: 11 a.m.–midnight Monday–Thursday; 10 a.m.–1 a.m. Friday and Saturday; 10 a.m.–midnight Sunday
Children: Yes, with an adult until 8 p.m.
Food: Full menu of pub fare, pizza and sandwiches
Entertainment: Extensive arcade of video, interactive and other games
Smoking: No
Payment: Debit, Visa, MC
Beer to go: No

DIRECTIONS: From I-5 Northbound, take the Seneca Street exit and turn right on 6th Avenue. Go 3 blocks to Pike Street and turn right. GameWorks is on the corner of 7th Avenue and Pike Street. From I-5 Southbound, take the Stewart Street/Denny Way exit. Follow Stewart Street to 7th Avenue and turn left. GameWorks is two blocks up 7th on your right.

Gordon Biersch Brewing Company

Established 1998

600 Pine Street, 4th Floor • Seattle WA 98101
(206) 405-4205 • www.gordonbiersch.com

Gordon Biersch Brewing Company was founded in 1987 in Palo Alto, California. Today, there are ten Gordon Biersch Brewery restaurants—including their first in the Pacific Northwest, located on the fourth floor of Pacific Place in downtown Seattle.

Owing to its California origins, and the Bavarian predilections of co-founder Dan Gordon, Gordon Biersch is unlike any other brewery or brewpub in the Washington. It is not the first "chain" brewery to come to the state—Rock Bottom, Ram Big Horn and even Oregon-based McMenamins have been serving beers throughout the region for years. Rather, Gordon Biersch is the first chain operation to offer both an upscale restaurant atmosphere and menu, along with a lager-only brewery. In this way, it is reminiscent of the Mark James Group's downtown Vancouver, B.C. brewpub, Dix BBQ amd Brewery.

Hours: Open 11 a.m.–1 a.m. daily
Children: Yes, in the restaurant
Food: Full upscale menu
Entertainment: Live music most evenings
Smoking: Yes in the the bar
Payment: Checks, Visa, MC, AmEx
Beer to go: No

The Gordon Biersch restaurant in Pacific Place is stunning. While the expansive bar faces the indoor courtyard with views of the movie theater and retail stores in one direction, and the brewery in the other, the restaurant offers impressive views onto the commercial buildings of downtown Seattle. A partially exposed kitchen serves up tempting dishes ranging from smoky portabella mushroom appetizers to brick oven pizzas and Pacific Rim, Cajun, and Northwest-inspired entrées. Live jazz music imbues the bar with an upbeat, urban atmosphere.

Bavarian-styled lagers are the brews of the house. The small brewhouse is visible through windows behind the bar. The Gordon Biersch flagship lagers are a Pilsner, the popular Märzen, and a dunkel (a dark, malty unfiltered lager). Seasonals rotate regularly and include a variety of bock-style lagers and a summertime hefeweizen. The brewery is also fairly unusual in that it offers recommended pairings for their lagers, suggesting the best complement of food and beer.

DIRECTIONS: From the left lane on I-5 in Seattle heading north, take the Seneca Street exit, which curves to the right. Take a right onto 6th Avenue and follow 6th to Pine. Gordon Biersch is on the fourth floor of the Pacific Place building. There is a parking garage in the building.

Hale's Ales

Established 1995

4301 Leary Way • Seattle, WA 98107
(206) 782-0737 • www.halesales.com

In 1983 Mike Hale opened Washington's third microbrewery, a one-man operation in the northeastern town of Colville. Between then and 1999, Hale's has opened, and then closed, brewing operations in Spokane and Kirkland, and is now located in the Fremont District of Seattle. The Fremont brewpub quickly became an anchor neighborhood establishment.

The pub, decorated with rich colors and wood trim, features a small stage for live music. A striking oval bar of Honduran mahogany defines the space lengthwise. To the rear is a separate family seating area. The tantalizing menu offers appetizers such as beer-boiled shrimp, a ploughman's platter and a brewer's grain soft pretzel. The pizzas are gourmet, with toppings such as spinach, garlic and blue cheese, or even barbecued chicken.

The midsection of the pub looks out through a glass wall to the "arcade," an enclosed central area between the pub and the brewery, used for standing room on busy nights. The impressive thirty-barrel brewhouse is visible beyond the arcade.

Hours: 11 a.m.–10 p.m. Monday–Thursday; 11 a.m.–11 p.m. Friday and Saturday
Children: Yes, except in the bar or during live music
Food: Upscale pub fare, pizzas with spent-grain crust
Entertainment: Live jazz and blues on Wednesday and Saturday
Smoking: No
Payment: Visa, MC
Beer to go: Yes, draft

The pub has both regular taps and beer engines, the latter pouring Hale's Dublin-style ales, with the rich creaminess achievable only via nitrogen dispense. Try the cream ale, special bitter, or the Moss Bay Stout on nitro. Also, look for seasonals on draft throughout Washington, and in limited bottling runs. Among the most notable of the seasonals are the full-flavored Celebration Porter and popular Drawbridge Blonde, named for the statue of Rapunzel on the Fremont Avenue Bridge. A visit to Hale's will leave not doubt as to why Northwest beer drinkers have long been enjoying Hale's flagship brews, especially their Moss Bay Extra, an exceptional brew, with the "extra" referring to the Northwest style of using huge amounts of malts and hops, lending great complexity.

DIRECTIONS: From I-5, take the 80th/85th Street exit. Take 85th west several blocks to 8th Avenue. Turn left on 8th and drive south approximately three miles. Here 8th meets Leary Way at a diagonal, with only a left-turn as an option. Once on Leary, the brewpub is on your right, about a block down.

Lunar Brewing Company

Established 1999

1605 S 93rd Street, Building E, Unit L • Seattle, WA 98108
(206) 764-1213

Frank Helderman was a brewer at the Pike Brewing Company prior to, and just following, its major pub expansion in the mid-'90s. Since then, he has struck out on his own—as have several other former Pike brewers. Helderman started Lunar Brewing Company in the late 1990s. He's making Northwest-style beers that take advantage of great Northwest ingredients, so you'll find big beers, with lots of hops in the nose and in the finish.

The pale ale is straw-colored and nicely hopped, with eight pounds of finishing hops in a seven-barrel batch. It's well-balanced, though, with good malt character and a creamy mouthfeel. The Porter, black and hoppy, is another Northwest interpretation of the English style, as is the Lunar IPA, with twenty-five percent higher gravity than the regular pale ale and lots of the hops' citrusy flavors. He also makes a lighter-gravity ESB, and watch for rotating seasonal brews as well. All the Lunar beers are unfiltered.

The Lunar Brewing Company is in a warehouse industrial space in the South Park area, across the Duwamish River from Boeing Field, not far from Pacific Crest's brewpub. If you'd like to visit the brewery for a tour and a tasting, call ahead for an appointment—you'll have to catch Frank between brewing and delivering batches of beer. He keeps pretty busy, brewing and self-distributing as a one-man show.

Look for Lunar primarily within Seattle city limits, with its tap-handles displaying realistic representations of the moon. Don't get Lunar Brewing Company confused with Moon Ales—different companies, different beers.

DIRECTIONS: Call for directions.

Hours: Call for appointment
Children: No
Food: No
Entertainment: No
Smoking: No
Payment: Checks
Beer to go: Yes, draft

Maritime Pacific Brewing Company

Established 1990

1514 NW Leary Way • Seattle, WA 98107
(206) 782-6181

What was once an auto shop in Ballard, the yachting and commercial fishing district of Seattle, has evolved over the years into the home of the Maritime Pacific Brewing Company. A brewery since 1990, Maritime Pacific opened the Jolly Roger Taproom in October of 1997, and added a full kitchen in 2000. The menu offers a range of appetizers, a combination of which can make a real meal. There are salads and shrimp plates—even burgers.

Maritime Pacific produces six standard ales. Flagship Red Ale, the first beer brewed by the company, is the brewery's most popular ale. Red amber color, a slightly nutty flavor, and a smooth finish make this an exceptional ale. The five other standards are Clipper Gold Hefeweizen (a golden, light wheat ale), Islander Pale Ale, lightly hopped Nightwatch Ale (a smooth, dark amber), Salmon Bay ESB (a hoppy, bitter English-style ale), and Bosun's Black Porter.

Hours: 3 p.m.–9 p.m. Monday–Thursday; noon–11 p.m. Friday and Saturday
Children: No
Food: Light pub fare
Entertainment: No
Smoking: No
Payment: Checks
Beer to go: Yes, bottles

Seasonal offerings include Windfest Ale, their Oktoberfest brew, Cape Lager, and Jolly Roger Christmas Ale (an English-style Strong Ale with a high alcohol content available in November/December). The Jolly Roger Taproom always offers three cask-conditioned ales drawn on antique beer engines, and is usually pouring thirteen different Maritime beers at any given time.

The taproom, named for their popular winter ale, fits in well with the subdued seafaring theme of the brewery. The floor is a hand-painted representation of an old pirate treasure map, while a Jolly Roger flag hangs opposite the bar. The old oak tables and chairs, diffused lighting through a long bar made up of glass blocks, and a simple, yet satisfying menu, all contribute to making the Jolly Roger a cozy place to launch a treasure hunt for your favorite Maritime Pacific brew.

DIRECTIONS: From I-5 in Seattle, take the 45th Street exit. Follow the exit signs to 45th Street and turn west at the stoplight. Go west on 45th Street, which will change into Market Street as it goes downhill into Ballard. Continue on Market Street to 15th Avenue NW. Turn left at 15th Avenue NW and stay in the right lane. Follow the Leary Way Exit sign to the stoplight and turn right at Leary Way. The brewery and taproom are on the right hand side of the street, second building from the corner.

Pacific Crest Brewing Company

Established 1996

10845 East Marginal Way South • Seattle, WA 98168
(206) 764-1731 • www.pacificcrestbrewing.com

The Pacific Crest Brewing Company is a place where you stop on the way home from work, or meet your friends for a game of cards or darts. It's a neighborly spot where you might strike up a conversation with a couple of guys at the bar, or find yourself suddenly playing dominoes with the folks working behind the counter.

Sparse decorations consist of a couple of baseball bats and paddles hang on the walls. The bar and seating area is small, with the brewing equipment, recycled from the original Thomas Kemper (Pyramid) brewery on Bainbridge Island and the Pike Brewing Company at the Pike Place Market in downtown Seattle, taking up most of the space.

Pacific Crest usually has six brews on tap. Hefeweizen, a straw-colored, citrusy wheat ale, is the lightest of the bunch. Trailhead Red, a malty, red-amber pale ale, is dry hopped to give it a little extra kick. The India Pale Ale is highly hopped and has a mildly fruity flavor like most of this style, but is refreshingly different from most IPA's brewed in the Northwest. Seasonals include Old Man Winter, a full-flavored, full-bodied winter ale, and a summer Golden Ale. Pacific Crest also lagers—a pilsner and the spring seasonal Weizenbock are the brewery's current offerings in this arena.

If a conversation with a new friend or the tasty beer doesn't convert you to the charms of the place, then the food should do the trick—Pacific Crest serves up a mean barbecue. Area food critics have showered praise on the pork ribs and sliced beef brisket sandwich. The shredded pork sandwich has become so famous the recipe was recently published in Sunset magazine.

DIRECTIONS: From I-5 heading north toward Seattle take exit #158, which is East Marginal Way/Airport Way S (also signed as the exit to the Museum of Flight/Boeing Field). Loop around onto S Boeing Access Road. Get into the left lane for E Marginal Way/Pacific Highway Southbound. At the next light, turn left onto E Marginal Way S. Go 1/2 block to Pacific Crest Brewing Company.

Hours: 3 p.m.–8 p.m. Monday–Thursday; 3 p.m.–10 p.m. Friday; 10 a.m.–6 p.m. Saturday
Children: No
Food: Bar snacks
Entertainment: Dominoes and darts, occasional televised sports
Smoking: No
Payment: Checks only
Beer to go: Yes, draft

Pacific Rim Brewing Company

Established 1997

9832 14th Avenue SW • Seattle, WA 98106
(206) 764-3844 • www.pacificrimbrewing.com

In case you were wondering what happened to the folks at California & Alaska Streets Brewpub (now the home of Elliott Bay Brewery & Pub, see page 122), they got out of the brewpub business and are now concentrating strictly on making beer—doing business as Pacific Rim Brewing in the White Center area of West Seattle. The principals of the business are Scott Lord, longtime homebrewer and homebrew-supply merchant, and Charles McElevey, the original Redhook brewer, and currently a brewery consultant.

The brewery is located in a nondescript warehouse space in a retail/warehouse neighborhood. The brewing system is a twenty-barrel prototype built by the New England Brewing Company, and is commercial in scale, but just quaint enough to still require hand-stirring of the mash tun. Drop in visitors are welcome.

The company features a standard collection of five ales, four of which take their names from local neighborhoods. Alki Ale is a light amber; Vashon Old Stock is a Northwest-style pale ale; Fauntleroy Stout is a fine dry stout you'll want to sample; and Admiral ESB is the best of the bunch—well-rounded and a traditional interpretation of the style. The fifth standard offering is Ringtale, a creamy, malty ale made with rye and wheat as well as barley.

Lord's many seasonal brews include Leprechaun Ale (a dark ale for St. Patrick's Day), Punkin' Patch Ale (with real pumpkin included in the brew), and Castaway Barley Wine (over nine percent alcohol, but smooth and silky).

The beers are marketed and on tap throughout King and Pierce Counties. Some accounts request dry-hopped versions of the above brews, so ask for that treat at local alehouses.

Hours: 11 a.m.–7 p.m. Monday–Thursday; 11 a.m.–6 p.m. Friday; Saturday by appointment
Children: Yes
Food: No
Entertainment: No
Smoking: No
Payment: Checks
Beer to go: Yes, draft

DIRECTIONS: From I-5 take Exit 163-B West Seattle Freeway. Before crossing the bridge to West Seattle, turn south on Highway 99. Cross the Duwamish Waterway and, at the Marginal Way exchange, take Highway 509 South. Take the first exit, Olson Place SW. At the top of the hill, turn right on SW Roxbury Street. Follow Roxbury 10 blocks and turn left on 14th Avenue SW. The brewery is one block down 14th Avenue, on the left.

The Pike Brewing Company

Established 1989

1432 Western Avenue • Seattle, WA 98101
(206) 622-3373 • www.pikebrewing.com

Pike Place Market, one of Seattle's premier attractions, is a regular stop for city natives, and a favored destination for visitors. The open-air produce and sea-food market is the kind of sight people come to the Pacific Northwest to experience.

The Pike Brewing Company has been a mainstay of Pike Place Market since the late 1980s. In the early days, this was a production-only brewery, and the Liberty Malt Supply homebrew store served as a tasting room. Today, the homebrew supplies are downstairs at the Market Cellar Winery, and Pike Brewing Company's large pub now serves as a centerpiece to the marketplace.

The pub offers dining-room seating on wide, graduated platforms, a horse-shoe-shaped bar, a game room with bar, and a cigar room. The pizzas are very good, as are the specialty pastas. The cigar room is a glass-enclosed snug with beer-related reading materials. Don't miss the tavern-like game room, with five pool tables and TV sports. Both bars pour Pike's beers, as well as several guest taps, notably European imports such as Celebrator of Germany and lambics by Lindeman.

Regular house ales include Pike Place Pale Ale, XXXXX Stout, East India Pale Ale and Pike Place Porter, often served up creamy and rich on nitro dispense. The pale ale, the brewery's most popular, is a slightly nutty, deep amber ale. Kiltlifter Scotch Ale, a savory, malty brew with subtle peat highlights, has been added to the brewery's list of regulars, and can be found in six-packs throughout the Northwest.

Many former Pike brewers have gone on to open other brewpubs and craft breweries around the region. Current Pike brewer Kim Brusco, formerly of Pacific Northwest Brewing Company, makes an extensive line of seasonals in addition to Pike's regular offerings. Auld Acquaintance (a spiced Christmas beer), and Old Bawdy (a barley wine), are available in the winter. In the spring, look for the mild and nutty Bootleg Brown; in the summer there's Cerveza Rosanna, a chili beer.

Hours: 11 a.m.–12 a.m. Sunday–Wednesday; 11 a.m.–2 a.m. Thursday–Saturday
Children: Yes, except in the bar
Food: Upscale pub fare, pizzas
Entertainment: Pool tables, video games, TV sports
Smoking: Yes, in the game room
Payment: Debit, Visa, MC, AmEx, Discover, Diners Club
Beer to go: Yes, bottles and draft

DIRECTIONS: From I-5 in Seattle, take any downtown exit. Drive west to 1st Avenue, follow signs to Pike Place Market. The Market is at the corner of Pike and 1st. The pub is on the second floor of the market, inside and one floor down from the street-level produce market.

Pyramid Ales/Pyramid Brewery & Alehouse

Established 1995

1201 1st Avenue South • Seattle, WA 98134
(206) 682-3377 • www.pyramidbrew.com

Located right across the street from the new Seattle Mariners stadium, Pyramid's large pub and brewing facility is housed in a brick and timber building marked by a prominent silo out front. Built in 1913 for the Washington and Oregon Railway and Navigation Company, the structure now houses the brewery, a two-story pub, and a retail store. Its center is dominated by a handsome, refurbished 1940s copper mash tun manufactured in Munich.

Pyramid is a popular and busy night spot. Relax on the open air patio, or, to order off the extensive menu, go inside, where the large pub has two balconies with additional seating. The whole interior has been rebuilt with handsome woodwork and massive timber beams. The brewery itself is an equally spacious facility, with multiple conditioning tanks and a full bottling and kegging operation. Founded in 1984, Pyramid Ales is the fusion of two early Puget Sound microbreweries: Hart Brewing of Kalama and Thomas-Kemper Lagers of Bainbridge Island/Poulsbo. Both Pyramid ales and Thomas-Kemper lagers are brewed at this Seattle location, as well as at Pyramid's other brewery and alehouse in Berkeley, California.

Pyramid's line of ales, produced by Brewery Manager Phil Phillips, runs the gambit, from the good old standbys of a hoppy pale ale and a rich well-balanced amber, to their Best Brown and an Espresso Stout. Northwest beer drinkers have long rallied around their signature Apricot Ale, pleasantly fruity, and Wheaten Ale, a bright, refreshing and crisp brew.

A few of the standard lagers available on the Thomas-Kemper label are a Münchener-style pale lager, a Bohemian dunkel with delectable malt character, and an amber lager that's smooth, but with spicy highlights from Saaz hops. Thomas Kemper is also the Northwest's premier craft soda company, selling draft kegs and six-packs of root beer, birch beer, and cream soda, at grocery stores around the region.

DIRECTIONS: From I-5, take the Stadium exit onto Royal Brougham Way and drive to the first traffic light at 1st Avenue. The brewpub is on your left.

Hours: Summer: 11 a.m.–11 p.m. daily (11 a.m.–midnight on Mariners' game days); winter: 11 a.m.–10 p.m. daily
Children: Yes
Food: Upscale pub fare
Entertainment: No
Smoking: No
Payment: Checks, Visa, MC
Beer to go: Yes, bottles and draft

Rock Bottom Restaurant & Brewery

Established 1996

1333 5th Avenue • Seattle, WA 98101
(206) 623-3070

Rock Bottom Restaurant & Brewery

550 10th Avenue NE, Suite 103 • Bellevue, WA 98004
(425) 462-9300 • www.rockbottom.com

The Washington Rock Bottom locations are among over twenty such restaurant/breweries sprinkled around the U.S., including property in Portland, Oregon (see page 64). Each of these brewpubs has both a restaurant and bar, which occupy separate spaces. At the Seattle location, the bar and restaurant, along with the brewhouse (JV Northwest, 12-barrel), are located on the ground floor of a bustling skyscraper complex.

The ambiance is urbane and handsome, with subdued lighting and wood paneling. High-backed booths create private seating areas. The bar is cigar-friendly and has a fairly sizable humidor. It's also sports-friendly, with many TVs and pool tables. The Bellevue location is even larger, with an upstairs game room and bar. The selection of upscale pub fare includes brick oven pizzas, pastas, and other entrée, and a long list of "Beerginnings."

Brewmaster David Meyers offers his own versions of the company-wide standard ales. Most of the ales are filtered and a shade on the malty side. The Peashooter Pale Ale, Raccoon Red Ale, Brown Bear Brown Ale, and Flying Salmon Stout are joined by the unfiltered Faller Wheat Ale, a golden, light-bodied wheat brew. The brown is a licoricey, porter-like ale, and the "Flying Salmon" is a nice, creamy English-style stout. An occasional lager finds its way into the seasonal rotation, including an Oktoberfest, and other specialty beers such as Morse Kölsch.

Hours: 11 a.m.–2 a.m. Monday–Saturday; 11 a.m.–midnight Sunday
Children: Yes, in restaurant
Food: Upscale eclectic American
Entertainment: Live music Wednesdays and Sundays; pool tables; TV sports events
Smoking: Yes, in the brewpub
Payment: Checks, Visa, MC, AmEx, Diners Club
Beer to go: Yes, draft

DIRECTIONS to the Seattle location: From I-5 take one of the downtown exits (such as southbound exit 164 James Street or northbound exit 165 Union Street). Head west toward the water and downtown, to 5th Avenue. Turn onto 5th toward Union and University Streets. The brewpub is on the west side of 5th between University and Union; look for the silo out front. Call the Bellevue Rock Bottom for directions and hours.

Tir Na Nog Brewpub

Established 1998

Seattle: 801 1st Avenue • Seattle, WA 98104
(206) 264-2700
Portland: 230 NW Westover • Portland, OR 97210
(503) 221-6621 • www.tirnanogpub.com

The Ram company's family of brewpubs now includes a series of meticulously replicated Irish pubs with miniature brewhouses. Both of the Pacific Northwest's Ram Irish pubs, located in downtown Seattle and Portland, are named Tir Na Nog. "Tir Na Nog" is Gaelic for "wonderland" or "faerie realm," and stepping into this brewpub in downtown Seattle is fantastic. In fact, the entire interior of the property was built in Ireland and shipped to the U.S. in forty-one container loads.

There are three separate environments at Tir Na Nog: the Country Cottage is a restaurant space, the Victorian Bar is a fully stocked bar featuring Irish and Scotch whiskeys with an elevated cigar room, and the Celtic Brewpub, a pub and live music venue, a great place to sip a draught Guinness. Its thrust bar area encompasses a tiny Newlands brewing system emblazoned with hammered-copper Celtic designs. The menu has traditional Irish shepherd's pies and corned beef, along with Pacific Northwest seafood and other regional favorites.

Tom Hoare, Washington Brewmaster for Ram, brews a single house ale at the Seattle Tir Na Nog property. The Lowlander Scottish Ale is light amber in color, nice 'n malty with a hint of peat. Other Big Horn beers on tap at Tir Na Nog include some standards with Celtic names attached, such as the Irish Blonde.

Hours: Summer, 11 a.m.–2 a.m. daily; winter: 11 a.m.–11 p.m. daily
Children: Yes, in some areas
Food: Upscale pub fare with many Irish dishes
Entertainment: Live music, usually Irish or Celtic, Thursday–Friday afternoons and Thursday–Saturday evenings
Smoking: Yes, in some areas
Payment: Visa, MC, AmEx, Discover, Diners Club
Beer to go: Yes, draft

DIRECTIONS: Tir Na Nog is at the foot of the Columbia Street off-ramp from the Alaska Way Viaduct. Or, from I-5 Southbound, take the Union Street exit and follow the off ramp as it becomes Union. Take Union to 1st Street and turn left. Follow 1st six blocks to Columbia Street. The brewpub is on the corner of 1st and Columbia on your right. From 1-5 Northbound, take the James Street exit, then follow James to 1st and turn right on 1st. Call the Portland Tir Na Nog for directions and hours.

Tapps Brewing Company

Established 1995

15625 Main Street • Sumner, WA 98390
(253) 863-8438 • www.brewingnw.com/tapps/Tapps1.htm

Tapps Brewing is a microbrewery crafting a variety of ales in their twenty-barrel brewhouse housed in a former machine shop. The brewery, located on a retail strip, has a tasting room with a dozen booths on the front of the building. Tours are available by calling ahead, or if you are visiting the tasting room, you may be able to enter the side of the building and stand in a foyer area to watch the brewing process.

Tapps offers a lineup of five standard ales. They include Paradise IPA (a true Northwest hop-head beer), and Amazon Amber (a malty brew with fruity highlights tempered with fresh hop flavors). The best of the bunch are Black Diamond Porter (robust and creamy, with a handful of rolled oats in the brew), and a Scotch ale called Frost Bite (ruby-colored, with caramel and other subtle malt flavors). Tapps also makes a unique multi-grain beer, with three types of specialty malted barley, as well as amaranth, triticale, rye, oats, wheat, and spelt. The beers are bottled and kegged, and are distributed throughout Western Washington.

The patio out front makes a good spot to enjoy a beer tasting session. You'll see locals bring fast food with them, or even have pizzas delivered to the diner-like seating area. When in doubt, do as the locals do—ask to use the phone to order a pizza if you get hungry while trying your Tapps beers.

DIRECTIONS: From I-5, take Highway 161, 167, or 512 to Highway 410 West. Follow 410 West to Sumner and exit onto Traffic Avenue. Follow Traffic to Main and turn right. Follow Main all the way through town to the 15000 block. The brewery is on your left in the strip.

Hours: 2-8 p.m. Thursday–Friday
Children: Yes
Food: No
Entertainment: No
Smoking: No
Payment: Checks, Visa, MC
Beer to go: Yes, bottles and draft

Redhook Ale Brewery & Forecasters Brewpub

Established 1994

14300 NE 145th Street • Woodinville, WA 98072
(425) 483-3232

Trolleyman Pub

3400 Phinney Avenue North • Seattle, WA 98103
(206) 548-8000 • www.redhook.com

Redhook, one of the Northwest's oldest microbreweries, sold its first beer in 1982. Redhook ales became cornerstone brews of the Northwest and were instrumental in fostering Seattle's love affair with assertively flavored craft beers.

The brewery grew rapidly in the 1990s, teaming up with Anheuser-Busch to take on the national market, and opening a second brewery in Portsmouth, New Hampshire. Redhook's original Ballard brewery was replaced by a brewery and taproom in the Fremont District in the late 1980s, called the Trolleyman Pub. Housed in an historic railcar barn, it still pours Redhook Ales, but no longer brews it.

The Forecasters Brewpub and bottling facility in Woodinville is the largest craft brewery in the area, with state-of-the-art equipment and nearly 100 conditioning tanks.

The 24-acre plot in the rolling foothills of Woodinville's wine country makes this a picturesque stop. The pub consists of an enormous common area with long tables, plenty of natural light, and high ceilings. The dark rafters against light plaster walls are reminiscent of Bavarian beer halls.

Redhook Ales' flagship beer is their India pale ale, a balanced, quaffable amber brew. Other standards include an ESB (caramelly, copper-colored, with plenty of Northwest hops), Blackhook Porter (dry and roasty), Doubleblack Stout (made with Starbucks coffee in the brew), and one of the original Northwest hefeweizens.

Hours: Brewery, call for tour times. Pub, 10 a.m.–10 p.m. Monday–Thursday; 10 a.m.–midnight Friday; 11 a.m.–midnight Saturday; noon–7 p.m. Sunday
Children: Yes, until 8 p.m.
Food: Pub fare
Entertainment: Live music Friday and Saturday
Smoking: No
Payment: Checks, Visa, MC, AmEx
Beer to go: Yes, bottles and draft

DIRECTIONS: From Highway 405, turn West on Highway 522. From 522, take the Woodinville exit onto 202 South. Follow 202 approximately two miles. The brewery is on the left, across the road from Chateau Ste. Michelle winery. Call the Trolleyman Pub for directions and hours.

Rogue Ales/Issaquah Brewing Company

Established 1995

35 W Sunset Way • Issaquah, WA 98027
(425) 557-1911

Issaquah is a quaint little town at the base of the Cascade foothills. An extensive trail system leads out of town onto nearby Tiger and Cougar Mountains. This is the last major town as you head east over the Cascades on Highway 90. For a nice, in-town walk, follow a salmon-spawning creek that flows through a fish hatchery in the city center.

Two doors down from the salmon hatchery is the Issaquah Brewing Company's restaurant and pub. The brewpub is large, with an additional restaurant area. The combination makes an attractive, comfortable space for family dinners, drinks with friends, or a spirited game of darts. The menu offers a range of pastas, seafood, and pub fare. The house specialty pizza is made with a thick, chewy crust heaped with delicious cheeses and toppings.

The brewery, now owned and operated by Rogue Ales of Oregon (see pages 19 and 20), offers five house standard ales. Bullfrog, a wheat ale with lemon and lime juices added to produce a mild citrus flavor, is the most popular. In addition to Bullfrog, you'll find Kodiak Jack Amber, Brass Rail Porter, and Old's (a light ale with a dry crisp finish that comes from brewing with honey). The Issaquah location also pours a complete lineup of Rogue Ales from a plethora of taps.

DIRECTIONS: From I-90, take exit 17 to Front Street. At the bottom of the exit get in the left lane and go forward to the second light. At the light, turn right onto Sunset. The brewery is on the left.

Hours: 11:30 a.m.–10 p.m. Monday–Friday, 1 p.m.–midnight Saturday–Sunday
Children: Yes
Food: Pub fare and pizzas
Entertainment: Darts, regularly televised sports events, live music
Smoking: No
Payment: Checks, Visa, MC
Beer to go: Yes, draft and bottles

Snoqualmie Falls Brewing Company

Established 1998

8032 Falls Avenue, SE • Snoqualmie, WA 98065
(425) 831-2337 • www.fallsbrew.com

Snoqualmie Falls Brewing Company is a slimmed-down brewery focused on quality beer production and draft market sales. With five local owners, this brewing venture is the brain-child of a group of businessmen whose passion for beer makes up for their lack of experience in the brewing business. The company landed brewer Rande Reed after his long-standing association with Pyramid Breweries. Reed, along with assistant Tom Muñoz, brews a line of hopped-up Northwest-style ales that are pouring from tap-handles throughout Snohomish, King and Pierce Counties.

The brewery is housed in a light industrial warehouse space in the darling town of Snoqualmie. Visitors are welcome for a tour and tastings anytime during regular business hours. The brewery is a seven-barrel system (ready for expansion).

The beer line, known as Falls Ales, includes four standards plus a contract brew made for Snoqualmie Summit ski area. Light from the Falls Cream Ale is smooth and mild, produced via a twist on the method for producing a Cream Ale—instead of fermenting with a bottom-fermenting yeast at ale temperatures, Reed uses a top-fermenting yeast at colder temperatures. In keeping with Reed's the-more-hops-the-merrier style, 24-Karate Golden Ale is not your typical mild-mannered Golden. Summit Ale is a slightly maltier version of 24K, and their best-seller is Copperhead Pale, an eminently drinkable, well-balanced beer. Also available are the malty Falls Amber, and the potent Wildcat IPA.

Reed also produces seasonal brews, including Avalanche Ale and Old Rattlesnake Barley Wine for the winter, Spring Fever Belgian-style Strong Ale for spring, and Harvest Moon Ale and Black Frog Stout for the autumn.

Hours: 8 a.m.–4 p.m. Monday–Friday; noon–5 p.m. Saturday
Children: Yes
Food: No
Entertainment: No
Smoking: No
Payment: Checks
Beer to go: Yes, draft

DIRECTIONS: From I-90 take Exit 27 North Bend/Snoqualmie. Turn north and head downhill bearing right (sign to Snoqualmie). One mile down the hill, turn left onto Meadowbrook Way (sign to Snoqualmie). Another mile downhill, turn left onto Highway 202/Railroad Avenue. After Railroad Avenue enters town, turn right onto King Street, across Railroad Avenue from the Old Railroad Depot. Follow King Street one block and turn right onto Falls Avenue. The brewery is on your left.

Twin Rivers Brewing Company/ Sailfish Bar & Grill

Established 1995

104 N Lewis Street • Monroe, WA 98272
(360) 794-4056 • www.eskimo.com/~jleybo/sailfish

The Sailfish Bar & Grill was originally located in Seattle; in 1993 it moved to Monroe, where it resumed its tradition of fine steaks, seafood, pasta and spirits. Chef/owner Tim Kovach teamed up with his bartender, Steve Ladenhauf, and began producing small batches of beer for sale in the restaurant, brewing on the stove in the kitchen. The reception was overwhelming, and they now have a four-barrel brewing system installed next door.

The restaurant is upscale, but not uptight, with dark wooden, high-backed booths, an open kitchen, and arching walls with handsome old brick supports. The menu is impressive, offering such appetizers as roasted garlic custard, Manila clams and Dungeness crabcakes. Traditional entrées include filet mignon, tiger prawns, and a few exotic choices, such as Thai stew.

Twin Rivers Brewing produces a collection of traditionally styled European ales and lagers, exploring all the great styles of German, English and Belgian brews, with recipes that are true to tradition, but often with their own twist. Some of the many styles brewed to date include an India pale ale, a Saison with unmistakable flavors from the added coriander and orange peel, a hoppy and light-bodied English brown ale, an English pale ale, a rich and perfectly hopped Imperial stout, and a German alt.

They are also kegging their beer for draft markets in the greater Seattle area, so seek out these bold, fine brews at your local restaurant or alehouse. Look for their prison tower tap-handles, harkening to Monroe's penitentiary.

DIRECTIONS: From Highway 522, turn east on Highway 2. From 2, turn south on Lewis Street and drive three blocks to Main Street. The restaurant is on the right, on the corner of Lewis and Main.

Hours: Restaurant, 5 p.m.–10 p.m. Tuesday–Saturday; brewery, tours by request
Children: Yes
Food: Fine dining
Entertainment: No
Smoking: Yes, in the bar
Payment: Checks, Visa, MC
Beer to go: Yes, draft

Northwest Brew-Wërks

Established 1997

12437 116th Avenue NE • Kirkland, WA 98034
(425) 821-6141 • www.brewwerks.com

Northwest Brew-Wërks is a unique hybrid in which brew-on-premise facility meets craft brewery taproom meets breweriana retail store. Many of the brew-on-premise establishments in the region offer retail sales of some homebrew and/or wine-making equipment, but this place goes one step further, offering a great collection of steins and gift baskets for the wine lover.

The interior is bright and cheery. A three-barrel kettle for microbrewing, and a half-dozen twenty-gallon copper kettles for you-brew clients line the front window. A small three-sided bar area is set up thrust-style in the center of the space. During nice weather, a few tables are placed out front along the parking lot for fresh air seating.

As with most of the finer you-brew facilities, Northwest Brew-Wërks offers a catalog of over sixty recipes for beer, cider, and wine. It also features templates and materials for customizing computer-printed bottle labels for the finished product.

The craft brewery part of the business rotates through most of the beer recipes offered for the brew-on-premise experience. Owner Ward Taylor sees offering craft beer for sale as another way of presenting the make-it-yourself opportunity as tangible as possible. You never know just what you'll find pouring at the three in-house tap-handles: perhaps an Oktoberfest, a hefeweizen, and a stout. The business also brews a contract IPA for the Rose Hill Alehouse in Kirkland. (See the Seattle Alehouse section for the address.)

Whether you're looking for another craft brew to try, curious about the brew-on-premise concept, or are shopping for a beer enthusiast on your Christmas gift list, Northwest Brew-Wërks is worth a stop.

Hours: 2 p.m.–9 p.m. Tuesday–Friday; 11 a.m.–9 p.m. Saturday, Sunday and Monday by appointment
Children: Yes
Food: Bar snacks
Entertainment: Occasional live music or cigar evening
Smoking: No
Payment: Visa, MC, Checks
Beer to go: Yes, draft

DIRECTIONS: From I-405, take Exit 20-B NE 124th Street Go west on NE 124th and turn right immediately on 116th Avenue NE, which runs between the highway on the right and a shopping center on the left. Turn left into the shopping center at the first entrance. The brewery is in the complex on the left, to the rear of the first parking area.

Mac & Jack's Brewery

Established 1994

17825 NE 65th Street, Suite B-110 • Redmond, WA 98052
(425) 558-9697

Malcom MacLean "Mac" Rankin and Jack Schraap share a devotion to craft beer. Jack used to run a boat restoration business, and they met the day Mac brought in an antique runabout to be restored. Soon thereafter, Mac took up homebrewing with a passion and when he ran out of space at home, the two teamed up to brew in Jack's garage. From there, the unforgettable name combo was born.

Business savvy and frugality enabled Mac and Jack to weather the storms of the Northwest craft beer scene during the '90s. With a focus on maintaining the uniqueness of flavor associated with small batch brewing as they grew, Mac, the brewmaster, is now using a 20-barrel system. This equipment, manufactured by Ripley Stainless and formerly the property of Granville Island Brewing Company (see page 201), now produces Mac & Jack's line of draft-only ales.

Hours: Call for appointment
Children: Yes
Food: No
Entertainment: No
Smoking: No
Payment: Checks
Beer to go: Yes, draft

The beer lineup is nice and straightforward: African Amber, Serengeti Wheat, and Mac & Jack's Porter. These are Northwest-style beers, with big hop flavors riding on big malt flavors. The amber is nicely balanced and the porter is roasty and smooth. The wheat beer is a hopped-up take on the creamy German weizen type.

The two brews sporting the African motif were originally contract brews for the Park Pub in Seattle, which is not far from the zoo. (See the Seattle Alehouse Scene, page 111.) A lion adorns the tap-handle for the amber, and a giraffe is the mascot for the Serengeti Wheat. Come taste the beers at the brewery and have a tour of the jam-packed brewhouse. Just make sure to call ahead to catch Mac and his assistant between brews. Larger groups are welcome, by appointment, too. Mac and Jack's beers are at restaurants and pubs throughout Seattle.

DIRECTIONS: Call for directions

Northwest Brewhouse & Grill

Established 1999

7950 164th Avenue NE • Redmond, WA 98052
(425) 498-2337 • www.bearcreekbrewing.com

Redmond, a young city just north of Lake Sammamish and Marymoor County Park, is home to the illustrious Microsoft Corporation and other software ventures, and to a large brewpub called the Northwest Brewhouse & Grill. Located in a building that was originally a bank, the site was also the location of the former Redmond Brewing Company, but it is now under different ownership, and sports a renovated interior.

An open counter kitchen and two-story, glassed-in brewhouse divide Northwest Brewhouse & Grill into a dining room and a pub. The dining room has a mellow atmosphere, with sandy-colored walls adorned with framed images by local photographers. The pub area features an island bar, as well as views of the fifteen-barrel brewhouse and cellaring operations. Come here for dart matches and cocktails, or for occasional live music.

The restaurant is an American grill, with ribs and steaks, as well as a few pastas, salads and soups. While you decide on dinner, order some hot wings with bleu cheese, or a tomato bruschetta appetizer, then perhaps a wood-fired pizza to accompany some beer. After dinner, for a stretch of the legs, walk the twenty-or-so blocks to Bear Creek Park, a small green space with the same name as the Brewhouse's parent corporation, Bear Creek Brewing Company.

The beers are brewed by Ted Palmer (formerly of Fish, Pyramid, and Redmond Brewing Companies), along with owner Michael Piechowiak. They make five standards, from a blonde on up through a Scottish-like amber, an IPA, and either a porter or a stout. The fifth regular beer here is a Northwest-style hefeweizen. Seasonally, they offer a Maibock, an Oktoberfest, and a Christmas beer.

Hours: 11 a.m.–midnight daily
Children: Yes, in the restaurant
Food: Upscale pub fare and wood-fired pizzas
Entertainment: Steel-tip darts, big-screen TVs with sports events
Smoking: No
Payment: Checks, Visa, MC, AmEx, Discover
Beer to go: Yes, draft

DIRECTIONS: From Highway 405, take Exit 18 Highway 908 (Redmond-Kirkland Way) and head west. As 908 enters Redmond, turn onto Redmond Way and cross the Sammamish River. From here, turn left on 164th, which becomes Highway 202 (Woodinville–Redmond Road). The brewpub is three blocks down 164th, on your right.

Gallagher's Where-U-Brew

Established 1995

120 5th Avenue South • Edmonds, WA 98020
(425) 776-4209 • inet-rendezvous.com/gallaghers

Edmonds is a charming little city just north of Seattle situated on the water. There is a ferry-boat terminal here for a major run to Kingston on the Olympic Peninsula. Public beaches by the ferry dock offer in-town nature fun for the family.

Dennis Gallagher established a brew-on-premise in Edmonds in the mid-'90s. Several such establishments opened in Washington during that time, but many have since closed. The key to success for Gallagher's came with an additional license—one to commercially brew and sell beer.

Gallagher's facility is now both a you-brew facility and a microbrewery. Customers can come in and try making their own beers, or sample Gallagher's commercial line of microbrews, called the Fifth Avenue series. The standard Fifth Avenue beers are a wheat ale, the Galley Mac Amber, Eddie Hop IPA, Abercrombie Special Porter, and Hal's Celebration Pale.

Hours: 2–8 p.m. Tuesday–Friday; 11 a.m.–5 p.m. Saturday; by appointment Sunday
Children: Yes
Food: No
Entertainment: Occasional special event
Smoking: No
Payment: Check, Visa, MC
Beer to go: Yes, draft

Gallagher, owner and brewer, is not afraid of hops, and he believes in adding more hops and wider varieties of malts to turn British types into potent Northwest-style ales. Three of his Fifth Avenue beers won medals at the first national brew-on-premise beer competition.

You can taste most of these full-character brews on-tap at any given time at Gallagher's small tasting facility. Stop in and see the mini-microbrewing system by Brew Pro of B.C. at Gallagher's in the middle of Edmonds' downtown. The city's shops are perfect for window shopping while waiting for a ferry.

Or, if you'd like to try Gallagher's beers in a restaurant atmosphere, you'll find the whole Fifth Avenue series on-tap at Café Pinso in Edmonds, in addition to various tap-handles at restaurants and taverns in the Edmonds/Mountlake Terrace area. Don't miss Gallagher's big special event, which has become a Halloween tradition: a brewing party in costume!

DIRECTIONS: From I-5, take the Mountlake Terrace/221st Street exit, and head west on 221st. Go about four miles until you reach 9th Avenue. Turn right on 9th and go about ten blocks to Dayton Street. Turn left on Dayton and go to 5th Avenue. The you-brew is at the intersection of 5th and Dayton in the Horizon Bank Building.

Ellersick Brewing Company

Established 1997

5505 216th Street • Mountlake Terrace, WA 98043
(425) 672-7051

Ellersick Brewing Company takes its name from owner and brewer, Rick Ellersick.It is the first licensed brewery in Washington state housed in a garage physically attached to a residence—Rick's and his family's. The brewery, while small, is neat and tidy. It was created by Ellersick's own metal-fabricating business, along with the creative use of various salvaged pieces of equipment. A six-barrel fermenter going on-line right around the turn of the millennium, will replace his original three-barrel one.

Converted grundies serve as the kettle, fermenter and bright tanks, while a bagel boiler makes a useful mash tun. A pair of ice cream coolers are the foundation of a homemade glycol coolant system. An industry-worthy set-up—once you're inside the brewery, the only reminder that you're in a residential neighborhood comes from a glance out the garage door, if it's open.

Ellersick's background in the grocery business and as a youth sports coach has provided his brewing business with an extensive word-of-mouth clientele. Most of his beer sales are tied up in private functions: weddings, sports events, birthday parties, and the like. Ellersick also supplies restaurant and alehouse accounts, though, so watch for his "Big E" tap handles in North King/South Snohomish counties.

In addition to making root beer for youth sports events, Ellersick brews a constantly evolving line of beers. Generally, you will find some variation on the following four-beer lineup: A light-bodied and citrusy amber, a very lightly hopped pale ale, and an American-style Honey Wheat. The best of the lot is a nut brown, approaching a porter, with complex flavors including hints of nuts, licorice, and charcoal. You might also happen to catch a helles bock or a Pilsner, as well as a seasonal ale, such as an apricot light ale, or a brew Ellersick calls Lawnmower Ale—a very light interpretation of the Scottish style, intended for easy consumption and refreshment while doing yard work.

DIRECTIONS: Call for directions

Hours: Tours by appointment
Children: Yes
Food: No
Entertainment: No
Smoking: No
Payment: Checks
Beer to go: Yes, draft

Diamond Knot Brewery & Alehouse

Established 1994

621 Front Street • Mukilteo, WA 98275
(425) 355-4488 • www.aa.net/diamondknot

Diamond Knot Brewery & Alehouse is a craft brewery and accompanying tap room situated right at the Mukilteo ferry dock for the run to Whidbey Island. The alehouse is located in a renovated bus barn and has a classic tavern feel.

The limited menu options are familiar companions to beer, such as bratwurst and BBQ wings. This is a smoking establishment, cigar-friendly too, with cigars for sale, along with ports and other wines. The once-a-week open microphone sessions feature antique films as a visual backdrop for the local musicians.

The company's name comes from a freighter that sank off the coast of Port Angeles in 1947. Ask the bartender for the full story of pluck and determination in the face of overwhelming odds. The brewery was founded in this same spirit by Bob Maphet and Brian Sollenberger. They are joined by brewer Eric Bean, trained at UC Davis. Together, this team produces a line of fine beers sold in many alehouses and restaurants throughout Puget Sound.

Hours: 11 a.m.–2 a.m. daily
Children: No
Food: Appetizers and snacks
Entertainment: Beer library, pool table, video games, darts, pull tabs; Monday open mike, occasional other live music; TV sports events
Smoking: Yes
Payment: Checks, Visa, MC
Beer to go: Yes, draft

Diamond Knot's lineup includes an IPA, and a super-strength version called the Industrial IPA, with twice the bitterness and half-again the gravity. Also available are a golden ale, a brown ale with a roasty edge to it, Possession Porter, and Icebreaker Barleywine—one of the few examples of this style available year-round. Diamond Knot seasonals have included a rich Oktoberfest-style Bavarian lager, a bold German-style hefeweizen, an amber hemp ale with ten-percent hemp seed in the grist, Steamglide Stout, and the Holiday Special Ale.

DIRECTIONS: From I-5, take Exit 189 Mukilteo-Whidbey Island Ferry and head west on Highway 526. Follow the ferry landing signs to the off-ramp on the right. Pass the exit ramp and proceed straight down the hill to Front Street. The brewpub is on your left.

Eagle Brewing Company/Riley's Pizza

Established 1995

645 4th Street • Mukilteo, WA 98275
(206) 348-8088

Mukilteo is a small town that serves as a bedroom community for Seattle and Everett. There's a ferry dock here for a run over to Whidbey Island. While waiting for a ferry, or at the end of a full day's excursion, you can make a stop at Riley's for some pizza and a pint of fresh Eagle beer.

Eagle Brewing is located in the basement of a converted house, with Riley's Pizza occupying the main floor. Both are owned by Brian Sullivan, an active political figure in Mukilteo, and erstwhile mayor of the town. Ask for a tour of the small brewery, pieced together to just fit in the house's small basement.

Riley's Pizza is a family establishment in a homey setting with a gorgeous, old wisteria vine over the arched entrance. The main dining area and deck share a lovely view over Puget Sound to Whidbey Island and beyond. Calzones are the house specialty, and the deep-crusted pizzas are also terrific. Order at the counter for delivery at your table.

Standard ales here include an amber, a golden, an Irish red, a porter and a stout. Golden Eagle Ale, their most popular beer, is a very light amber with a full hop aroma and a crisp finish. Cole's Porter is a rich, strong brew with robust charcoal flavor, named after Brian's father, who was the general manager of the Butte Brewery in Montana.

Hours: 11 a.m.–9 p.m. Sunday–Thursday; noon–10 p.m. Friday and Saturday
Children: Yes
Food: Pizzas, calzones and sandwiches
Entertainment: Bands on special occasions, including St. Patrick's Day
Smoking: No
Payment: Checks, Visa, MC, AmEx, Discover
Beer to go: Yes, draft (bring your own container)

DIRECTIONS: From I-5, take the Mukilteo–Whidbey Island Ferry exit and proceed west on Highway 526. After entering the town, drive down the hill toward the ferry dock and turn right on 4th. The brewery and pizza parlor are one block up 4th on the right. From the ferry, head straight up the hill and turn left on 4th.

Captains City Brewery

Established 1996

23 NW Front Street • Coupeville, WA 98239
(360) 678-9080

Coupeville is a charming Whidbey Island town, smaller than Langley to the south. Situated right on the water, facing the mainland, this hamlet's cove has long given shelter to seafarers. Due to its central location on Whidbey Island, Coupeville makes a good stop for lunch during a day on the island.

Captains City Brewery was named for Coupeville's original nickname, the City of Captains. You'll find this venue in the Mariner's Court Building, overlooking the water at the edge of town. It is tucked in the back of the building, but is visible from the side street and the entrance corridor. Also housed in this weathered structure are a couple of gift shops, along with Christopher's, a restaurant of some sophistication.

Hours: Call for appointment
Children: Yes
Food: No
Entertainment: No
Smoking: No
Payment: Checks
Beer to go: Yes, draft

Captains City's owner/brewer Kevin Locke comes from Napa Valley Brewing Company via an American Brewer's Guild apprenticeship. Locke likes to brew big, full-flavored beers including Coupe's Success Cream Ale, Barry Burton's Roof Top Red, Ray's Copperpipe Porter, and the award-winning Skookum Stout. He's known for his Public House Red, a tasty brew with complex malts and a gentle body. Look for his beers on tap throughout the Puget Sound area, and in 22-oz bottles for sale in Seattle and Whidbey Island retail stores.

Locke also brews house beers on contract for several Washington alehouses. You'll find variations of his red ale on tap under the house banner at places such as the Whistle Stop Alehouse in Renton, the Port Townsend Public Grill & Alehouse, Nickerson Street Pub in Fremont, and Toby's Tavern in Coupeville.

DIRECTIONS: From Highway 20, turn east toward Coupeville City Center at the light by the pedestrian overpass. This becomes Main Street. Follow Main Street all the way to the water and turn left on Front Street. The brewery and restaurant are in the gray building on the left, at the far end of Front Street.

Whidbey Island Brewing Company/ Oak Harbor Pub & Brewery

Established 1996

6405 NW 60th Avenue • Oak Harbor, WA 98277
(360) 675-7408 • www.whidbey.net/whidbrew

Oak Harbor is ten minutes south of breathtaking Deception Pass, the water channel that separates Whidbey Island and Fidalgo Island. If you're planning a trip to Whidbey, consider a lengthy stop at the shores of this scenic wonderland. You can picnic on a secluded beach, hike on rocky bluffs, even camp at Rosario Beach. Bring your binoculars for viewing marine mammals and birds frolicking off shore.

Oak Harbor Pub is a multiple-environment brewpub with something for everyone. Located on the main strip of the town, it's an ideal stop for island explorers. The facility is divided into a restaurant area and a pub. The restaurant has tables, a lunch counter, a live music stage, and a fenced-in patio. The menu includes pastas, steaks, seafood, and sandwiches, with a specialty assortment of sausage sandwiches.

Next door, the pub offers sports on the TV, a jukebox, pool and darts, a snug area with cozy furniture, a wood-burning stove, and board games. The bar sports twenty-eight taps, including the full Whidbey Island line of beers, and many others, from Bud to Fuller's ESB. Regulars, many of them from the local naval air base, have an extensive mug-club collection on display, with a bell they ring upon arriving. There's even a game room in back with pool tables and pinball machines.

The brewpub's parent company, Whidbey Island Brewing Company, originally produced most of its beer in a Langley brewing facility. The company has subsequently consolidated its operation at the Oak Harbor premises. The small brewhouse is visible through windows by the pub's entrance.

House beer selections include Whidbey Ale, Island Stout, Cascade Pale Ale, Bayview Blackberry, and Langley Light. Owner and brewer Jim Grimes also makes seasonals such as the Oak Harbor Dutch Style Ale (made with Belgian yeast and rock candy), an Irish red ale, a smooth and delectable oatmeal stout, and an India pale ale.

DIRECTIONS: From I-5, take Highway 20 west to Oak Harbor. The brewery is on the west side of 20, just north of 70th Avenue West.

Hours: 7 a.m.–10 p.m. Sunday; 10 a.m.–11 p.m. Monday–Friday; 7 a.m.–11 p.m. Saturday
Children: Yes, in the restaurant
Food: Pub fare
Entertainment: Live music, pool, darts, pinball, TV sports
Smoking: No
Payment: Checks, Visa, MC, Discover
Beer to go: Yes, draft

San Juan Brewing Company & Front Street Ale House

Established 1993

1 Front Street • Friday Harbor, WA 98250
(360) 378-2337

When docking at Friday Harbor on San Juan Island, one of the first establish ments you'll notice in this summer-resort town is the Front Street Ale House, home of the San Juan Brewing Company. San Juan Island offers a host of other attractions as well, including San Juan Island National Historical Park, with its two locations: American Camp on its southern end, and British Camp on its west side.

After exploring cute, bustling, Friday Harbor, stop into the Front Street brewpub before catching a return ferry. Head upstairs for views of the water and surrounding islands—a very scenic place to sip the only local suds on the islands.

Owner and brewer, Oren Combs, produces about thirty different beers in a slow year, and close to seventy in a busy one, approximately a quarter of them first-timers—that is, beers or blends he and Phil Murphy, assistant brewer, have not made before. All this in a small brewhouse tucked next door to the dining room. One crowd favorite is the Eichenberger Hefeweizen, an authentic, estery Bavarian-style brew. Other beers that frequent the pub's taps include Raging Main Ale, Haro Straight Pale Ale, Brown Island Bitter, and Starboard Porter.

Hours: 8 a.m.–midnight Sunday–Thursday; 8 a.m.–1 a.m. Friday and Saturday
Children: Yes, in the restaurant
Food: English and American pub fare; breakfast through dinner
Entertainment: Steel-tip darts, TV sports, pull tabs, occasional acoustic live music, trivia game on Tuesdays in winter
Smoking: Yes, in the upstairs pub
Payment: Visa, MC
Beer to go: Yes, draft and bottles

For something offbeat, look for one of their laced beers, such as No Vamp Ale, (flavored with elephant garlic and served around Halloween), Hot Harry's Pepper Beer, (seasoned with jalapeños); or Java Ale (a coffee-infused brown ale). You can find San Juan's twenty-two-ounce limited bottlings at select retail stores on the islands and along the Puget Sound shores.

In addition to beer, the pub offers a huge sixteen-page menu covering everything from French toast to bangers and mash. The predominantly English fare includes many American standbys, and is available for breakfast, lunch, or dinner.

DIRECTIONS: Take the ferry from Anacortes to Friday Harbor. The pub and brewery are located on the corner of Main and Front streets, one block from the ferry landing.

Washington's "Fourth Corner" Brew Tour

The Northwest corner of Washington is home to a remarkable cluster of breweries, well worth an excursion to this area known by residents as "The Fourth Corner" of Washington, due to their feeling of residing in a forgotten quadrant of the state. This is a region of stunning natural beauty, where the Cascade Mountains meet the sea.

The urban center of this area between Seattle, Washington, and Vancouver, B.C., is Bellingham, an eclectic city of 60,000, and home to a pair of brewpubs and a distribution-only microbrewery. Start a brew tour at Boundary Bay Brewing & Bistro, located on the main bike trail route at the edge of downtown. Don't leave without trying the outstanding Scotch ale. In Bellingham's historic Fairhaven District, at the entrance to scenic Chuckanut Drive, the Archer Alehouse offers an unrivaled selection of Belgian and other European bottled and draft beers.

Quality beers are served at several other restaurants and taverns in downtown Bellingham. You will want to sample Lowefield Ales, crafted by the North Cascades Brewing Company, at one of these establishments, since you cannot visit the brewery to taste their beers. Look around town for their Bellingham ESB, their London-style porter, and their Rebel Ale, a dark mild ale. On the north side of Bellingham, lies Orchard Street Brewery. This is a good stop for a nice dinner and a sampling of classic European and English-style beers in traditional glassware.

Whatcom Brewery of Ferndale, the area's oldest brewing operation, does not offer scheduled tours; call for an appointment, or look for their ESB and IPA at area taverns. Just east of Bellingham, on the Mount Baker Highway, lies the Beer Shrine. Home of the North Fork Brewing Company and their line of Frog Ales, this funky roadhouse shouldn't be missed if you're a pizza lover.

One of the Northwest's most delightful brew tours follows Chuckanut Drive out of Whatcom County to the idyllic Skagit Valley, stopping along the way for island views. Visit the rustic Skagit River Brewing in Mount Vernon for a barbecue dinner and some live music. Make time to drive to the spiffy La Conner Brewing Company for a craft beer and a wood-fired pizza, followed by a peek around an antique shop or two.

A bit farther to the south, in Everett, you'll find a pair of brewpubs a short distance off the interstate. Downtown, the Flying Pig Brewing Company serves up fresh beer and good pub fare. Down by the waterfront, Scuttlebutt Brewing Company's small taproom offers Scuttlebutt's beers and a full pub menu.

Scuttlebutt Brewing Company

Established 1996

1524 West Marine View Drive • Everett, WA 98201
(425) 257-9316 • www.scuttlebuttbrewing.com

Located on Everett's working waterfront, Scuttlebutt, a little brewery with café-like pub, offers fresh beer and a pleasant repast to a mix of locals, tourists, and boaters. This family-owned and -operated craft brewery runs a full-service pub, albeit with limited hours. The small dining room is built into the corner of a warehouse space that used to be a fish-processing plant, with the brewery (twenty-barrel, Specific Mechanical Systems) sitting on display on the other side of a windowed wall from the restaurant. You'll note that there's an ocean notion at the Scuttlebutt brewpub: nautical knick-knacks inside and views of the docks outside remind you that you're near saltwater.

Hours: 11:30 a.m.–8 p.m. Tuesday–Saturday
Children: Yes
Food: Pub fare and sandwiches
Entertainment: No
Smoking: Yes, on the patio
Payment: Checks, Visa, MC
Beer to go: Yes, draft

From the menu, you might start with the Texas Toothpicks—tasty onions and jalapeños dipped in batter, and deep-fried. After a pint to cool the jalapeño burn, move on to one of the many sandwiches offered for lunch, or ask about their daily pasta specials for dinner. Kids are welcome, and will enjoy saying the name of Scuttlebutt homemade root beer almost as much as they'll enjoy drinking it!

Pat Doud is the brewer, and he's making an assortment of ales—most unfiltered, largely of the Pacific Northwest styles. The Scuttlebutt regular lineup is a hefeweizen, an amber ale, and a porter. Seasonal offerings have included a pair of high-gravity top-fermented interpretations of the bock style for spring and fall, as well as a Scotch ale and the Winter Warmer Weizen, made with tangerine zest. There will be a Millenium Barleywine release in the winter of 2000. If you don't make it to Scuttlebutt's Everett brewpub, look for their mermaid tap handles at restaurants and taverns throughout the Puget Sound region.

DIRECTIONS: From I-5, take the Everett Avenue/Junction Highway 2 exit. Turn west on Everett Avenue toward downtown. Proceed about 3 miles as Everett Avenue enters, and passes through, downtown, and takes you downhill toward the water. At the foot of the hill, turn right on Marine Drive. Follow Marine Drive north to 1/4 mile past the Navy Base's main gate. The brewpub is on your left.

The Flying Pig Brewing Company

Established 1997

2929 Colby Avenue • Everett, WA 98201
(425) 339-1393

The Flying Pig is the brewpub hub of the bustling downtown core of Everett. Located on the main street of town, the Pig is poised to serve this working town with a restaurant-style dining experience in a brewery setting. The Flying Pig is a popular business lunch spot, while afternoons lend themselves to contemplative time in the dining area, before it fills again with busy pub energy in the evenings.

The lunch menu is pub fare with a spotlight on grilled sandwiches—the Rueben is much-praised. The dinner menu has the pub grub too, but also includes an array of pastas, chops and steaks, with a smattering of something for most everyone.

The ornately carved, cross-shaped bar sits in the middle of the restaurant and, houses an almost-hidden staircase in the rear. This staircase descends to a basement-level banquet room with views of the lower level brewhouse and cellaring operations. The main brewhouse (a copper and stainless fifteen-barrel system by Newlands Services) is visible from the dining area upstairs behind floor-length windows. The décor emphasizes the establishment's theme of flying and pigs, and includes "pigphrenalia" large and small. Be on the lookout for seasonal special events from the crazy uncles at the Pig. For instance, on Saint Patrick's Day, the downstairs banquet room is transformed into Uncle Leeham's Rec Room, and in October it becomes Uncle Gunther's Polka Palace for an Octoberfest.

The Flying Pig's brewer, Paul Scott, is a hop enthusiast. You won't find his beers dull. The regular beer lineup includes either a roasty smoked porter or an American-style brown ale, as well as Curly Tails Golden (a revved up example of a golden with citrus highlights); Hogwild Hefeweizen (authentic German flavor zapped with extra hops); and Big Pig IPA (the best of the batch, with good malt depths and hop heights). Seasonals include an English-style bitter and a Belgian-style wit in the warm months, and a barleywine when the weather turns chill.

Hours: 11 a.m.–10 p.m. Sunday–Thursday; 11 a.m.–Midnight Friday and Saturday
Children: Yes
Food: Pub fare lunches, steaks, and pasta dinners
Entertainment: Occasional live music: jazz/Celtic/acoustic; seasonal special events
Smoking: No
Payment: Checks, Visa, MC, AmEx, Diners Club
Beer to go: No

DIRECTIONS: From I-5, take the Everett Avenue and Junction Highway 2 exit. Turn west on Everett Avenue toward downtown and the water, and drive to Colby Avenue. Turn left (south) on Colby. The brewpub is three blocks down on the left, three doors south of the Everett Theater.

La Conner Brewing Company

Established 1995

117 South 1st Street • La Conner, WA 98257
(360) 466-1415

The town of La Conner is an historic centerpiece to the area known as the Skagit Flats. With its stately old houses and antique shops, La Conner feels like a Western town caught sometime in the early part of the twentieth century. The Skagit Valley Tulip Festival, held annually in the spring, is a major tourist attraction to the area.

The La Conner brewpub is housed in a striking, dark wood structure at the edge of town near the small marina on the Swinomish Channel. The brewpub's interior is small and upscale. The magnificent light pine columns and façades, and the open kitchen with its wood-fired oven give the brewpub a pleasant ambiance. In nice weather, there is outdoor seating on a small private patio. Or, if you've been out birdwatching in the chilly rain, you can warm up by a cozy fireplace.

Hours: 11:30 a.m.–10 p.m. Sunday–Thursday; 11:30 a.m.–11 p.m. Friday and Saturday
Children: Yes
Food: Wood-fired pizzas, pub fare
Entertainment: Television at the bar
Smoking: No
Payment: Visa, MC
Beer to go: Yes, bottles

The menu focuses on pizzas and offers a variety of toppings, from feta and calamata olives to smoked salmon, roasted chicken, and spinach. You can sit at a counter and watch the pizzas being made while enjoying a glass of house beer and playing one of the woodcrafted board games.

The ten-barrel brewery is in the same building as the pub, but is not visible. The beers are bottled and available in many Western Washington retail locations. In the pub, they're all served in traditional European glassware, including schooners, Imperial pints and many others.

Owner and brewer Scott Abrahmson's beers include a light, creamy Pilsner with a crisp finish, a smooth and smoky stout, a brown ale that's light-bodied and nicely balanced between sweet and dry, a refreshing wheat, and a root beer. Seasonal brews include an IPA, a spring bock, and for the winter holidays, Tannenbaum Ale, a spicy and nutty English-style old ale.

DIRECTIONS: From I-5, take Exit 221 and head west. Take the first right to Conway. Go through Conway and cross the Skagit River onto Fir Island Road. Proceed as it becomes Best Road, then turn left onto Chilberg Road. Go to the stop sign and turn left on La Conner/Whitney Road, which becomes Morris Avenue as it heads into La Conner. Follow Morris to the end of town and turn left on 1st Street. The brewpub is on the left.

Skagit River Brewing Company

Established 1994

404 3rd Street • Mount Vernon, WA 98273
(360) 336-2884

Mount Vernon is a delightful town in the Skagit Valley's farmbelt. Come here during the Tulip Festival in April, or stop at Mount Vernon when you are headed west on Highway 20 toward Anacortes, or east toward Diablo and points beyond. The Skagit River Brewing Company is housed in what was once the Pacific Fruit & Produce Company, a handsome brick building near the railroad tracks at the edge of downtown. This microbrewery has a large taproom adjoining the impressive brewhouse (AAA Metal Fabricating and Newlands Services equipment), with brewing and cellaring operations visible from the dining area.

The brewpub is a nice place for folks to gather inside, or outside on the roofed back porch. Art that changes with the seasons lends a warm atmosphere to the main seating area; massive beam and timber construction supports a balcony seating area suitable for private parties. The open kitchen serves soups, salads, and pub fare, and specializes in barbecue. Try the Brewer's Melt—house-smoked brisket grilled with onions, mushrooms, and cheese. For a romping good time, dance to live music on the hardwood floor.

Brewer Charlie Sullivan worked at McMenamins for three years prior to opening Skagit River Brewing. He brews several standard ales, including a lager-like Skagit Golden Ale (flavorful without the assertiveness of most ales); an English-style nut brown called Skagit Brown (brewed with a touch of oats in the mix); and Yellowjacket Pale Ale (a golden pale with intense hop character from all-Northwest hops). Other brews include Highwater Porter (a light-bodied porter with plenty of hops), and a very smooth, roasty and strong Russian Imperial Stout. Skagit also makes a contract brew available only at the Snoqualmie Pass Ski Area that is fifty percent rye, light, and very quaffable.

Hours: 11 a.m.–10 p.m. Monday–Thursday; 11 a.m.–midnight Friday; 11 a.m.–11 p.m. Saturday; 11 a.m.–9 p.m. Sunday
Children: Yes, except during live music
Food: Pub fare, barbecue
Entertainment: Live acoustic and full band music on weekends, occasional swing dance classes
Smoking: No
Payment: Checks, Visa, MC, AmEx
Beer to go: Yes, draft and bottles

DIRECTIONS: From I-5, take the Mount Vernon City Center/Kincaid Street exit and turn west on Kincaid. Turn right on 3rd and drive two blocks. The brewery is on your right.

Boundary Bay Brewery & Bistro

Established 1995

1107 Railroad Avenue • Bellingham, WA 98225
(360) 647-5593

At the end of Bellingham's eclectic collection of shops and eateries on Railroad Avenue, you'll find the Farmer's Market on Saturdays and Sundays, April through October, and next to the market is Boundary Bay Brewery and Bistro. Named for the bay at the Canadian–American border, this brewery-pub is a gem: a true hometown pub and restaurant in a refurbished warehouse space at the edge of downtown. The interior is divided into the taproom—a pub-like area with many tables and a bar, and the bistro—a high-ceilinged dining room with sconce-like lighting, old bricks, local artwork, and woodwork.

Boundary Bay's menu offers a mix of Northwest cuisine and pub fare. House specialties also include fajitas and wraps, pasta dishes, and specialty pizzas—including a sausage and potato pizza. Enjoy lunch on the expansive deck.

The handsome seventeen-barrel brewhouse stretches the length of the building. Brewers Skip Madsen and David Morales make an extensive line of quality, unfiltered beers that have garnered national attention under the supervision of proprieter Ed Bennett. The widely known Scotch ale, thoroughly malted with lots of fruit esters, is very tasty. The amber is also an excellent, fully hopped example of the style.

There's also a classic best bitter, a full-bodied golden, an IPA, and the Reefnetter Ale—a delicious dry-hopped version of the best bitter. Seasonals have included a Pilsner, a doppelbock, and Cabin Fever, a wee heavy ale. Look for the "BB" logo on tap handles around the region.

DIRECTIONS: From I-5, take Exit 253 Lakeway Drive. From I-5 Northbound, the ramp merges right onto King Street. In a block, turn right on Lakeway Drive, pass under the highway. (From I-5 Southbound, at the end of the ramp turn right.) Follow Lakeway to a five-way intersection. Go straight, onto Holly, and drive five blocks. Turn left on Railroad Avenue and go two blocks to the end of the street; the brewpub is on your right.

Hours: 11 a.m.–11 p.m. Monday–Wednesday; 11 a.m.–midnight Thursday–Friday; 10 a.m.–midnight Saturday; 10 a.m.–10 p.m. Sunday
Children: Yes, in the Bistro
Food: Northwest cuisine
Entertainment: TV sports events; live music in the Bistro on Thursdays, occasional other live music, classic movies on the deck
Smoking: No
Payment: Checks, Visa, MC, Discover
Beer to go: Yes, draft and bottles

Orchard Street Brewery

Established 1995

709 W Orchard Drive, Suite 1 • Bellingham, WA 98225
(360) 647-1614

Bellingham is home to the Bellis Fair mall a retail mecca that attracts shoppers from around B.C.'s Lower Mainland and Northwest Washington. While you're out this way, stop into the Orchard Street Brewery for some fine food and beer.

Orchard Street is a microbrewery and restaurant located in a mixed-zone area just off this commercial strip. An upscale restaurant with brightly colored walls, folks meet at the brewery for a business lunch, or gather at the end of the day for a nice dinner accompanied by good wines, as well as quality house brews.

The menu offers several appetizers, including baked brie and the popular tapenade bread dip. Entrées range from steaks to pastas; the specialty, however, is wood-fired pizza. Try the Thai Chicken Pizza or the zesty roasted garlic pie! The twenty-barrel brewhouse is visible behind the rear glass wall of the bar area.

Owner/brewer Christian Krogstad comes from a long tenure at McMenamins, where he managed several of the breweries, including Edgefield. He makes an assortment of unfiltered beers true-to-style, using a variety of yeast strains. You can enjoy Orchard Street beers without coming to Bellingham, though, on tap throughout Western Washington, and in widely available six-packs.

The standard beer lineup includes a Bavarian-style hefeweizen with true banana aroma, a complex and malty stock ale made to be enjoyed with food, a Northwest-style pale flavored with Cascade hops for a lip-smacking finish, and Christina Porter (named for Christian's wife) with intriguing highlights of chocolate, licorice and other malt flavors. Seasonal brews have been a Kölsch-style ale with twenty percent wheat in the grist, a raspberry wheat ale, and Jingle Ale—a strong, spicy winter brew. All the beers at the restaurant are served in traditional glassware, and there's usually a guest cider on tap.

Hours: 11:30 a.m.–10 p.m. Monday–Thursday; 11:30 a.m.–11 p.m. Friday; 3-11 p.m. Saturday
Children: Yes
Food: Northwest cuisine
Entertainment: No
Smoking: No
Payment: Checks, Visa, MC, AmEx
Beer to go: Yes, draft and bottles

DIRECTIONS: From I-5, take the Meridian Street exit and turn south toward the city center on Guide-Meridian Street. Go two blocks and turn left on Orchard Street. Follow Orchard about three blocks to West Orchard Drive. Turn right and enter the parking lot on your right. The brewery and restaurant are at the end of the building.

Whatcom Brewery

Established 1994

P.O. Box 427 • Ferndale, WA 98248
(360) 380-6969

The Whatcom Brewery produces ales from a truly bioregional perspective. Owner Lloyd Zimmerman and brewers John Hudson and Tony Reetz are joined by brewmaster, Adam Goldstein, formerly of Skagit River Brewing Company, Hales Ales, and breweries in Scotland prior to becoming a Pacific Northwest transplant. Together this team is using the cobbled-together brewhouse, "made from ninety-seven percent recycled materials," to produce a limited line of yummy ales. The system is completely gravity fed, from the mill tucked away under the rafters, to the open fermenter on the ground floor of the early 1900s pioneer cabin.

Hours: Tours by appointment
Children: No
Food: No
Entertainment: No
Smoking: No
Payment: Checks
Beer to go: Yes, draft

It's worth a trip to see this brewery, so call ahead for an appointment. One day Zimmerman hopes to open a tasting room in downtown Ferndale. Until then, it's a matter of catching one of the brewers when they're available for a tour. The top floor of the small brewery, located behind Zimmerman's house, is an elaborate brewer's quarters, complete with a sliding bookcase and totem-style wood carvings crafted by Lloyd himself.

While you're visiting, ask Lloyd to tell you about how they work with local hop growers to produce a strain of Czech Saaz hops that will grow in Western Washington. His holistic operation even trades spent grains to a local pig farmer in return for pork.

Whatcom Brewery's standard beers are a Northwest-type IPA and an ESB with a hearty mouthfeel and balanced flavor. These are bold, assertive ales, in keeping with Lloyd's latest motto, "Our beer's not for everyone—we just couldn't make enough for them all."

The beers are primarily available on draft at regional establishments in Whatcom County, but have been sighted on tap in Seattle and Mount Vernon. Look for Zimmerman's hand-carved tap handles. Whatcom also makes a pale ale, straw in color and light in body, for the Workshop Pub in the small town of Birch Bay. Ask for the Workshop Pale Ale if you put in at Birch Bay.

DIRECTIONS: Call for directions

The North Fork Brewery/Pizza/Beer Shrine

Established 1997

6186 Mount Baker Highway • Deming, WA 98244
(360) 599-2337

A beer and pizza shrine located just before the final outpost of civilization on your way out the Mount Baker Highway for a back-country trek—or, more likely, the final stop on your way home . . . what more could a group of skiers, hikers, kayakers, or any other band of roving travelers hope for? Between the foothills and the Nooksack River, the icy runoff of majestic Mount Baker, the North Fork Brewery is a worthy stop. Its funk factor is high, its beer brewed true to traditional styles, and its pizza worth the drive alone.

The "beer shrine" title comes to mind as you view a behind-the-bar area decorated with a random assortment of bottles, steins, beer trays and knick-knacks that make up an actual shrine. You will be impressed by the beer bottle collection displayed in glass cases set into the dividing wall between the two seating areas. The main seating area includes the long bar (made from the floor boards of a nearby dancehall), and a dozen tables and booths.

You can expect three or four house beers on tap to warm your bones as you seek refuge here from the elements. The brewer and proprietor, Sanford Savage (formerly of the Triple Rock Brewery in Berkeley, California), strives for beers that achieve a traditional profile. The American Wheat is a quaffable, almost lager-like light ale. To round out a typical day's brew lineup, add a strong entry into the IPA arena and a robust stout. You may be lucky enough to find that your visit coincides with a batch of the English Mild, with its fruity malts and caramelly highlights. Seasonal brews have frog names, such as the rich and flavorful Tree Frog Ale.

Hours: Summer: 4 p.m.–11 p.m. Monday–Thursday; 2 p.m.–11 p.m. Friday; noon–11 p.m. Saturday–Sunday winter, call for hours
Children: Yes, until 9 p.m.
Food: Full menu, pizza
Entertainment: Open mike on Mondays, Grateful Dead Tuesdays
Smoking: Yes, except in non-smoking room
Payment: Checks, Visa, MC, AmEx, Discover
Beer to go: Yes, draft

The pizza is big, East Coast thin-crust and is served on a handy elevated serving pan in the center of the table. A touch of fennel makes the sauce a bit more exciting than the average pie.

DIRECTIONS: From Bellingham, take I-5 exit 254 Sunset Drive. Turn east onto Sunset, which becomes the Mount Baker Highway. Travel exactly 20 miles, and the Beer Shrine is on your left, at mile-marker 20 (between the towns of Deming and Kendall).

Yakima Valley Brew Tour

The Yakima Valley accounts for seventy-five percent of the hops grown in the United States today. Thus, it was only a matter of time before breweries appeared in what is more widely known as Washington's wine country. A tour of the Yakima Valley breweries provides insight into the history of this region, as well as an education on the influence hops have had on Pacific Northwest ales and lagers.

The tour begins, appropriately enough, with Bert Grant and the Yakima Brewing Company. Bert Grant worked for thirty-six years in the brewing and hop-producing industries until 1982, when he opened the first modern brewpub in the U.S. Stop by the pub for a pint of cask-conditioned Scottish Ale, or a sample of the seasonal Fresh Hop Ale, brewed with the first Cascade hops of each year's harvest.

Next stop is Snipes Mountain. The Yakima Valley, with an average of 300 days of sunshine each year, and plentiful water from the nearby Yakima River, is ideal area for farming. Snipes Mountain of Sunnyside, Washington, is located right in the middle of the farmbelt. Stop by for a nut brown ale, with its rich malty flavor balanced out by Yakima Valley hops.

A short drive brings you to Prosser, and a rather ingenious project: a small business "incubator park" that gives start-up enterprises certain incentives during the first few years of operation. The five-unit complex houses the Whitstran Brewing Company. Try comparing Whitstran's Highlander Ale to Grant's Scottish.

The Tri-Cities of Richland, Kennewick, and Pasco sit at the junction of the Yakima and Columbia Rivers. Three breweries also reside here: Atomic Ale, Rattlesnake Mountain and Ice Harbor. Atomic Ale Brewpub and Eatery takes its theme from nearby Hanford Nuclear Reservation. Get a pint of Atomic Amber or

Plutonium Porter and see if you can figure out the half-life of a beer atom!

Rattlesnake Mountain Brewing Company sits right next to the Columbia River and offers beautiful views of the river from both the indoor and outdoor eating areas. Try the hoppy Rattlesnake Pale Ale or pub favorite Honey Red Ale while enjoying the local scenery. Just down the road from Rattlesnake is The Brew Garden, a retail store with six tap handles so you can sample before you buy. They also sell tons of microbrew paraphernalia and over 250 different bottled brews, including offerings from all of the locals breweries.

Across the river, in Pasco, is the Ice Harbor Brewing Company, a bottling and distribution operation. Try their best-selling Kölsch-style ale or the seasonal Extra Special Bitter. If time permits, head over to Walla Walla for a final stop—the Mill Creek Brewpub, home of Big House Brewing. A little off the beaten path, Walla Walla played an important role early on in the formation of the Northwest Territories, and later in the history of the state of Washington. You can try a pint of their widely known Penitentiary Porter, and at the same time get an interesting Northwest history lesson.

Roslyn Brewing Company

Established 1990

208 Pennsylvania Avenue • Roslyn, WA 98941
(509) 649-2232

The Roslyn Brewing Company, located in the quiet town made famous as the filming location for the "Northern Exposure" TV series, is an historically rooted brewery. The Roslyn Brewing and Malting Company, founded in 1889, and operating until Prohibition closed it in 1913, brewed beer for the locals working in the booming coal mines. Brewers Roger Beardsley and Dino Enrico opened the Roslyn Brewing Company in 1990 to rekindle the tastes, styles, and traditions of the former brewery.

Beardsley and Enrico brew two beers, both lagers—a rarity among modern craft breweries. Roslyn Beer is a smooth, dark lager; Brookside Beer is a pale lager. The longer and colder conditioning of these lagers produces beers that will appeal to novice beer drinkers as well as ale lovers. These brews prove that fine, handcrafted lagers do exist in the Pacific Northwest.

The tasting room is decorated with photos and memorabilia from early 1900s Roslyn. Look at the pictures of Pennsylvania Avenue and then step outside. Very little has changed over the years—one of the main reasons the town was chosen as the site of "Northern Exposure." After you enjoy the beauty of Roslyn, be sure to visit the Cle Elum River valley, one of the largest recreation areas in the region, and site of Lemah Mountain, located only a few miles away. Lemah, which roughly translated, means "the hand" in French, refers to the five peaks of this mountain—captured in the logo and bottle labels of Roslyn beer.

Directions: From I-90, take exit 80. Follow signs 3 miles to Roslyn. Turn left at Pennsylvania Avenue. The brewery is $1^{1}/_{2}$ blocks down, on the left.

Hours: Noon–5 p.m. Saturday and Sunday all year; noon–6 p.m. Friday–Sunday in the summer
Children: No
Food: No
Entertainment: Acoustic musicians play occasionally
Smoking: No
Payment: Checks, Visa, MC
Beer to go: Yes

Grant's Brewery Pub/
Yakima Brewing Company

Established 1982

32 N Front Street • Yakima, WA 98901
(509) 575-2922 • www.grants.com

Grant's Brewery Pub began brewing beer in 1982. For head brewer Bert Grant, whose brewing career began in 1945, the goal has always been to produce high-quality, traditional-styled ales. And, even though the ownership of Grant's has recently changed hands, the Brewery Pub is still Bert's domain—a place to spin out delightfully rich and full-bodied ales.

The pub is located in the northern half of the old Yakima train station. The inside of the building has been refinished to create a warm, relaxing pub split into two rooms, divided by a small brewing operation used to produce the cask-conditioned ales served at the pub. The main brewing and bottling is done in a large warehouse on the edge of town. Tours are available by appointment, or you can find Grant's beers widely distributed in six-packs.

The cozy atmosphere of the pub is ideal for sampling Bert Grant's ales. The ales generally are very hoppy, and are served at cellar temperature to bring out their best characteristics. Grant's Scottish Ale, the flagship product, is a strong, hoppy, traditional ale that tastes even better when cask-conditioned. The Perfect Porter and Imperial Stout, the darkest ales, are both thick and rich with varying degrees of chocolate flavor. Grant's India Pale Ale is a light-colored ale with very hoppy bitterness and aroma. Although all of Grant's Ales are bottled, the true flavors and delights of the ales really come out when tasted direct from the brewery, in the comfort of the Brewery Pub.

Hours: 11:30 a.m.–midnight Monday–Thursday; 11:30 a.m.–1 a.m. Friday and Saturday; 11:30 a.m.–9 p.m. Sunday; closed Sundays in winter
Children: Yes
Food: Standard pub fare
Entertainment: Darts, board games, television, live jazz and blues
Smoking: No
Payment: Checks, Visa, MC
Beer to go: Yes

DIRECTIONS: From I-82, take the 1st Street exit. Follow 1st Street all the way into town to Yakima Avenue. Turn right on Yakima, and then right onto Front Street. The pub is on the left, in an old train depot.

Snipes Mountain Microbrewery & Restaurant

Established 1997

905 Yakima Valley Highway • Sunnyside, WA 98944
(509) 837-2739

The first thing that hits you when you get off the Interstate and go into Sunnyside, in search of Snipes Mountain, is the fact that you are most definitely in the country. This is working agricultural land. Everything seems to grow here—fruits, vegetables, grains.

Snipes Mountain Microbrewery and Restaurant added another product to the local economy in July of 1997—beer. The brewery takes its name from nearby Snipes Mountain, which, in turn, was named for Ben Snipes, the first white settler to come to this area. The building that houses Snipes Mountain Microbrewery is one of the largest in town. The exterior is reminiscent of a very large log cabin, while the interior walls and ceiling are similarly rustic, with rough-cut, exposed studs and beams providing support for the structure. An upstairs balcony offers a good view of the entire restaurant, a large separate dining area, and a spacious outdoor seating area that takes advantage of the 300-plus days of sunshine in the area.

The menu at Snipes Mountain is extensive. Pub fare includes the calzone of the day, tasty wood fired pizzas, or beer-battered fish and chips. Entrées range from a lighter salmon pasta to weekend-only prime rib. Snipes Mountain ales figure prominently in the menu, and are used to create their Beer-B-Q sauce, and other marinades.

Of course, you can drink beer, too. Standards include an extra special bitter, a Northwest-style hefeweizen, a slightly sweet nut brown ale, or the dark roasted and somewhat smoky porter. Seasonals have included an India pale ale, wintertime barley wine, and a fall Harvest Ale. All of the beers are served with a CO_2/nitrogen mix, giving the drawn pint a creamy head and a smooth texture.

Hours: 10 a.m.–11 p.m. Sunday–Thursday; 11 a.m.–11 p.m. Friday and Saturday
Children: Yes, except in the bar
Food: Upscale pub fare; wood-fired pizza
Entertainment: Televised sports in bar area
Smoking: No
Payment: Checks, Visa, MC, AmEx, Discover
Beer to go: Yes, draft

DIRECTIONS: From Yakima on I-82 take exit 63 to Outlook and Sunnyside. At the stop sign turn left and cross over the freeway. At the next stop sign turn left onto the Yakima Valley Highway and go one mile into Sunnyside. The second stop light will be 9th Street. The restaurant is on the right.

Whitstran Brewing Company

Established 1996

3800 Lee Road, Suite B • Prosser, WA 99350
(509) 786-3883

Whitstran Brewing Company is a small brewery located in the heart of Yakima Valley wine country. It currently resides in the Port of Benton "Incubator Suites," a small collection of start up businesses. Whitstran is focused on distribution of bottles and kegs throughout the Yakima Valley.

Using a fairly small brewing system—the brewery operates with two four-barrel fermenters, Whitstran offers a variety of ales both in bottles and on tap. Highlander Ale, a Scottish-style ale—and the brewery's best seller—is dark amber in color with a pleasant, slightly sweet flavor. The favorite of brewer and co-owner John Paul Estey is 11th Hour Pale Ale. Seasonal ales have included a Spiced Holiday Ale, an India pale ale, and a Belgian-style brown ale.

Whitstran likes to experiment with its beers, and the size of the brewery makes it easier to try out different recipes. Estey is a long-time homebrewer, and likes the trial-and-error approach to brewing. The brewery is divided into two rooms, with the brewery in back and the tasting room in front. Several ales will always be on tap, where guests can sample the latest experiment, or one of the flavorful standards.

In an area long known for hops production, it is fitting that a brewery should carve out a niche among the many wineries of the region. In addition to Whitstran, the "incubator suite" has two wineries and is just 100 yards away from regional giant, Hogue Winery's tasting room. A trip to Whitstran could quickly turn into a full afternoon of beer and wine tasting!

Hours: 1 p.m.–5 p.m. Friday; 11 a.m.–5 p.m. Saturday and Sunday
Children: No
Food: No
Entertainment: No
Smoking: No
Payment: Checks, Visa, MC
Beer to go: Yes, bottles

DIRECTIONS: From I-82 take exit 82. Go east on Wine Country Road (right from I-82 South, left and back over I-82 from the north). Turn left on Lee Lane, then right on Lee Road.

Atomic Ale Brewpub & Eatery

Established 1997

1015 Lee Boulevard • Richland, WA 99352
(509) 946-5465

The Atomic Ale Brewpub and Eatery both pays homage to, and pokes fun at the history of this area. The tri-cities of Richland, Kennewick and Pasco are famous (or perhaps infamous) as the home of the Hanford nuclear reservation, site of the world's first operating plutonium reactor. The Atomic Ale Brewpub shares in some of that history—it sits across the street from the former site of the Hanford Camp women's barracks. The pub has captured slices of that history in framed photographs scattered along the walls.

The Atomic Ale building is something of an icon itself. Originally an A&W drive-in restaurant (complete with roller-skating servers), it has been modified a little over the years, but you'll still wonder whether you're in the right place when you park under the drive-up awning.

It is good to honor the past, and it's also okay to have a little fun with it. The brewery produces several standard ales, and almost all have names appropriate for the region. Plutonium Porter, Half-Life Hefeweizen, and Proton Pale Ale are a few of the standards from which to choose. Atomic Amber, the pub's biggest seller, is a flavorful, amber-colored ale with a smooth malt flavor balanced well with a hop finish and aroma. Waynier Isotope Ale, named for their first homebrew contest winner, is a hoppy India pale ale and worth sampling if on tap. Check out the designs for the beer labels as well; many are available as T-shirts to purchase. Nearly every brewery offers T-shirts, but you'll definitely regret it if you pass up one of these!

The menu favors gourmet wood-fired pizzas that are very high quality. The Godfather pizza is especially popular, but if you're feeling adventurous try the spicy Thai Bangkok Chicken pizza. With or without the chicken, it is extremely good.

Hours: 11 a.m.–10 p.m. Monday–Thursday; 11 a.m.–11 p.m. Friday and Saturday
Children: Yes
Food: Pub fare, wood-fired pizzas
Entertainment: Games, Monday night blues
Smoking: No
Payment: Checks, Visa, MC, AmEx, Discover
Beer to go: No

DIRECTIONS: From I-82 heading east, take exit 102 to I-182. From I-182 take the George Washington Way exit. Follow George Washington Way to Lee Boulevard and turn left onto Lee; the brewpub is $2^1/2$ blocks down, on the left.

Rattlesnake Mountain Brewing Company

Established 1997

1250 Columbia Center Boulevard • Richland, WA 99352
(509) 783-5747 • members.home.net/rattlesnake-mtn

One novel way of touring the breweries and brewpubs of the Pacific Northwest would be to travel down the Columbia River, stopping for supplies (and beer tastings) along the way. If you were to choose this method, the first brewpub you would come to would be the Rattlesnake Mountain Brewing Company in Richland, Washington.

Rattlesnake Mountain Brewing Company, sitting on the south bank of the majestic Columbia, takes ample advantage of its location. Ever since Steve and Renea Metzger opened the brewery in July of 1997, outdoor music has always been part of the venue. They now host a monthly concert series during the summer. The main dining room of the somewhat medieval-styled restaurant faces out to the river, providing expansive views.

In the middle of the dining room is the brewery, enclosed by glass, but completely visible to patrons. Steve and his brewers produce seven standard ales and a variety of seasonals for both in-house consumption and local distribution. Honey Red Ale, a reddish-brown ale with a lightly sweet, nutty flavor and a crisp finish, is a local favorite. Other standards include a rich and dark oatmeal stout, a fairly hoppy Rattlesnake Pale Ale, a golden, and a wheat. Seasonals have included a Scottish ale and a winter brew.

Hours: 11:30 a.m.–11:30 p.m. Sunday–Thursday; 11:30 a.m.–12:30 p.m. Friday and Saturday
Children: Yes, except in the bar
Food: Pub fare and entrées
Entertainment: Weekend music, televised sports, board games
Smoking: Yes, at the bar
Payment: Checks, Visa, MC
Beer to go: Yes, draft

The menu includes a wide range of burgers and sandwiches, including Ruebens, fish and chips, both regular and vegetarian Philly-style cheese steaks, and dinner entrées. Come on a special night and you might end up choosing from a Cajun-influenced menu, or something altogether different. If you are doing a beer tour by boat you should be sure to stock up—it's a long way to your destination, the Pacific Rim Brewing Company in Astoria, Oregon, at the mouth of the Columbia River.

DIRECTIONS: From I-82 heading east take exit 102 onto I-182. Take exit 5 to Highway 240 East/South. From Highway 240 take the Columbia Center Boulevard exit. At the left go left (north) onto Columbia Center. Rattlesnake is at the corner of Columbia Center and Columbia Drive overlooking…the Columbia River.

Ice Harbor Brewing Company

Established 1997

415 W Columbia Street • Pasco, WA 99301
(509) 545-0927 • www.iceharbor.com

Ice Harbor Brewing Company opened on January 1, 1997, in downtown Pasco next to the Pasco Farmer's Market. Owners Bill Jaquish and Mike Hall purchased the then Meheen & Collins Brewing Company, renaming it to reflect the history of the region. The bottle labels are inspired by the region's railroad, river, and agricultural history. Meheen & Collins still run a bottling equipment plant next door—perfect neighbors for a microbrewery focusing on distribution.

The ten-barrel brewhouse is located in the back of the building. The brewery utilizes old dairy equipment for significant portions of the brewing process, including dairy tanks used as open fermenters. If you've never seen the fermentation process done in open containers, to get a good look at fermenting beer in horizontal vats, ask for a tour. It is absolutely worth the visit.

The brewery produces a variety of ales for bottling. Their initial three bottled products include Runaway Red Ale (a full-bodied amber colored ale with a slightly fruity flavor), Sternwheeler Stout (a dark ale with strong mocha flavors and a rich aroma), and Harvest Pale Ale (a medium-bodied, golden-colored ale with mild hop characteristics). They also produce a Kölsch-style ale and a barley wine-style ale, available in bottles and on draft. Other seasonals, including an extra special bitter, a Christmas ale, and an alt-style ale, are available only on draft.

Around the corner from Ice Harbor is Alchemy Brew and Wine, a homebrew supply store, as well as a good source for regional bottled beers and wines. In summer you can also enjoy the Pasco Farmer's Market, open most Wednesdays, Thursdays, and Saturdays.

DIRECTIONS: From I-82 heading west take exit 102 to I-182. Take exit 13 to 4th Avenue. Take 4th Avenue south to Columbia Street. Turn left onto Columbia. Ice Harbor is $1/2$ block down on the left.

Hours: Noon–6 p.m. Monday–Friday; 9 a.m.–3 p.m. Saturday
Children: No
Food: No
Entertainment: No
Smoking: No
Payment: Checks, Visa, MC
Beer to go: Yes, bottles, liters, cases

Big House Brewing/Mill Creek Brewpub

Established 1997

11 S Palouse • Walla Walla, WA 99362
(509) 522-2440 • www.wallawallawa.com/millcreekbrewpub.htm

Although Walla Walla, Washington, is probably best known for producing a particularly good sweet onion, there is a lot more to this town than just onions. The area was first explored and mapped when the Lewis and Clark expedition traveled through here in 1806. Whitman College, one of the region's best private undergraduate schools, was founded in 1859. One of the oldest breweries in the Pacific Northwest opened in Walla Walla in 1855.

This area is also home to the Walla Walla Penitentiary, which inspired the name of owner Gary Johnson's brewery when he opened Big House Brewing in June of 1997. He would actually have opened earlier except for an unfortunate fire that completely demolished the building shortly before they were due to open. Johnson was determined, however, and other than some burn marks that remain around the fireplace and on a telephone pole on the sidewalk, the fire is a thing of the past.

The local prison also provides the name for Big House Brewing's most well known ale, the Penitentiary Porter. Other standard brews include Brew 22 (a slightly sweet lager), the Institutional Pale Ale (full of hops in the brewing and dry-hopped for extra bitterness), and Riehl Light (a very light American-style lager).

The pub attracts students from Whitman and the other local colleges as well as loyal regulars, and the menu reflects the financial and gastronomic interests of both crowds. Entrées include beer-battered fish and chips and bratwurst, while the sandwich menu ranges from the Five Alarm Arson Burger—a nod to the building's recent history—to the Grilled Yellowfin Tuna Steak sandwich.

Hours: 11 a.m.–midnight Monday–Saturday; noon–9 p.m. Sunday
Children: Yes
Food: Pub fare
Entertainment: Occasional live music
Smoking: Yes, in the bar
Payment: Checks, Visa, MC
Beer to go: Yes, bottles

DIRECTIONS: From Highway 12 heading east take the 2nd Street exit, turning right onto 2nd and following it to Main. Turn left onto Main and go three blocks to the five-way intersection of Main, Boyer, and Palouse. The brewpub is on the corner of Palouse and Main.

Northern Lights Brewing Company

Established 1993

1701 S Lawson Road • Airway Heights, WA 99001
(509) 244-4909

Northern Lights Brewing Company is located in a big storage building in the Spokane suburb of Airway Heights. With its quality ales, it makes up for what it may lack in ambiance. The brewery focuses on draft distribution—the extent of the entertainment provided is the music pounding out of brewer Mark Irvin's radio. If you stop by, look for a new facility, however, as increased distribution and demand will likely force Northern Lights to soon move to more spacious quarters.

Irvin spent several years working for Hale's Ales, and he has blended the finest of the Hale's traditions with his own to produce six wonderful creations. He lager-conditions all of his ales, letting colder temperatures and time produce smooth, full-bodied ales with deep, complex flavors. The brewery is mostly made up of old dairy equipment, which is remarkably well suited for the production of beer.

Lightest of the Northern Lights ales are the Creme Ale and Blueberry Creme Ale. Fermented with huge quantities of Oregon blueberries (instead of extract—an easier, but less-flavorful alternative), the Blueberry Creme Ale is an excellent dessert ale, with the smell and taste of fresh berries. Crystal Bitter, the most popular Northern Lights ale, is a very hoppy extra special bitter-styled ale, dry-hopped for an extra punch of herbal hop aroma and flavor. Chocolate Dunkel, a rich dark ale brewed with plenty of chocolate malt and roasted barley, is simply a wonderful brew. If you visit in winter, look for the Northern Lights Winter Ale, a very hoppy, dark amber brew with a high alcohol content sure to warm you to your toes.

DIRECTIONS: Call for directions.

Hours: 9 a.m.–5 p.m. Monday–Saturday. Tours by appointment.
Children: Yes
Food: No
Entertainment: No
Smoking: No
Payment: Checks
Beer to go: Yes, draft

Bayou Brewing Company

Established 1997

1003 East Trent • Spokane, WA 99202
(509) 484-4818

The Bayou Brewing Company is basically one continuous Mardi Gras celebration...every night of the week, every day of the year. You walk in, get your complimentary string of beads, and the night has begun. Bayou Brewing is several different restaurants at the same time. The Mardi Gras Restaurant is a formal dining room with views of the Spokane River. The VooDoo Lounge is a hopping bar designed to Hollywood-caliber detail. Fat Tuesday's is a dance and entertainment room that features comedians and performers several nights a week.

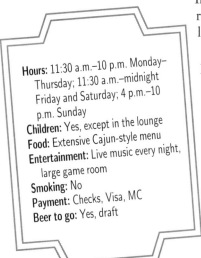

Hours: 11:30 a.m.–10 p.m. Monday–Thursday; 11:30 a.m.–midnight Friday and Saturday; 4 p.m.–10 p.m. Sunday
Children: Yes, except in the lounge
Food: Extensive Cajun-style menu
Entertainment: Live music every night, large game room
Smoking: No
Payment: Checks, Visa, MC
Beer to go: Yes, draft

If that isn't enough, a video arcade and pool room is available if you want still more stimulation.

In short, Bayou Brewing is great fun. The place is designed to look like the inside and outside of an up-tempo New Orleans French Quarter restaurant and bar. You'd never suspect from its current look that the building was long used as an automotive and bus repair shop.

The menu is nearly all Southern and Cajun-influenced, from the Bayou gumbo and étouffée to hickory smoked baby back ribs and peach cobbler for dessert. The VooDoo Lounge and Fat Tuesday's both have a shorter appetizer menu.

The beers are appropriately named in keeping with the Southern theme, but are definitely Northwest-style. Gator Ale is an amber-colored pale ale with a moderate hop profile, while Mugbug IPA is full of hops. VooDoo Dark is a rich tasting porter. Crystal-Weizen is a clear, light tasting wheat ale and pleasantly refreshing. Seasonals rotate through, but one of the best times to visit is around St. Patrick's day when the very Irish town of Spokane goes a bit crazy, and beer has a habit of changing its color to match the occasion.

DIRECTIONS: From I-90 take exit 282, the Hamilton Street exit. Go across the river and through one light. At the next street, turn right on Trent. Bayou Brewing is at the end of the block.

Fort Spokane Brewery

Established 1989

401 West Spokane Falls Boulevard • Spokane WA 99201
(509) 838-3809

The original Fort Spokane Brewery, constructed in 1889, was operated by brothers Bernard and Max Bockemuehl, and supplied beer to the U.S. Cavalry troops stationed at the fort. The present-day brewery has revived the traditions of the Bockemuehl brothers and brews a German-style alt, a top-fermenting beer finished in a lager-like environment. The result is a beer with complex flavors and a clean, smooth finish.

The pub is a marvelous place, located in one of the many early 1900s buildings still standing in downtown Spokane; an original stamped-tin ceiling and an absolutely stunning antique back bar are two of the brewpub's charms. The labyrinthine cellar, which houses the fermenters, conditioners, and kegs, was once the site of a Prohibition speakeasy; tunnels connected the site to the basements of other prominent buildings of the time.

Brewer Jeb Wilson produces four standard ales and a series of seasonal products. Flagship ale, Border Run, an amber with a smooth, malty flavor, is rivaled in popularity by the seasonal rye, an increasingly fashionable style with a distinctive spicy flavor. Red Alt, a sweet, medium-bodied ale brewed with caramel malts to produce the red color and smooth flavor, is a must-try. Bulldog Stout, Godzilla (a "big" India pale ale) and an Octoberfest are a few of the other Fort Spokane brews.

The Fort Spokane Brewery, with its distinctive brewing style and beautiful building, is a treat for any fan of microbrewing. The pub is also one of the best places to hear a sampling from Spokane's hot music scene; it offers live music several nights a week.

DIRECTIONS: From I-90 in Spokane, take exit 281 and head north to Spokane Falls Boulevard. Turn left onto Spokane Falls and go four blocks to Washington. The brewery is on the SW corner of Washington and Spokane Falls.

Hours: 11 a.m.–midnight Sunday–Thursday; 11 a.m.–2 a.m. Friday and Saturday
Children: Yes
Food: Eclectic lunch and dinner menu
Entertainment: Big screen TV's, weekend live music
Smoking: Yes
Payment: Checks, Visa, MC, AmEx
Beer to go: Yes, draft

Sweetwater Brewing Company/ Solicitor's Corner Restaurant and Bar

Established 1996

6301 N Division • Spokane, WA 99208
(509) 465-9554

Solicitor's Corner Restaurant feels quite a bit like an old Irish or English pub—something unexpected at this very busy intersection in northern Spokane. Once you appreciate that fully one-quarter of the people living in Spokane are of Irish decent, however, it seems fairly natural. Dark, old wooden tables and chairs are set up under subdued, antique-style lighting. Large photos of old Spokane breweries from pre-Prohibition times, when more than ten breweries operated in Spokane, hang on the walls. The overall feeling is snug and relaxed.

In contrast to this general simplicity, however, are the outrageous logos for the Sweetwater ales. Cartoonish in nature, they are reminiscent of characters out of The Canterbury Tales or another old English humorous story. The names of the beers are themselves suggestive of the logos: Laughing Horse Stout, Pot Belly Porter, Cock and Bull Amber, and Jack Ass Domestic are all names crying out for a joke to be made.

The quality of the beers, on the other hand, is no joke. Tall Tale Pale is a refreshing, lightly hopped pale ale with a seductively fruity flavor. Cock and Bull Amber is a full-flavored amber with hints of caramel. Howdy's Scottish Red, their best seller, offers an even bigger malty flavor. Cahill's Irish Ale, brewed for St. Patrick's Day, is a full-bodied ale, dry hopped for a strong finish.

Hours: 7 a.m.–midnight Monday–Friday, 7 a.m.–11 p.m. Sunday
Children: Yes, in the restaurant
Food: Full breakfast menu and extensive pub fare
Entertainment: Live music on Saturdays, televised sports events in the bar
Smoking: Yes, in the bar
Payment: Checks, Visa, MC
Beer to go: Yes, draft

Unique to Solicitor's Corner is their full breakfast menu, complete with hardy options you might expect of a pub or restaurant in Ireland. Be careful, though. You might find yourself doing a beer tasting along with your morning eggs and sausages!

DIRECTIONS: From I-90 take exit 281 to Highway 395/Division Street. Stay on Division Street approximately four miles. The restaurant and brewery are at the northwest corner of Division and Francis Avenue (Highway 291).

The Leavenworth Brewery

Established 1992

636 Front Street • Leavenworth, WA 98826
(509) 548-4545 • www.leavenworthbrewery.com

Visconti's at the Brewery

636 Front Street • Leavenworth, WA 98826
(509) 548-1213 • www.viscontis.com

What could be better after enjoying the spectacular outdoors of Eastern Washington than savoring a fresh, hand-crafted brew? Leavenworth has the makings for just such a combination. Head up Icicle Creek for some excellent rock climbing and backpacking opportunities. There's also ample cross-country skiing and snowshoeing to be had here on the North Cascades' east slope, as well as some of the best mountain biking in the state. Afterwards, come to the stylized Bavarian hamlet of Leavenworth, and to Visconti's at the Brewery.

Visconti's is upstairs in a quasi-European, alpine-style building; as you enter, the spiral staircase up provides a view of the large copper brew tanks. The crowd is a nice blend of locals and tourists, and the food is Italian and American fare. Enjoy a pizza, one of the many pastas, or one of the zesty baked entrées.

Visconti's serves as a taproom for the Leavenworth Brewery, offering all the brewery's beers on tap in both its downstairs pub-like area, and its more upscale second-floor dining room. You can also find Leavenworth beers available throughout Eastern and Central Washington, so keep your eyes open.

Hours: Winter: 11 a.m.–10 p.m. Sunday–Thursday; 11 a.m.–midnight Friday and Saturday; summer, 11 a.m.–midnight Sunday–Thursday; 11 a.m.–1 a.m. Friday and Saturday
Children: Yes, in the restaurant
Food: Italian fare
Entertainment: Monthly Brewmaster and Winemaker Dinners
Smoking: No
Payment: Checks, Visa, MC
Beer to go: Yes, draft

The regular beer lineup includes the always-popular Whistling Pig Wheat, as well as Escape Altbier, Dirty Face Stout, Friesian Pilsner, and Hodgson's India Pale Ale. Past seasonals have included the potent, malty and smooth Blind Pig Dunkelweizen, in addition to Bull's Tooth Porter, an Oktoberfest, and variations on the bock theme. If you want a brewery tour, call ahead for an appointment.

DIRECTIONS: Follow Highway 2 as it passes through the heart of Leavenworth. The brewery is on the south side of the highway, upstairs in a three-story building.

Winthrop Brewing Company

Established 1993

P.O. Box 112 • Winthrop, WA 98862
(509) 996-3183

If you've never been to Winthrop, you've missed a town that feels as if it belongs in the Old West. It's done up for tourists, with the plank sidewalks and the roughcut siding on the buildings' façades making the place look like a set from a classic Hollywood western. The Methow and Chewuch River Valleys offer great camping, horseback riding trails, and unparalleled cross-country skiing.

The Winthrop Brewing Company is set in an old, red schoolhouse right downtown. The funky interior of the brewpub looks like an old saloon, with four-inch thick wooden tables and a hefty bar. You can't miss the collections of 600 cigarette lighters and 300 lipstick kisses on the backs of coasters that adorn the walls.

During Eastern Washington's long summers you can enjoy the extensive outdoor seating overlooking the Chewuch River. Order from the menu's selection of good pub fare, and watch the cooks prepare it in the kitchen situated underneath the main deck level. Then, relax on the patio at the river's edge and enjoy a good burger and brew, or a pizza with dough made from the brewery's spent grains.

Owner and brewer Dan Yingling, who brings a background of brewery apprenticeships and professional training to his craft, has created a line of beers that is wildly popular with the locals. The establishment's standard brews include Outlaw Pale Ale (the local favorite), Hopalong Red Ale (a nice, well-balanced beer of this less common type), Grampa Clem's Brown Ale, and Black Canyon Porter (a full-bodied porter with a smooth, roasty aftertaste).

Seasonal Winthrop brews include Boulder Creek Golden Bock, Grizzly Paw Honey Rye, OktoberWest, Jingle Bell Ale and Uncle Buford's Scottish Ale. The brewery offers samples of the OktoberWest at its annual autumn beer festival, also attended by numerous other Northwest breweries.

DIRECTIONS: As Highway 20 passes through Winthrop, it angles and crosses the Chewuch River, and serves as main street east of the river. The western block of Winthrop's main street leaves Highway 20 at its elbow curve. The brewpub is half a block down this section of the main street, on your left.

Hours: Summer, 11 a.m.–midnight daily; winter, call for hours
Children: Yes
Food: Pub fare
Entertainment: Board games, TV, live music
Smoking: No
Payment: Checks, Visa, MC, Discover
Beer to go: Yes, draft

Methow Valley Brewing Company

Established 1998

209 East 2nd Avenue • Twisp, WA 98856
(509) 997-6822 • www.methowbrewing.com

This upscale brewpub is located in the small town of Twisp at the foot of the east slope of the North Cascades. The Methow Valley Brewing Company's building, dating from the 1930s, was originally the town creamery. Extensive renovations didn't diminish the building's fun, old character. You'll find the brewery across the street from the town's historic inn.

One large dining room wraps around a horseshoe-shaped bar, which gives an intimate feel to each portion of the room. The walls of the pub serve as a rotating gallery for Methow Valley artists' work. Watch for the addition of a patio in the near future. Bring the kids and order a house-made root beer for them.

The bar serves quality wines to accompany your meal, in addition to the fresh-brewed house beers. For meals, there are close to ten burgers to choose from, in addition to some finer fare. Try the rustic tart with roma tomatoes, basil pesto, mushrooms, and cheeses, or ask about the daily pasta and seafood specials. Save room to try one of the mouthwatering desserts.

Owner and brewer Aaron Studen makes a three-beer standard line for Methow Valley. The three house mainstays are a cream ale, an extra special bitter, and a porter. The ESB is traditional English-style and the porter is black, smooth, and brewed with five different malts. There's a fourth tap that rotates through the many seasonal beers Studen creates. In their first year of operation, the seasonal list included a Pilsner, a Vienna lager, a bock, an oatmeal stout, a brown ale, a hefeweizen, an altbier, a Scottish ale, an India pale ale, and a Christmas ale.

DIRECTIONS: From Highway 20, turn at the Fire Hall onto E 2nd Avenue and head east. Go two blocks on 2nd, and the brewpub is on your right.

Hours: Summer, 11 a.m.–11 p.m. Monday and Wednesday–Friday; 8 a.m.–11 p.m. Saturday and Sunday; winter, 3-11 p.m. Wednesday–Friday; 11:30 a.m.–11 p.m. Saturday–Sunday
Children: Yes, except bar area
Food: Pub fare and eclectic fare
Entertainment: Board games, live music on Fridays and Saturdays, acoustic open mike most Saturdays
Smoking: No
Payment: Checks, Visa, MC, AmEx, Discover, Diners Club
Beer to go: Yes, draft

Lake Chelan's Deep Water Brewing & Public House

Established 1999

225 Highway 150 • Chelan, WA 98816
(509) 682-2720 • www.deepwaterbrewing.com

L ake Chelan is one of Washington state's most striking destinations, with the town of Chelan at the south end of its narrow, fifty-five-mile length, and the Stehekin rustic resort settlement at the northern end. This is a paradise for backpackers, canoeists, and other outdoors enthusiasts. From here you can easily access the North Cascades National Park, Glacier Peak Wilderness Area, Lake Chelan–Sawtooth Wilderness Area, and the Lake Chelan National Recreation Area.

Located at the edge of town, Deep Water Brewing Company and Public House offers multiple environments for your leisure time pleasure, including a pair of lounges and a pair of dining rooms. Split between two floors, the restaurant areas are family oriented. Both bars are handsome spaces, with full-liquor complements and a nice wine list. Check out the deck if weather permits, and enjoy the brewpub's unparalleled views of the lake and mountains.

Appetizers at the restaurant include brandy-fired button mushrooms, calamari focaccia, and a ploughman's platter. Entrées include an extensive selection of ribs: beef, pork, and more exotic game, and such dishes as a cioppino stew and Pasta Chelan, with asparagus and toasted pine nuts in a garlic cream sauce. Or, for a pepped-up version of a pub classic, try the prosciutto and smoked gouda burger.

Scott Dietrich, formerly of Hales Ales, is the proprietor and brewmaster. He uses two rare yeast strains from English breweries to produce a collection of English-type ales, as well as a wheat beer that is made with nothing but wheat in the mash. Dietrich uses an English-made, seven-barrel brewhouse. Generally, a pale ale, a brown or red ale, and a porter or stout are available in addition to the wheat. Also, look for guest tap handles and a wildcard tap offering a beer made from the recipe of a homebrew contest winner or a guest professional brewer.

Hours: Summer, 11 a.m.–12:30 a.m. daily; winter, call for hours
Children: Yes, in the dining areas; no, in the lounges
Food: Steaks, seafood and pastas
Entertainment: Video golf, trivia games, pool and darts, occasional live music or DJ
Smoking: Yes, in the lounges
Payment: Checks, Visa, MC, AmEx
Beer to go: Yes, draft

DIRECTIONS: From Highway 97, turn west onto Highway 150, the North Shore Highway. The brewpub is 2.5 miles from the junction with 97, on your left (the lake side of the road).

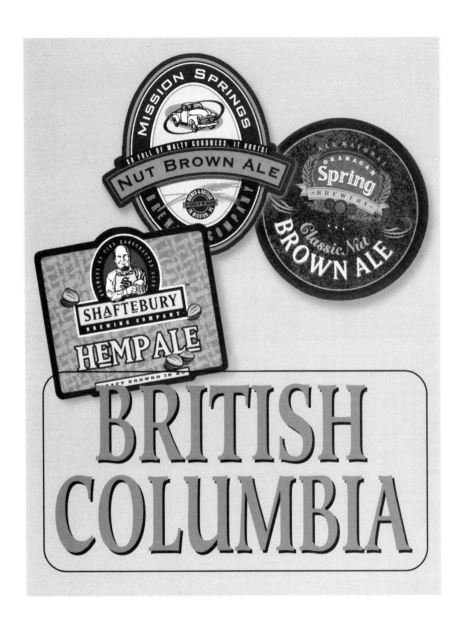

BRITISH COLUMBIA

The cycle of high demand for craft beer and high supply of the same, which kick-started almost overnight in Oregon and Washington during the 1980s, has only begun to be matched by British Columbia. While all three have experienced their shares of modern craft brewery closures, B.C. saw more ventures close early on than either Oregon or Washington. In the late 1990s, however, the Province's craft brewing industry began to gain momentum.

Governmental regulation can be held somewhat culpable for B.C.'s torpid craft

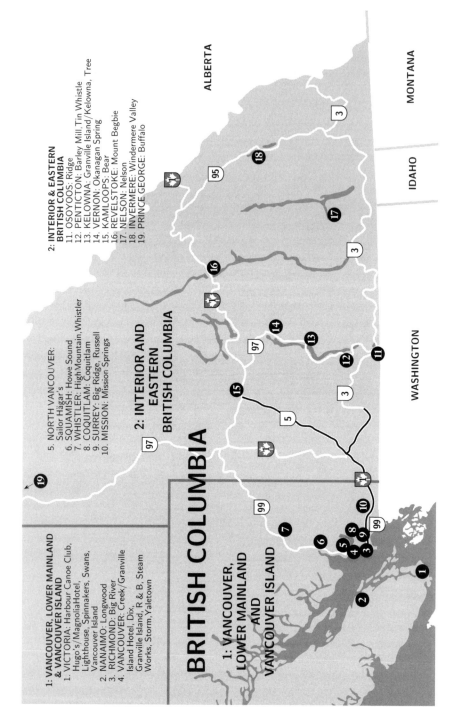

BRITISH COLUMBIA

1: VANCOUVER, LOWER MAINLAND AND VANCOUVER ISLAND

1: VANCOUVER, LOWER MAINLAND & VANCOUVER ISLAND
1. VICTORIA: Harbour Canoe Club, Hugo's/Magnolia Hotel, Lighthouse, Spinnakers, Swans, Vancouver Island
2. NANAIMO: Longwood
3. RICHMOND: Big River
4. VANCOUVER: Creek/Granville Island Hotel, Dix, Granville Island, R & B, Steam Works, Storm, Yaletown
5. NORTH VANCOUVER: Sailor Hägar's
6. SQUAMISH: Howe Sound
7. WHISTLER: High Mountain, Whistler
8. COQUITLAM: Coquitlam
9. SURREY: Big Ridge, Russell
10. MISSION: Mission Springs

2: INTERIOR AND EASTERN BRITISH COLUMBIA

2: INTERIOR & EASTERN BRITISH COLUMBIA
11. OSOYOOS: Ridge
12. PENTICTON: Barley Mill, Tin Whistle
13. KELOWNA: Granville Island/Kelowna, Tree
14. VERNON: Okanagan Spring
15. KAMLOOPS: Bear
16. REVELSTOKE: Mount Begbie
17. NELSON: Nelson
18. INVERMERE: Windermere Valley
19. PRINCE GEORGE: Buffalo

ALBERTA

MONTANA

IDAHO

WASHINGTON

brewing history. At the time of this printing, British Columbia still forbids brewpubs to sell their beers to other retail outlets. In-house sales volumes at brewpubs must therefore be high to warrant either the capital investment needed to open a brewpub or the subsequent brewing of much beer. These realities explain the trend in B.C. toward massive brewpubs with extensive seating areas and in-house restaurants, many in new, high-end developments.

Another interesting fact of B.C.'s craft beer market, which in part might be a result of its delayed penetration of the mainstream beer market, is that lagers and lightly hopped ales are more prevalent among craft breweries in B.C. than in Washington and Oregon. Craft beer enthusiasts in the Pacific Northwestern U.S. dived head first (so to speak) into full-flavored, hoppy ales—a wholesale departure from the American mass-produced, weak-bodied lagers they had been drinking. Often, the "crossover" style first enjoyed by Americans new to craft beers is a golden (or blonde) ale or a Weizen—something with a color similar to the standard industrial lager, since color is the novice's primary criterion for judging beer.

Meanwhile, to a great extent, British Columbia's beer consumers eased themselves into the craft beer scene with microbrewed lagers, and continue to embrace them more than their beer-quaffing counterparts have in Washington or Oregon. There are several all-lager microbreweries and brewpubs in B.C., and many other B.C. craft breweries offer at least one house Pilsner, or other lager. Other styles of beer that are less hoppy than pale ales and porters have flourished in the nascent B.C. craft breweries as well. Note the numerous altbiers (The Creek Brewery's True Creek Alt for instance) and cream ales (such as Russell Brewing Company's cream ale) that abound in this province. These cream ales vary quite a bit in brewing methods—from ales that are lagered following fermentation (or "cold-conditioned"), to ales fermented with a lager yeast. The main thing these various concoctions have in common is a malt flavor predominance and an absence of hoppy bitterness.

While the city of Vancouver and the surrounding Lower Mainland have the highest concentrations of craft breweries in the province, brewing establishments dot the entire B.C. landscape. These far-flung beer havens are worthy pilgrimages for outdoor enthusiasts and travelers of all sorts. As we enter the new century, B.C.'s interior is well-supplied with good beer. Craft beer is being brewed fresh in such outlying hamlets as Rossland and Kamloops, and brewpubs as far afield as Kelowna and Prince George offer a welcome haven to the intrepid adventurer. In the far eastern reaches of B.C., toward the foot of the Rockies, there are breweries in Nelson, Invermere, and Revelstoke. And, on Vancouver Island, Nanaimo offers an "up-island" brewpub stop with the arrival of Longwood Brewpub.

If you're traveling to B.C. from the U.S. to sample some Canadian craft beers, be sure to note the unique fact that with brewpubs in Bellingham, Washington, and Richmond, B.C. (or for that matter, in Winthrop, Washington and Osoyoos, B.C.), you can fit an international brew-tour into a single day!

Big River Brewing Company

Established 1998

Riverport Centre #180 • 14200 Entertainment Way
Richmond, B.C. V6W 1K3
(604) 271-2739 • www.zone-entertainment.com

Is there a new movie out that you're itching to see on a big screen? Consider the Riverport sports and entertainment center in Richmond—and stop into the Big River Brewing Company for dinner beforehand. Actually, there are a lot of reasons to visit Riverport—from hockey leagues in the winter, to fun at the waterpark in the summer, to extreme "cosmic" bowling year-round.

The Big River brewpub is nothing if not eye-catching—larger-than-life images from the history of the mighty Fraser River live up to the company's name. Take, for example, the twenty-five-foot canoe crashing through the wall from the brewpub into the bowling alley.

Choose between an intimate, dark-wood pub area offering views of the brewhouse or a brightly painted restaurant dining room. You can even order food and beer in the bowling area, which is bedecked with massive models of biplanes and steam ships. The menu includes burgers, pastas, and steaks.

Brewer Vern Lambourne, formerly of the Orange Brewery in London, utilizes the English-like tiled brewhouse to make an assortment of unfiltered British, Continental, and Canadian styles of beer. The standards include the ever-popular blonde ale, a Pilsner lager, a Vienna lager, an ESB, a pale ale, and a stout. There's usually a guest tap, along with a seasonal house beer or two, such as a brown ale, a hefeweizen, or a blueberry ale. Ask for a brewery tour while you're here.

DIRECTIONS: From I-99 take Exit 32, Steveston Highway. Head east on Steveston Highway about a mile. The entertainment complex is on your left. When you turn in on Entertainment Way, the brewpub is on your right.

Hours: 11:30 a.m.–midnight Sunday–Thursday, 11:30-1 a.m. Friday and Saturday
Children: Yes, in restaurant
Food: Restaurant, eclectic Northwest; pub, upscale pub fare
Entertainment: Cineplex with an IMAX and 18 other big screens, water park, basketball gym, hockey rink and sports shop, bowling lanes, video arcade; brewpub has a pool table
Smoking: Yes, in the pub
Payment: Visa, MC, AmEx, Interac
Beer to go: No

Russell Brewing Company

Established 1995

Unit 202, 13018 80th Avenue • Surrey, B.C. V3W 3A8
(604) 599-1190

In 1995 Peter and Mark Russell launched one of Canada's few single-family-owned cottage breweries with a little help from their relatives. The company is quite successful, producing about 300 kegs per month for distribution all over lower mainland B.C. You can arrange for a brewery tour and beer sampling by calling ahead.

Russell Brewing's equipment includes a twenty-hectoliter open-fermentation system and four conditioning tanks in a cold room. Brewer Mark Russell uses cold-conditioning to achieve an unparalleled level of smoothness in his beers.

Before he and his brother opened their brewery, Mark was a long-time brewer at Granville Island Brewing. At Russell Brewing he brews traditional English-style ales with British yeast and imported British malts. To suit the local palate, the beers are filtered for clarity and aged for fairly long periods of time—often a month in the cold room.

Two standard offerings are a medium-hopped amber ale that is light in color, but not in body or flavor, and a cream ale that you've got to taste to believe. This dark cream ale is an excellent beer in terms of complex malt flavors, smoothness and drinkability. Seasonal brews include a blonde ale and a golden ale, a deliciously malty Christmas ale, and a refreshing lemon ale.

Note that Surrey is quite close to the U.S. border. If you're planning a tour of B.C. breweries and will be coming from the States, make an effort to build a visit to the Russell brothers' brewery into your visit. Or else seek out a Russell beer on tap, available at many restaurants and taverns all around Vancouver and the Lower Mainland.

DIRECTIONS: From 91 (Annacis Highway), take the 72nd Street exit and follow 72nd east to 99A (King George Highway). From 99, turn north on 99A (King George Highway). From 99A, turn west on 80th Street. Follow 80th to the intersection with 132nd. Cross 132nd and take the next left. The brewery is in the second white building on the left.

Hours: Call to arrange a tour
Children: Yes
Food: No
Entertainment: No
Smoking: No
Payment: Cash only
Beer to go: Yes, draft

BigRidge Brewing Company

Established 1999

15133 Highway 10 • Surrey, B.C. V6B 2S2
(604) 574-2739 • www.markjamesgroup.com or
www.bigridgebrewing.com

The BigRidge brewpub lies between Cloverdale and White Rock, in an area known as South Surrey. It shares the shopping center called Panorama Village with an assortment of movie theaters, fast food, and retail shops. Rolling farmland and housing developments make up the landscape.

BigRidge has two areas, a restaurant and a separate pub. Enter the pub beside the fully functional silo, complete with an auger that pipes grain into the brewhouse. Both the pub and restaurant feature reused timbers. Vivid paintings memorialize BigRidge's brews. The restaurant's patio, with its brick fireplace, is a nice place to sit.

Choose from various food styles on the menu, from brick oven pizzas to steaks to stirfrys. Try the Thai chicken sticks with peanut sauce, then have an authentically prepared wok meal, such as Calico Bay scallops and asparagus with a ginger-black bean sauce. In addition to the house beers, there's also a full bar with cocktails and espresso drinks.

David Varga, a transplant from Alberta's craft beer scene, is at the helm of BigRidge's fifteen-hectoliter Ripley Stainless brewhouse. He's producing a line of quality, unfiltered beers including: Clover Ale, an English-style pale ale named for the local district; Old Sullivan Porter, ruby-colored and made with Northwest hops and Belgian specialty malts; and Harvest Lager, a North American-style craft Pilsner. The pale ale's nitro dispense lends it an appealing creaminess. Varga also offers a house mixed beer, entitled Bootheroyd Black & Tan, combining the pale and the porter. Look for a weekly cask-conditioned ale, and a house-sponsored homebrew contest, with the winning recipe on-tap at the brewpub.

Hours: 11:30 a.m.–midnight Sunday, 11:30 a.m.–1 a.m. Monday–Saturday
Children: Yes, in the restaurant
Food: Eclectic Northwest cuisine
Entertainment: Pool tables, steel-tip darts, big screen TVs with televised sports events, occasional live music
Smoking: Yes, in the pub
Payment: Visa, MC, AmEx, ATM on property
Beer to go: No

DIRECTIONS: From Highway 99 or Highway 91, take the Highway 10 Surrey exit and head east on Highway 10. Follow 10 about five miles until you come to 152nd Street. The brewpub is in the Panorama Village shopping center on your left at the corner of Highway 10 and 152nd.

VICTORIA'S CHARMS

The City of Victoria, capital of British Columbia, lies on the southern tip of Vancouver Island, and is home to Canada's oldest operating brewpub, the famous Spinnakers in the Esquimalt district. Victoria is one of the prettiest cities in North America, with exquisite nineteenth century architecture, and is a popular port-of-call for Northwest boaters.

The fact that the city is in the "Blue Hole," the rainshadow from the Olympic Mountains that makes southern Vancouver Island and the San Juans famously sunny, is part of its appeal. With an excellent public bus system and miles of relatively flat bicycling and walking trails, Victoria can be pleasantly explored without a car. And, leaving your car behind makes the ferry passage from the mainland much less costly. Several public and privately operated ferries run between Victoria and the mainland, so inquire ahead as to which one suits your needs and schedule.

Victoria is known as the Garden City, owing to its year-round temperate climate, the resultant extended growing season, and the city's lush, sometimes tropical foliage. One of the most renowned flower gardens in the world is in the Victoria area, the Butchart Gardens, which gloriously occupies a former quarry in the countryside between Victoria and Sidney. But Victoria itself should be the primary destination for any brief visit, with its splendid Parliament buildings and Empress Hotel, its delightful waterfront plazas and clusters of boutiques, and its collection of tearooms that feel more "English" than England.

Plan to stay at one of the numerous brewing-and-lodging establishments in Victoria: Spinnakers Brewpub and Guesthouse, Swans Suite Hotel, and Buckerfield's Brewery, or the Magnolia Hotel and Hugo's Brew Club. Or, if you're looking for moorage for your boat, put in at the Harbour Canoe Club's Brewhouse, Restaurant and Marina. Each of these resort-like properties allow the traveler to relax and enjoy craft brewed beer made on premise, with creature comforts ranging from Jacuzzi tubs at Spinnakers to live music at Hugo's Brew Club.

Swans Suite Hotel, with its fine restaurant, brewpub, and nightclub, is just a couple of blocks from the Harbour Canoe Club. Each property offers multiple environments to suit various occasions. For a stretch of the legs after a session at Swans, you can explore the fun Olde Town district and Victoria's small Chinatown. If you're up for a long ramble, take Pandora Street from the Swans Hotel straight across Victoria, all the way to Oak Bay, widely held to be Victoria's most "British" neighborhood. If you're at the

Canoe Club, you can catch a mini Harbour Taxi and enjoy a boat ride through the Upper or Inner Harbour. Stop at Spinnakers, near the mouth of the Upper Harbour, for a pint of fine ale and a basket of fresh baked bread—and sit on the balcony upstairs, overlooking the water.

With all the craft-brewed beer on hand at Victoria's hotel-brewpubs, you hardly need to explore to find more good beer. However, among the neat shop windows full of china, kilts, chocolates, and tea, you'll find alehouses, such as Christie's Carriage House, which serves locally brewed beers such as Lighthouse Brewing Company's Race Rocks Amber. The Strathcona Hotel's popular Sticky Wicket bar is a good place to try the latest local beers, too. Or, choose from among the four other bars at Strathcona, starting with the Sailor Tavern on the ground floor that has a sign proclaiming "A dirty dog lives here," to the rooftop lounge and volleyball courts that offer panoramic views of the Victoria cityscape.

There are many excellent restaurants in Victoria, with a wide array of cuisines. While you're dining out, look for the full line of Vancouver Island Brewing Company products on tap around Victoria. Or; plan to stop at their facility for a tour of their enormous copper brewing vessels, and a tasting in their comfortable tasting room.

It's nice to know that charming Victoria is there for a getaway. It's as close to visiting Britain as you can get in North America, from the distinctly British accent spoken in the pubs to the fire-engine-red double-decker buses lined up in front of the majestic Parliament Building. For those who associate a visit to Britain with a chance to drink some quality real ales, Victoria now can offer an excellent experience in that regard as well.

Spinnakers
ALES
308 Catherine Street, Victoria, British Columia, Canada
phone: (250) 384-2739
email: spinnakers@spinnakers.com

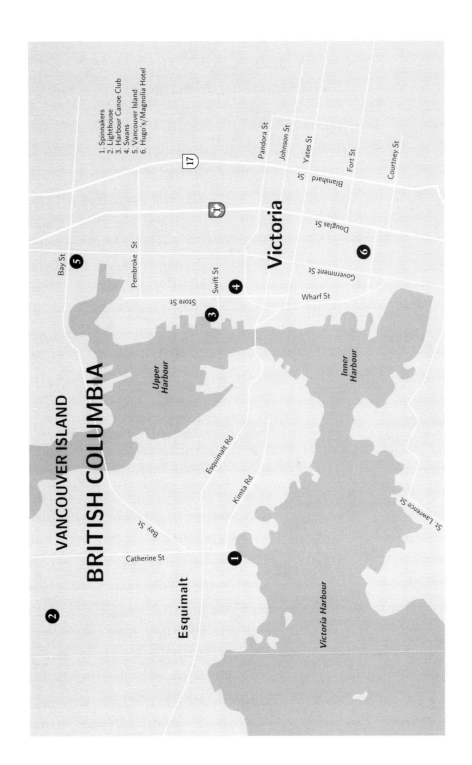

1. Spinnakers
2. Lighthouse
3. Harbour Canoe Club
4. Swans
5. Vancouver Island
6. Hugo's/Magnolia Hotel

VANCOUVER ISLAND

BRITISH COLUMBIA

Victoria

Esquimalt

Upper Harbour

Inner Harbour

Victoria Harbour

Bay St
Pembroke St
Store St
Swift St
Wharf St
Government St
Douglas St
Blanshard St
Pandora St
Johnson St
Yates St
Fort St
Courtney St

Esquimalt Rd
Kimta Rd
St. Lawrence St
Bay St
Catherine St

17

Harbour Canoe Club Brewhouse, Restaurant, Marina

Established 1998

450 Swift Street • Victoria, B.C. V8W 1S3
(250) 361-1940 • Marina: (250) 386-2277
www.greatpacificadventures.com

If you're planning to visit Victoria by boat, be sure to put in at the Harbour Canoe Club for a unique marina and brewpub experience. The full-service marina, run by Great Pacific Adventures, offers great opportunities, whether you have your own boat or are looking for a getaway experience. You can rent a rowboat or kayak to tool about the harbors, or a tandem bicycle to explore the greater Saanich Peninsula.

Located in the old City Lights power utility building, this unique destination serves as anchor for the Upper Harbour, where this area shifts from working waterfront to restaurant/retail businesses.

Its brick structure and massive ramping beams have been left to speak for themselves, adorned only with some understated paintings. The restaurant's loft is the smoking dining room, and there's a relaxing smoke-free lounge area below; the pub's open seating area is complemented by two snugs for intimate occasions; a large, sweeping patio overlooks the harbor and marina.

The menus at the Harbour Club eateries include pizzas, pub snacks and burgers, as well as a great array of entrées such as spanakopita, shellfish dishes, and a top sirloin sandwich. Brewer Sean Hoyne is crafting several different ales and lagers. Davey Jones Lager is nicely carbonated in the North American style, Pacific Fog Pale Ale is very pale, Dry Dock Bitter has a robust malt lineup, and Jack Tar Brown Ale is a ruby porter.

Hours: 11 a.m.–11 p.m. Sunday–Thursday; 11 a.m.–midnight Friday and Saturday
Children: Yes, in the restaurant
Food: Restaurant, West Coast comfort food; pub, upscale pub fare
Entertainment: Pub, live music, Sundays rhythm & blues, Wednesdays swing, occasional other bands or DJ
Smoking: Yes, in the pub
Payment: Pub/Restaurant, Interac, Visa, MC, AmEx
Beer to go: Yes, bottles

DIRECTIONS: From the Sidney ferries, take Highway 17 into Victoria, where it becomes Blanshard. Turn right on Pandora Avenue and go five blocks to Store Street. Turn right on Store Street and take the first left, Swift Street. From the Inner Harbour, proceed north on Wharf Street Wharf, which merges with Store Street. Continue on Store another three blocks to Swift Street (just past the entrance to the Johnson Street Bridge). Turn left on Swift and go one block down; the brewpub/marina is on your right.

Magnolia Hotel/Hugo's Brew Club

Established 1998

625 Courteney Street • Victoria, B.C. V8W 1B8
Hugo's Brew Club: (250) 920-4844 • Magnolia Hotel: (250) 381-0999
Capital Steak House: (250) 920-4846

The Hugos' Brew Club and Magnolia Hotel complex make a lively destination for a Victoria vacation. Just a few blocks from the waterfront, this new property offers a homebase located squarely in the midst of Victoria's small, but bustling, retail district. This boutique hotel, and the uptown-feeling Capital City Steakhouse that occupies its ground floor, make a handsome, late-'90s addition to the Victoria skyline.

Hugo's Brew Club, owned by the folks who bring you the Strathcona Hotel and its mind-boggling five-bar complex just a block away, is in a renovated Legion Hall located next door to the Magnolia Hotel. With the Strathcona and the Magnolia a stone's throw from each other, this portion of Victoria's downtown district has become a veritable craft beer wonderland.

If you're scheduling a visit to this fun city, plan to stop into Hugo's Brew Club for a pint and a steak sandwich, made with the same great steak served in the restaurant next door. Or, plan a dinner at the Steak House, which also serves Hugo's beers, then drop by next door to catch some DJ-spun music on the Hugo's dance floor.

Hours: Hugo's Brew Club, noon–2 a.m. Monday–Friday, 4:30 p.m.–2 a.m. Saturday, 4:30 p.m.–midnight Sunday; Capital Steak House, 4:30-11 p.m. daily
Children: Yes, in the steak house
Food: Hugo's Brew Club, pub fare, pizzas; Capital Steak House, steak and seafood
Entertainment: Hugo's Brew Club, DJ seven nights, TVs; Capital Steak House, pianist Friday and Saturday
Smoking: Mostly no
Payment: Interac, Visa, MC, AmEx, Discover, EnRoute, Diners Club
Beer to go: No

Of course, the best way to experience the Magnolia Hotel is by staying the night. The suite rooms are spacious and simply elegant, with views of the Victoria skyline and the harbor. Ask about the many services they offer. From computer ports to deep-soaking tubs, the suites at the Magnolia are fully appointed.

The hotel is an easy walk from all the attractions of the city center—shops, restaurants and nightlife. Almost as close is the harbor's waterfront, with European open air merchant's stalls, artists, and acrobats. From here you can rent a bicycle to explore the miles of harbor-front paths, catch a mini-Harbour Ferry to another point of interest, or just relax on one of the many water-view benches.

Hugo's Brew Club has a subdued feeling overall, patrons are a nice blend of business folks, other locals, and tourists, Canadian and American alike. Only the façade of the original Legion Hall remains, but the rebuilt interior feels old in its own way, with salvaged brickwork throughout, and a reclaimed wood floor.

The Newlands-manufactured brewhouse is split level, with brewing equipment poised above the dining room in all its splendor. Eye-catching murals grace the walls—and brew tanks as well! Exposed beams and a high ceiling give the place an elegant style with a modern industrial feel. Curves are the architectural theme here, with brick-laid sweeping lines leading to elevated brick platforms that support a DJ booth and a stage for musicians.

The Capital Steak House is a lovely restaurant with tremendous architecture as well. The menu ranges from steaks to pastas to seafoods, with an array of appetizers and decadent desserts. Be sure to include a bottle of wine from their extensive elevated wine cellar. The Brew Club next door specializes in great sandwiches, but they are also known for their gourmet pizzas.

Brewer Benjamin Shottle makes four standard beers: three ales and a lager. He brews Northwest interpretations of classic styles using Northwest ingredients. The Czech Pilsner and blonde ale are popular with the locals, while American tourists tend to gravitate more toward the pale ale and the porter. Shottle is constantly trying new brews, such as a bock in the springtime; more daring beers include a cream ale spiced with ginseng and a lager laced with lemon.

DIRECTIONS: From the Sidney ferries, take Highway 17 into Victoria, where it becomes Blanshard. Turn right on Broughton, then left on Gordon. From Gordon, turn left on Courteney Street; the brewpub-hotel is on your right.

Spinnakers Brewpub & Guesthouse

Established 1984

308 Catherine Street • Victoria, B.C. V9A 3S8
Taproom: (250) 384-6613 • Restaurant: (250) 386-2739 • Guest House:
(250) 384-0332 • www.spinakers.com

A lovely property that sits on a bluff overlooking the water at the edge of Victoria, Spinnakers is Canada's oldest operating post-Prohibition brewpub. Proprietor Paul Hadfield, an accomplished architect, along with John Mitchell, original brewer for both Spinnakers and Horseshoe Bay, and Frank Appleton, now a legendary brewery consultant, spearheaded the effort to establish a brewpub in modern B.C. It wasn't called a microbrewing revolution for nothing—the laws that prohibit brewing and selling beer on the same premises do not change easily. Hadfield continues to this day to be at the forefront of lobbying on behalf of the province's fledgling brewpub industry.

Spinnakers set—and exceeds—the standard for B.C. brewpubs, creating the pub/restaurant combination, and the expectation for a high-quality dining experience as a part of the high-quality beer experience. This excellence is reflected in their latest addition—elegant overnight accommodations in two newly acquired, handsome guest houses on either side of the main building. Spinnakers brewpub offers multiple environments that make it feel at times like a gabled mansion, a British pub, or a country club. On its ground floor are the restaurant (with split-level dining and two decks), the brewhouse, and a retail store. Upstairs is the taproom, with more deck seating that provides views of the harbor, Race Rocks and the open sea beyond.

Hours: Taproom, 11 a.m.–11 p.m. daily; restaurant: 7 a.m.–11 p.m. Monday–Sunday
Children: Yes, in the restaurant
Food: Taproom, upscale pub fare; restaurant, eclectic Northwest cuisine
Entertainment: Live acoustic and jazz music Friday and Saturday, pool tables, steel-tip darts
Smoking: Yes, in a section of the taproom
Payment: Visa, MC, AmEx
Beer to go: Yes, bottles

The nine guest suites are divided between two charming houses. The first is a nineteenth century fully restored heritage house, with a culinary herb garden and a private patio. The suites include such enticing comforts as wood- or gas-burning fireplaces, Jacuzzi bathtubs, and exquisite period furnishings. Tucked behind this house is the Spinnakers Vinegar Shed, where the ever-experimental Hadfield has recreated the classic vinegar-making processes of the Old World. Make sure to try some house vinegar on your fish and chips at the restaurant. The other guest house is down a little path from the main building, nestled behind a trellised entrance that opens to a small, but well-appointed, garden of flowers and herbs. The house's four suites are furnished in a garden motif and have patios amidst quaint planting areas, as well as two fireplaces apiece.

The Spinnakers restaurant offers excellent food and unbeatable views. Be sure to snatch a peek at the brewhouse (eight-hectoliter system by SPR of Ramsbottom, England), visible briefly on your way in the front door. An open kitchen gives a warmth to the busy dining room. The menu features many ingredients made on-premise such as beers, breads, and vinegars, and items obtained through direct exchange with farmers, with an emphasis placed on utilizing seasonal foods and items such as free-range eggs and local beef. Breakfast delights include French toast and fish cakes, while dinner features Cajun halibut, a curry of the day, or other specialties. The taproom upstairs is laid out in sections to facilitate groups of guests, and has a menu of traditional coastal pub fare. The gabled space is full of character, as are the beers pouring from the cold-taps and cellar temperature cask handles.

Spinnakers has been home to a long line of Northwest brewers, including Barry Ladell, now with the Longwood Brewpub in Nanaimo, and his son Lon Ladell. Matt Phillips, formerly of Wildhorse Brewing Company is at the helm today, hand-crafting an extensive line of beers. Beers on tap include Spinnakers Ale (a malty light ale with delightful fruity highlights), Doc Hadfield's Pale Ale (made with all Kent Goldings hops), a lovely Mild Brown with a soft texture and subtle chocolate malts; a nicely balanced oatmeal stout, a roast-a-riffic porter, and a Scotch ale with nine varieties of malts, including a touch of peat malt. When fresh, organically grown berries are in season, look for such delights as a cranberry hefeweizen and a blueberry weizen. Be sure to check the bottled beer selection on your way out for such gems as the bottle-conditioned IPA.

DIRECTIONS: From the Sidney ferry docks, take Highway 17 into Victoria, where it becomes Blanshard Avenue. Follow Blanshard to Bay Street. Turn right on Bay Street and go over the bridge. Bay ends at a diagonal intersection with Catherine. Turn left on Catherine, cross over Esquimalt Street. The brewpub/guest house is on your right, at the end of the street.

Swans Suite Hotel & Brewpub

Established 1989

506 Pandora Avenue • Victoria, B.C. V8W 1N6
Swans Brewpub/Fowl & Fish Café: (250) 361-3310 • Swans Suite Hotel:
(800) 668-7926 • www.islandnet.com/~swans

Swans is situated just off the Upper Harbour in Victoria's Olde Town, amidst storefronts and businesses, close to all the attractions of China Town and the growing bustle and excitement of Olde Town. Its restoration has made it an anchor in Olde Town, along with the restored Market Square, a collection of delightful shops and eateries across the street. The Swans Hotel is also within reasonable walking distance of Victoria's harbor-front and downtown attractions.

On the ground floor of the Swans building are Buckerfield's Brewery and accompanying pub and retail store, as well as the Fowl & Fish Café. The Swans Brewpub has become a local destination for good music and good beer. The hotel's suites occupy the upper three storys, and the basement level is home to a nightclub called the Millennium Jazz Club. All the venues serve Buckerfield's ales and lagers.

The brewpub is a veritable art gallery, with a collection of First Nations weavings and carvings, including a traditional dance mask, a contemporary totem pole, and a century-old Tlingit weaving, all interspersed with paintings of distinctly contemporary character that are rotated seasonally. At the bar, note the train tracks serving as foot-rests; they date from the building's history on the Olde Town train line. The large brewpub space is divided into cozy sections, including a wrap-around, solarium-style enclosed patio and a stand-up bar with full liquor complement. The beer is served both on cold-taps and beer engines—appropriate to the traditional British dark-wood pub feel. An eclectic menu offers such options as pan-fried personal pizzas and roasted eggplant-portabella foccaccia sandwiches.

The Fowl & Fish Café is a fine-dining establishment, with a wide selection of seafood, from trout to oysters, and a similarly varied list of pastas, chicken, and other entrées. Fresh flowers burst from enormous vases throughout this romantic venue. There are plenty of dimly lit booths for private evenings.

Hours: Swans Brewpub: 7 a.m.–2 a.m. Monday–Saturday, 7 a.m.–midnight Sunday
Children: Yes, in the café
Food: Swans Brewpub, upscale pub fare; Fowl & Fish Café, eclectic Northwest cuisine
Entertainment: Swans Brewpub, live blues and jazz Monday–Wednesday; Millennium Jazz Club, live jazz Thursday–Sunday
Smoking: Yes, in the brewpub
Payment: Visa, MC, AmEx, Diners Club, Interac
Beer to go: Yes, bottles

The hotel offers travelers pleasant suite-style accommodations in an intimate setting, which includes room-service and housekeeping. Most of the twenty-nine suites are suitable for up to six people, and have kitchens, living/dining areas, and private patios; many are split-level, with skylights and panoramic views of the city. Given its strategic Olde Town location, near both harbors and the financial district, the Swans Hotel makes a great destination for a Victoria getaway.

Downstairs at Buckerfield's Brewery, brewer Chris Johnson uses only imported British malts and brews an extensive line of unfiltered beers. The standard choices are Arctic Ale, Buckerfield's Bitter, Pandora Pale Ale, Swans Oatmeal Stout, Appleton Brown Ale, Olde Town Bavarian Lager, and Riley's Scotch Ale, which is of the wee heavy style—rich, potent, and sweet, with a hint of peat. The bitter is also recommended, with its ample hop flavor and a lightness of body and alcohol that invites you to go ahead and have another pint.

Seasonal brews include an aged IPA with complex flavors in the fall, a barley wine in the winter, and cherry and raspberry ales in the warmer months. Look for a cask-conditioned version of the bitter on Friday nights at the brewpub. If you want to take some Buckerfield brews home with you, there's a beer and wine store right in the Swans building offering the full line.

DIRECTIONS: From the Sidney ferries, take Highway 17 into Victoria, where it becomes Blanshard. Turn right on Pandora Avenue and go five blocks to Store Street. From the Inner Harbour, proceed north on Wharf Street to where it merges with Store Street Continue on Store another two blocks to Pandora Street (just past the entrance to the Johnson Street Bridge). The hotel/brewpub is on the corner of Store and Pandora.

Vancouver Island Brewing Company

Established 1984

2330 Government Street • Victoria, B.C. V8T 5G5
(250) 361-0007

Vancouver Island Brewing Company is located in a handsome, modern facility in downtown Victoria. Given its central location, the brewery and retail store are a convenient stop from any part of Victoria. So, if you're in the Victoria area, make a point of coming into the brewery for a tour and tasting.

You'll not get a chance to see enormous brewing vessels such as these anywhere nearby. The place has an overall feel of German efficiency and engineering; fittingly, the massive mash and lauter tuns were fabricated in Germany. This brewery produces a sizable output of beer for the local and regional marketplace. With distribution across the province and beyond, Vancouver Island Brewing Company is one of B.C.'s foremost regional breweries.

Tours are offered regularly at the end of the week, but call ahead for a reservation, because they can fill up. The spacious interior of the brewery houses a two-story system, a sizable bottling area, and a classy tasting room, offering the brewery's wares on draft at the end of a tour. There's also a retail store on premise, selling a full line of merchandise—all the beers, and the clothing and keepsakes to go with them.

The beer line consists of Vancouver Island Blonde Ale, West Coast Lager, and Wolf's Scottish Cream Ale, brewed with an ale yeast at lager temperatures, for a silky quaffability despite its strength (six percent alcohol/volume). Brewmaster Wolfgang Hoess continues to brew the winter seasonal developed by Vancouver Island Brewing's first brewmaster, Don Harmes. Known as Hermannator, it's a triple bock that is sure to warm whatever part of your body is chilled. Also watch for a reissue of Hermann's Bavarian Dark Lager.

DIRECTIONS: From the Sidney ferries, take Highway 17 into Victoria, where it becomes Blanshard. Pass two shopping centers and turn right on Bay Street. Turn left on Government and the brewery is on your right, half a block down.

Hours: Retail Store: 11 a.m.–6 p.m. Monday–Thursday, 11 a.m.–7 p.m. Friday and Saturday; Brewery tours: Summer: 3 p.m. Friday and Saturday, winter: 3 p.m. Saturday
Children: Yes
Food: No
Entertainment: No
Smoking: No
Payment: Visa, MC, AmEx, Interac
Beer to go: Yes, bottles

Lighthouse Brewing Company

Established 1998

Unit 2, 836 Devonshire Road • Victoria, B.C. V9Z 4T4
(250) 383-6500

O wner Gerry Hieter and Head Brewer/Owner Paul Hoyne have a combined history of over forty years in the brewing business. However, they have returned to their roots by opening a microbrewery in Victoria, Lighthouse Brewing Company, whose focus is on serving the local market with fresh, non-filtered craft beers. Look for their tap handles throughout the south island area, whether you're taking in Victoria's charms, or heading off on a Gulf Islands exploration.

Their flagship ale is Race Rocks Amber, a big, malty brew reminiscent of a Scottish ale. Its five-malt lineup keeps you interested with an evolving taste that is rare in its complexity, with crisp heights and roasty depths. Made with imported English Maris Otter malt, it is an Old World-type brew, with a balanced, smooth hop flavor. Race Rocks is the name of a reef that sports a lighthouse at the entrance to Victoria's Upper Harbour, and is a landmark in the annual sailboat race. The brewery's second offering is an IPA, similarly of Old World style.

The brewery is minimalist in style, and boasts such rarities as a three-tiered water filter and an electric-heated kettle. The emphasis throughout the process is on minimal beer handling and pumping to produce a pampered final product.

Lighthouse Brewing's ales are available only on draft. The kegs are distributed strictly on Vancouver Island, since Hoyne and Heiter believe that real ales should be non-filtered and fresh, characteristics that don't lend themselves to far-flung distribution. Future plans include bottling such high-octane brews as a barley wine and a Russian imperial stout. Whatever Lighthouse produces, it will be hearty; Heiter and Hoyne like to refer to their brewery as a "blonde-free zone."

DIRECTIONS: From the Sidney ferries, take Highway 17 into Victoria, where it becomes Blanshard Avenue. Follow Blanshard turning right on Bay Street, and go over the bridge. Bay ends at a diagonal intersection with Catherine Street. Turn right and take Catherine to Wilson Street. From Inner Harbour, turn left and follow Wilson, turn right on Hereward, then left on Devonshire and go about two blocks. The brewery is on the right, tucked in the back of the warehouse building. Go around the building to unit No. 2.

Hours: Call ahead to arrange a tour
Children: No
Food: No
Entertainment: No
Smoking: No
Payment: Cash only
Beer to go: Yes, draft

Longwood Brewpub

Established 2000

5775 Turner Road • Nanaimo, B.C. V9T 6L8
(250) 729-8225 • www.longwoodbrewpub.com

The classy Longwood Brewpub gives you reason enough to take a jaunt "up island" away from the hustle of the Victoria/Sidney metro area. The town of Nanaimo serves as a port-of-call for B.C. Ferries bound for Horseshoe Bay. Relax on Longwood's deck to watch boats in the Strait of Georgia.

Proprietor and head brewer, Barry Ladell, formerly the brewmaster at Spinnakers, is joined by brewer Harley Smith, formerly of SteamWorks, to offer eight house draft selections at all times. The mainstays are Longwood Ale (a blonde, cold-conditioned ale), an ESB, an Imperial stout, an IPA, and a dunkelweizen. The daily lineup is completed by a Scottish ale, and either a dark mild ale or porter. You'll also find one of an assortment of lagers—from bocks to alts, and from a Pilsner to a Dortmunder Export. The beers are unfiltered, and are made from specially imported English malts.

Hours: 11 a.m.–1:30 a.m. daily
Children: Yes, in the restaurant
Food: Casual and fine dining
Entertainment: TVs, pool table
Smoking: No
Payment: Visa, MC, AmEx, Interac/Debit
Beer to go: Yes, bottles

The brewpub occupies a large, freestanding building in the center of the Longwood Station shopping center, right on the edge of town. The building houses a restaurant and a pub, each with a full bar, as well as a retail wine boutique that sells Longwood's beers in bottles. The brewpub's interior décor of rich carpeting and hardwood cherry floors evokes a classic New Orleans French Provincial style. Wood burning fireplaces on both levels lend a cozy feel. Visit the downstairs pub for a game of pool, or to sample some fine wines.

The fairly formal menu in the main dining room focuses on fresh, local ingredients. Appetizers range from crabcakes to Indian pakoras and chutney. For dinner, choose from an assortment of salads, gourmet burgers, and entrées featuring halibut, lamb, and steaks. All breads, pastas, and desserts are made in-house.

DIRECTIONS: From the Departure Bay ferry dock in Nanaimo, drive north six miles on the Island Highway and watch for the grain silo on the right. Turn onto Turner Road and enter the shopping center parking area. From Victoria, drive north on the New Island Highway to Mostar Road. Turn right and follow Mostar to the Old Island Highway. Turn left and drive three blocks to Turner Road; the brewpub is on your left.

VANCOUVER, B. (BEER) C. (CITY)

The city of Vancouver is the focus of a sprawling region known as the Lower Mainland of British Columbia. The majestic drive up Highway 99 to Whistler delineates the area's northwest boundary, and the great Fraser Valley draws the southern border. Vancouver is nestled between the Strait of Georgia, busy with ocean-bound freighters, and the Lillooet Range, the northern continuation of Oregon and Washington's Cascade Mountains. This expansive metro area serves as a nexus for international trade, and is home to quality beers and a cosmopolitan population of beer drinkers.

The Vancouver region is the birthplace of British Columbia's current microbrewing renaissance. The metro area's brewing scene today resembles Seattle or Portland in the early 1990s—a handful of brewpubs and production-oriented craft breweries sprinkled all around the city. Recent years have seen many new operations open in the area, including several new brewpubs.

Yaletown Brewing Company and Sailor Hagar's Brewpub both opened in 1994, followed by SteamWorks Brewing Company in 1995. The wild popularity of these establishments indicates a growing enthusiasm for brewpubs in general, and also for the hearty flavors of ales. This is a shift from Vancouver's deeply rooted tradition of lagers; although many of the city's craft breweries also produce lager beers to satisfy the locals.

Given its success, Yaletown's management has moved forward with other brewpub developments. Across the street from the B.C. Place civic complex, you'll find Dix BBQ and Brewery, an all-lager house. The same folks administer the High Mountain Brewhouse in Whistler and the BigRidge Brewing Company east of Whiterock. Other companies are opening destination-type brewpubs in the Vancouver suburbs, including the Coquitlam Brewing Company to the east, and the Big River entertainment complex in Richmond.

In Vancouver you can also make a point of visiting some excellent production-focused breweries by calling to arrange a tour. Go to Storm Brewing and try their unusual lambic-type beers, or to R&B for a taste of their pair of award-winning flagship beers. Of course, the Granville Island Brewing Company's facility on Granville Island is a must-stop if you're in the area. And, Vancouver's first brewpub-hotel, The Creek Brewery/Granville Island Hotel, offers great accommodations for the overnight brew tour.

Wherever you go in Vancouver, you'll find many good beers on tap. The alehouse phenomenon has spread over the border from Washington, so you're sure to have a great craft beer selection. Given the large population of Vancouver, and the resulting strong marketplace for craft beers, you can also find many of the province's other craft beers on tap around town as well.

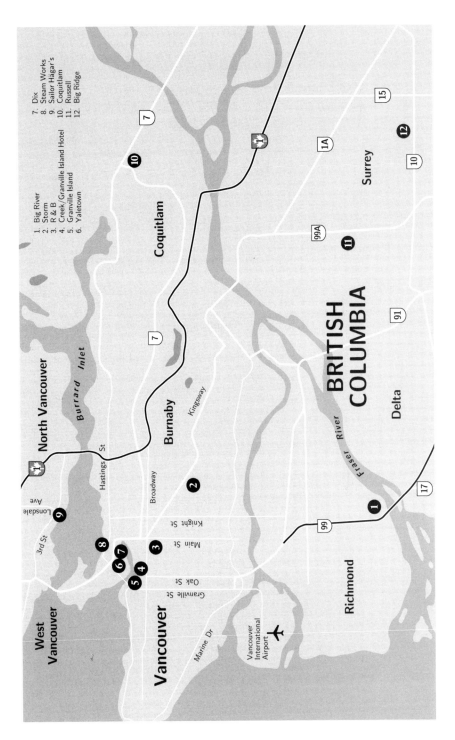

1. Big River
2. Storm
3. R & B
4. Creek/Granville Island Hotel
5. Granville Island
6. Yaletown
7. Dix
8. Steam Works
9. Sailor Hagar's
10. Coquitlam
11. Russell
12. Big Ridge

North Vancouver

West Vancouver

Vancouver

Burnaby

Coquitlam

Richmond

Delta

Surrey

BRITISH COLUMBIA

Burrard Inlet

Fraser River

Kingsway

Lonsdale Ave

3rd St

Hastings St

Broadway

Knight St

Main St

Oak St

Granville St

Marine Dr

Vancouver International Airport

7

7

7

1

1

1

10

11

12

15

1A

99A

99

91

10

17

The Creek Brewery/Granville Island Hotel

Established 1998

1253 Johnston Street • Vancouver, B.C. V6H 3R9
The Creek Restaurant/Lounge: (604) 685-7070 • Granville Island
Hotel: (604) 683-7373 • www.the-creek.com

Granville Island is a must-see part of Vancouver. Tucked away below the bridge spanning the False Creek waterway, the "island," which is really a peninsula, bustles with a marina and a Euro-style open-air market by day, and restaurants, clubs and a theater company by night. The whole area is quite small and is a vibrant urban mix of industry, the arts, retail spaces, and residences, all strung around a circular waterfront.

The Granville Island boutique hotel occupies one section of waterfront, offering views of water birds and watercraft traversing the narrow passage, and of downtown Vancouver's sparkling night lights. The Creek Brewery's equipment figures prominently in the architecture of the hotel, with the brewhouse (by Specific Mechanical Systems) displayed on both sides of the entryway (with connective piping underneath the walkway), and twenty massive conditioning tanks visible in the building's central solarium area from the balcony-like hallways leading to the guest rooms.

The fifty guest rooms in the hotel are elegantly furnished, done up in mahogany and wall-length mirrors, with each room featuring a floor of unique marble or stone tiles. The bedrooms have vaulted ceilings and the bathrooms have soaking tubs. Most rooms have queen beds, and all are equipped with wooden shutters that afford a stately sense of privacy.

Whether you have spent your day exploring the island's markets and shops, or have enjoyed an evening out on a sunset cruise, the Creek Brewery's restaurant can provide a suitable repast. Stop in for brunch, and refuel with wild mushroom eggs Benedict or spit-roasted breast of turkey, portabella and brie on sourdough. Or, if an evening visit to the dining room suits you, choose from appetizers such as new potato and prosciutto pizza, and main courses such as wood-grilled sea scallops and mesquite-grilled New York steak.

The long bar, with its high ceiling and panoramic views of the marina, is very inviting for a nightcap, and also is a great place to meet some friends to watch a big NFL game—the house team is the Minnesota Vikings. The 300-seat patio is a nice spot on warm days, and is equipped with heat lamps for chillier ones. The Creek's lounge sports a sizable humidor for cigar aficionados as well as a pool table and another fully stocked bar.

The Creek Brewery's beers are all unfiltered and are made in keeping with German traditions—including the Rheinheitsgebot law mandating the exclusive use of malted barley, whole hops, water, and yeast. Brewer Don Harmes was trained in Bavaria, and has built a local reputation at the Vancouver Island Brewing Company. The Creek's lounge and restaurant serve up samplers in handy little carriers, so you can try all of Harmes' tasty brews.

Hours: The Creek Restaurant, 11:30 a.m.–11 p.m. Monday–Friday, 10:30 a.m.–11 p.m. Saturday–Sunday; lounge, 4 p.m.–2 a.m. Monday–Saturday, 4 p.m.–midnight Sunday
Children: Yes, in the restaurant
Food: The Creek Restaurant, eclectic Northwest Cuisine; lounge, upscale pub fare
Entertainment: The Creek Restaurant: Big screen TV sports events; Occasional patio parties; Lounge: DJ Thursday–Saturday, and occasional cigar nights
Smoking: Yes, in most areas
Payment: Visa, MC, AmEx, ATM on premise
Beer to go: Yes, bottles

The Creek offers an extensive line of German-style beers made with three different yeasts—most are true-to-style with a couple of Northwest-style interpretations thrown in. The wide-ranging lager selections carry equally wide-roving titles: Donny's Dortmunder, Farrbuilder Dunkel, UpYourHeiny Pils, and Salzburger Lager (a very popular Vienna-style beer), as well as one or more of the Koolsch (an interpretation of the Cologne style), True Creek Alt (nicely balanced, rich, and amber), and the Hellava Hefeweizen.

Harmes also keeps a foothold in the English-style arena, with a couple of English ales available hand-drawn. Seasonal examples have included his Master Bitter (an ESB), Broadway Porter (a ruby, light-bodied interpretation), the Tremendous Ale (a mild that is indeed a good session beer), and the popular Roggen Stout (brewed with a dash of rye in the grist). Bottles of the beers are available at a retail space off the hotel lobby.

DIRECTIONS: From Highway 99, follow signs to the Granville Island exit just south of the Granville Street Bridge to downtown. Go down the ramp and pull onto the "island." Turn right into the shopping district and look for parking on the street, in the green parking garage (warehouse) or in the Granville Island Hotel's lot. The hotel/brewpub is on the east side of the island.

Dix BBQ & Brewery

Established 1999

871 Beatty Street • Vancouver, B.C. V6B 2M6
(604) 682-2739 • www.markjamesgroup.com

D ix BBQ and Brewery is right across the street from the GM Place civic arena, making it an ideal destination for meeting up with friends before or after a function. Dix is also close to the waterfront on False Creek, near the Plaza of Nations, and within a reasonable walk of the Yaletown Brewing Company (see page 205).

The Dix brewpub is full of character, with dark beam-and-timber construction and black-and-white tile flooring. A great collection of historic photos of the early Vancouver brewing industry decorates the walls: brewery workers, saloons, beer trucks. The impressive twelve-hectoliter brewhouse by Ripley Stainless is on display in the establishment's center. Along with the ten-seat bar, it serves as a division between the restaurant and pub. The pub is a fun place, with rock music on a good sound system, and a young, urbane crowd. The fully stocked bar features five TV screens, side-by-side, each tuned to a different channel.

The barbecue theme, known as "Dixperience BBQ," is an all-encompassing approach to barbecue. The kitchen does slow roasting, and offers a full range of barbecued beef, pork and chicken, as well as such attractions as Texas beef brisket and hickory smoked salmon. Try the portabella burger or one of the "Fancy Schmanzy" pastas.

This is an all-lager brewpub, with four standard beers brewed by Iain Hill, who also is brewmaster at Yaletown. You'll find a helles with nice malt depths and citrusy hop-highlights, and a dunkel with a rich hue and a quaffable creamy body. The Bohemian Pilsner is a well-balanced lager, though darker than most; and the Belgian Wit is reason enough to visit Dix, with its full yeast character and hints of coriander and orange. Ask what seasonal beer is on tap as well—perhaps a bock or an Octoberfest lager.

DIRECTIONS: On Highway 99 northbound, follow as 99 becomes Oak Street, turns left on Broadway and right on Hemlock, then goes over the Granville Street Bridge. Six blocks after the foot of the bridge, turn right on Nelson. Just before Nelson goes over the Cambie Street Bridge, turn left on Beatty Street. The brewpub is two blocks up Beatty, across the street from B.C. Place.

Hours: 11:30 a.m.–midnight, daily
Children: Yes, in the restaurant
Food: Upscale pub fare and Texan cuisine
Entertainment: Pool tables, many TVs, with sports events, occasional live music
Smoking: Yes, in the pub
Payment: Visa, MC, AmEx, ATM on premise
Beer to go: No

Granville Island Brewing Company

Established 1984

1441 Cartwright Street, Granville Island • Vancouver, B.C. V6H 3R7
(604) 687-2739

Granville Island Brewing Company occupies a large building in the center of the "island," which is really a tiny peninsula. The building's front corner is a retail store, well-stocked with beer and all types of beerphrenalia. Next door is a handsome tasting facility, including a board room for events. An impressive, two-story brewing system towers in the facility's main area. The brewery was one of the first wave of British Columbia craft breweries in the mid-1980s, and is an anchor to the island's open air market.

Hours: 9 a.m.–7 p.m. daily; brewery tours, 12 p.m., 2 p.m., 4 p.m.
Children: Yes
Food: No
Entertainment: No
Smoking: No
Payment: Checks, Interac, Visa, MC, AmEx
Beer to go: Yes, bottles and draft

They offer Canada's first micro in a can—cold-filtered Natural Draft. The other standards, available in cans or bottles, as well as on draft across B.C., are English Bay Pale Ale, Gastown Amber Ale, and Cypress Honey Lager. A couple of specialty, bottles-only beers are Brockton Black Lager and Kitsilano Light. Seasonal offerings, their "prototaps," are small (200-case) batches developed at their facility on Granville Island by Mark Simpson, plant manager, and then used for test-marketing. If the public embraces a new beer, it could become a regular, as happened with the Cypress Honey Lager. Recent prototaps have included a Märzen, a hefeweizen, and a Christmas beer.

Granville Island Brewing Company is a subsidiary of Cascadia Brands, a conglomerate which includes Calona Wines and Potter's Distilleries. The majority of Granville Island's production occurs at a plant in Kelowna, B.C., that adjoins a Calona Winery. The retail store in Kelowna offers tastings of Granville Island's main product line anytime during business hours. No tours of the Kelowna brewery are offered, but you can take a regularly scheduled tour of the winery.

DIRECTIONS: Follow Highway 99 as it heads north to downtown Vancouver. Follow the left-hand exit ramp to Granville Island just before the Granville Street Bridge to downtown. From Highway 1, take the Grandview Highway exit. Turn right on 12th Avenue and follow it to Hemlock. Turn right on Hemlock and follow signs to Granville Island. When you pull onto the island, go forward, then right, and the brewery is on your left.

R&B Brewing Company

Established 1997

54 E 4th Avenue • Vancouver, B.C. V5T 1E8
(604) 874-2537 • www.r-and-b.com

Owner/brewers Barry Benson and Rick Dellow sport a combined history of over thirty-five years in the brewing trade, having brewed for major companies internationally and having designed a hundred brewhouses. Benson is a graduate of the Siebel Institute in Chicaco, and veteran of Molson and Shaftebury, while Dellow holds a degree in brewing from Edinburgh's Heriot Watt University and brewed for Carlsberg and Bass before returning with Benson to Burnaby to open a microbrewery. Their initials combine to make for a brewery name with a groove.

Their flagship brew is Red Devil Ale, whose coppery hue is the result of a blend of domestic and imported malts, and whose flavor is appealing in its clean, smooth finish. Raven Cream Ale is an English Dark Mild spiced up with Northwest hops for a very quaffable twist on a traditional winner. The two seasonals rolled out in their first years of business include Sun God Wheat Ale (a very light blonde ale without the expected wheat haze), and Old Nick Winter Ale (a strong ale in the tradition of a wee heavy).

The brewhouse is a twenty-hectoliter steam-jacketed system from Newlands Services, and the cellar features reclaimed dairy tanks used for fermenters. The partners' long-time do-it-yourself style is borne out by the home-rigged grain mill, while the commercial scale is demonstrated by a double-boiler for the kettle. Despite the spartan feel lying behind the roll-up garage door, Dellow and Benson offer seminars on the finer points of craft brewing in their warehouse brewery.

R&B is focused on servicing the local market with fresh, consistent, filtered ales, and their beers are available only on draft. The kegs are distributed throughout the Lower Mainland, centered in Vancouver. Watch for their distinctive tap handles, sculpted by a local artist, with the unmistakable visages of a devil, a raven, and the sun.

DIRECTIONS: Call for directions

Hours: Call ahead to arrange a tour
Children: Yes
Food: No
Entertainment: No
Smoking: No
Payment: Checks
Beer to go: Yes, draft

SteamWorks Brewing Company

Established 1995

375 Water Street • Vancouver, B.C. V6B 5C6
(604) 689-2739 • www.steamworks.com

SteamWorks is an outstanding downtown Vancouver destination, featuring various environments on the ground floor and basement of The Landing, a cornerstone building on Vancouver's waterfront. Its downtown location and access to city transportation makes SteamWorks a perfect stopping point on most any tour of the city. While you're here, be sure to take a walk through Gastown to take in the sights, sounds, and smells of one of Vancouver's oldest and most characterful districts.

The Landing is the largest heavy timber-constructed building in Western Canada. The original massive wooden beams are visible inside, while the walls feature beautiful new wainscoting in the bright and cheery upstairs dining room and bar. A trip down the central spiral staircase leads to the pub, which has a fireplace, pool tables, and a softly lit dining room. The fermenters are separated from the dining area by a low, wrought-iron fence, and the ten-barrel brewhouse is set behind glass at the restaurant's rear. The brewery is called SteamWorks because the heat for the brewing kettle comes from tapping into the city's steam lines.

Hours: 11:30 a.m.–1 a.m. Monday–Saturday; 11:30 a.m.–midnight Sunday
Children: Yes, in the restaurant
Food: Casual and fine dining
Entertainment: Pool tables, library, live jazz 2–5 p.m. Saturday and Sunday, TVs
Smoking: Yes, in the pub
Payment: Visa, MC, AmEx
Beer to go: No

The savory menu is comprised of Pacific Northwest comfort food, and offers wood-fired pizzas, as well as numerous other fine entrées. For a quick bite, try the black bean cakes, the onion tarts, or the jambalaya.

Brewer Conrad Gmoser was previously the assistant when Shirley Warner was head brewer for SteamWorks. He makes several standards, including Lion's Gate Lager, Signature Pale Ale, Nutbrown Nirvana, and Empress India Pale Ale. You'll also find either Heroica Oatmeal Stout or the Cole Porter on tap. An eclectic array of seasonals has been served at Steamworks. Most recently these have been Cascadia Cream Ale, Ipanema Summer White, and raspberry-flavored Frambozen. For the holidays, Gmoser makes the Great Pumpkin Ale and Blitzen Christmas Ale.

DIRECTIONS: Follow Highway 99 across Granville Island into the heart of downtown Vancouver, where it becomes Seymour Street. Follow Seymour until it ends at Hastings. Go right one block, then left to the beginning of Water Street. The brewpub is on your left.

Storm Brewing Company

Established 1995

310 Commercial Drive • Vancouver, B.C. V5L 3V6
(604) 255-9119

Storm Brewing is one of the city's best-kept secrets, and is an example of minimalist, quality brewing at its finest. Brewer James Walton, with personal background in both homebrewing and welding, is a natural commercial brewer—though certainly not a typical one. He believes in pushing the exploration of Europe's classic beer styles as far as British Columbia's beer drinkers want to go.

Storm's brewery consists of a combination of old pharmaceutical, dairy, and pulp mill equipment pieced together just-so by Walton himself. Though it's not much to look at, it works magic under Walton's careful crafting. You'll find his beers on tap throughout Vancouver proper, but not far beyond the city limits. The centralized market focus of his beer production allows Walton to continue operating primarily as a one-man brewery.

Many of the city's finest restaurants carry Storm beers on tap. They are well worth seeking out, so look for the distinctive metal tap handles that are vaguely reminiscent of electrical coils. The standard lineup is Hurricane IPA (an intense entry into the style, copiously hopped), Highland Scottish Ale (creamy and nutty), and Black Plague Stout (an outstanding Irish-type dry stout). Look for various seasonals, such as Twister Wheat Ale, with a weissebier tanginess.

Storm continues to explore uncharted waters with its interpretations of the lambic traditional beers. You might find a raspberry, a blackberry, or a black cherry brew, each aged in oak casks for over a year. Each lambic-type seasonal is infused with some whole, unpasteurized fruit. The naturally occurring wild yeasts present in the fruit cause a slow, secondary fermentation that yields unique flavors.

DIRECTIONS: Call for directions.

Hours: Call ahead to arrange a tour
Children: No
Food: No
Entertainment: No
Smoking: No
Payment: N/A
Beer to go: No

Yaletown Brewing Company

Established 1994

1111 Mainland Street • Vancouver, B.C. V6B 2T9
(604) 681-2739

This, Vancouver's premier brewpub, serves as the anchor establishment for the trendy Yaletown district. Surrounded by a few choice retail shops, Yaletown Brewing Company's brewpub is located in one of the neighborhood's converted warehouses and is divided into a pub, on the left, and a restaurant, on the right,. The pub has a long, handsome bar, pool tables, and dart lanes, and a large sandstone fireplace and hearth. The brewhouse is visible through the rear glass wall.

The restaurant is adorned with colorful paintings by a local artist who once lived in the old warehouse. By day, the place is bright and cheery; by night, it's bustling. In nice weather, outdoor seating is available on a broad, raised sidewalk. Menu offerings include wood-fired pizzas, tempting pastas, pound-size T-bone steaks, seafood, and pub fare. For a quick bite to go with your pint, try a blackened chicken burger or a bowl of the clam-and-corn chowder.

The brewhouse features a seventeen-hectoliter system by Ripley Stainless, along with three closed fermenters and eighteen conditioning tanks. Brewmaster Iain Hill, formerly of Shaftebury, exercises his creativity in a wide range of beers, guided by customer feedback. Standards include the best-selling Munich-style Mainland Lager (delightfully bitter with a hint of peat), Indian Arm Pale Ale (a name taken from nearby Indian Arm Bay), a Pilsner-style Harbour Light Lager, and Hill's Special Wheat (a Bavarian-style hefeweizen).

Seasonals include variations on the hefeweizen, such as a cherry and a raspberry version; as well as a dunkel lager, a smoked lager, a Belgian-style Grand Cru, and Old Hooligan's Christmas Ale which is tart, fruity and brewed with juniper berries. Yaltetown's two bars pour the brews from both cold-taps and beer engines for your sipping pleasure.

Hours: 11:30 a.m.–midnight Sunday–Wednesday; 11:30 a.m.–1 a.m. Thursday–Saturday
Children: Yes, in the restaurant
Food: Full menu of nouveau pub fare
Entertainment: Multiple TVs, pool and steel-tip darts, club dancing Thursday–Saturday, live music Tuesday
Smoking: Yes, in the pub and at the restaurant's bar
Payment: Visa, MC, AmEx
Beer to go: No

DIRECTIONS: From Highway 99, cross Oak Street Bridge, take the first right down to Cambie. Turn left on Cambie and follow it across the Cambie Street Bridge. Turn left on Mainland. Drive two blocks, and the brewpub is on the right, on the corner of Mainland and Helmcken.

Sailor Hägar's Brewpub

Established 1994

86 Semisch Avenue N • North Vancouver, B.C. V7M 3H8
(604) 984-3087

Sailor Hägar's, North Vancouver's only brewpub, is an excellent destination for the brew tourist. A SeaBus ride from downtown Vancouver over to NorthVancouver is worth the trip for this fine establishment in itself. The pub sits on a hillside overlooking the water, with a panoramic view of the city from inside the pub or out on the spacious wrap-around deck. The interior is lavishly decorated with sailing accoutrements and oak and brass fixtures. Be sure to note the carved dolphins bas relief over the fireplace.

The menu offers some good burgers and fish and chips. But it also features some unusual options, such as the peanut satay chicken pizza. Or, try the chicken strips, with a coating using the brewery's spent grains. For an adventuresome variation on a ploughman's platter, order the Scandinavian Platter.

Brewer Gary Lohin is a self-trained homebrewer who convinced owner Al Riedlinger to install the brewhouse next door to his existing neighborhood pub. Since the four fermenters and assorted ale and lager conditioning tanks were installed, Lohin has been brewing a wide variety of unfiltered beers.

Regular offerings include Hägar's Honey Pilsner, Scandinavian Amber Lager, Narwhal Pale Ale, Lohin's Extra Special Bitter, a Belgian-style wit brewed with coriander and orange peel, and the outstanding Grizzly Nut brown. Past seasonals include the IRA (Irish Red Ale, a twist on the classic English export type), a maple oatmeal stout, a Maibock, a wee heavy ale with distinct peat flavor, and a spiced blueberry wheat. Beers are served both on tap and from a beer engine. The brewhouse is in a separate building from the pub, and tours are conducted on request.

Hours: 11 a.m.–midnight, daily
Children: No
Food: Extensive pub fare with a Norwegian flair
Entertainment: Darts, television
Smoking: Yes
Payment: Visa, MC, AmEx, Interac
Beer to go: Yes, bottles

DIRECTIONS: From the SeaBus terminal, walk straight off the dock up the hill three blocks. From Highway 99 take the first exit on the north side of the Lion's Gate Bridge. Stay in the right lane as it loops under the highway. As you head into North Vancouver, follow Low Level Road, and take the left fork, Marine Drive, around the hill by the railroad tracks, which puts you on Esplanade. Follow Esplanade across Lonsdale and turn right on Semische. Drive two blocks and the brewpub is on your right.

SATURDAY 16
MARCH

Howe Sound Inn & Brewing Company

Established 1996

37801 Cleveland Avenue • Squamish, B.C. V0N 3G0
Pub/Red Heather Grill: 605/892-2603 • Inn: (800) 919-2537
www.howesound.com

A ny trip up the Sea to Sky Highway (99) takes you around the foot of a striking small mountain with an awesome rock face towering directly over the road, the Stawamus Chief. "The Chief," as it is known locally, is on the international must-climb list for zealous rock climbers. Lying directly at the Chief's foot, the town of Squamish serves as basecamp to a veritable amusement park for outdoor enthusiasts.

Besides the climbers, hikers and bikers come for the Garibaldi Highlands; kayakers and windsurfers take delight in the Squamish River and Porteau Cove; sport anglers and cross-country skiers frequent Alice Lake Park, birders make pilgrimages to Brackendale to witness the largest congregations of bald eagles anywhere south of Alaska, and skiers traveling to and from Whistler Village form a steady stream. Many of these recreationists find their way to Howe Sound Inn & Brewing Company.

If you're planning any such recreational activities, Howe Sound makes a comfortable homebase, with its elegant cuisine, comfortable furnishings, and rustic mountain lodge architecture. Built-to-spec as a "character Northwest inn, restaurant, brewpub and meeting house," it delivers a quality package. Amenities include a sauna, an exercise room, a small outdoor climbing wall, a large patio off the brewpub, a couple of meeting rooms, and even a bakery serving up breads and muffins baked fresh in-house for breakfast and dinner.

Hours: Howe Sound Brewpub, 11:30 a.m.–midnight Sunday–Thursday, 11:30 a.m.–1 a.m. Friday and Saturday; Red Heather Grill Restaurant, 11 a.m.–2:30 p.m. and 5:30–10 p.m. Monday–Friday, 10 a.m.–2:30 p.m. and 5:30-11 p.m. Saturday and Sunday
Children: Yes, in the Red Heather Grill
Food: Brewpub, upscale pub fare and West Coast comfort food; Red Heather Grill, NW fine-dining, including in-house bakery
Entertainment: Brewpub, pool table, steel-tip darts, TV sports events, live music on most weekends, Vancouver rock bands or local folk artists, frequent films, occasional indoor beach parties; inn, exterior granite climbing wall
Smoking: Yes, in the brewpub
Payment: Visa, MC, AmEx
Beer to go: Yes, draft

The twenty guest rooms are comfy and understated, with day bed/window seat nooks for lounging (ask for a room facing the Chief), plush down comforters, and framed historic photos on the walls. In the morning, you can walk out the door of

the inn and down the street to the Squamish Estuary trail system for a stretch of the legs and a peek at the scenery before brunch at the Red Heather.

The Red Heather Grill offers a mixed clientele of locals and internationally diverse tourist groups Northwest-style casual fine dining in a simply elegant room of light fir (reclaimed wood). The menu includes such choice items as grilled peppercorn steak, fresh salmon, and penne with grilled vegetables in roasted garlic-tomato-goat cheese sauce, as well as a variety of decadent desserts.

The brewpub, which sits across the lobby from the restaurant, is a large, fun pub, with high ceilings; a fireplace at one end has couches that form an intimate conversation area. Ask about the nightly food specials, or order a bite off the menu—hot sandwiches, salads, pastas, pizzas. Maybe you'll play some darts, or check out the mural of "the Chief" that shows the climbing routes—including the one used by the first to climb it, Jim Baldwin and Ed Cooper. And, be sure to look up to see the mountain bikes and wind-surfboards dangling from the rafters.

The spacious brewhouse (eleven-hectoliter, Ripley Stainless) is largely set up in a traditional gravity-fed arrangement and is situated above, behind, and below the pub's bar area. If you ask for a tour you'll get a chance to climb the spiral staircases while you sample the draft lineup: their best-selling Whitecap Wheat Ale, as well as well as Garibaldi Ale, Baldwin & Cooper Best Bitter, Britannia Mild, Diamond Head Stout, and a Scotch ale. Most of the beers' names are drawn from local places, except for the B&C Bitter, which is named for the climbers who first scaled the Chief.

In the summer, Howe Sound brewer Nigel Roberts brews the eminently malty Rail Ale (proceeds go to a local organization of steam train enthusiasts), and a hemp ale made with hemp seeds and organically grown malts in the mash, called Mettleman (offered at the party following the local "Test of Mettle" bike race). In the fall, look for the smooth Harvest Lager. In the winter you'll find Sahib IPA, Milennium Barley Wine (in a limited bottling), and Father John's Christmas Ale (named for legendary B.C. brewer, John Mitchell, who consulted on the brewhouse).

DIRECTIONS: From Highway 99, turn west onto Cleveland Avenue at the sign for Squamish City Center. Follow Cleveland all the way through downtown until it ends at Vancouver Street near the Mamquam Blind Channel. The brewpub/hotel is on the right; covered parking is under the building.

Whistler Brewing Company

Established 1989

1209 Alpha Lake Road • Whistler, B.C. V0N 1B1
(604) 932-6185

Whistler Brewing Company is one of B.C.'s largest craft breweries, located in the tourist haven at the culmination of the "Sea to Sky" stretch of Highway 99. The mountains are breathtaking here, with Whistler Mountain looming above, and other mountains such as Black Tusk completing the high alpine feel of the area.

The brewery at Whistler Village includes a charming little tasting room, but regular tour times are not scheduled; you are welcome to call ahead to arrange a tour and tasting. If you do take a tour, you'll see the impressive pair of copper mash and lauter tuns built in 1954 and acquired from the Mîssingen Brewery in Germany.

Whistler absorbed other craft beer start-ups in the late 1990s, including Bowen Island Brewing Company and Coquihalla Brewing Company. The plant at Whistler now produces all the product lines from these former breweries, in addition to the original Whistler line, under the direction of Dennis Johnson

Whistler's first beer (and still its flagship label), Whistler Premium Lager, is a golden German-type lager. Whistler's Mother Pale Ale is a lager that is similar to an American Pale Ale, with a floral aroma and a touch of caramel. Black Tusk, first released in 1990, was changed to endow it with a malty character ending in a full hops celebration, much like a porter. Rounding out the Whistler line is Avalanche Pilsner.

The two surviving Coquihalla beers are the Canadian classic Coquihalla Lager, and Tatoo, a very pale and low-gravity lager. Bowen Island beers continue to pour on tap at many accounts around the Lower Mainland as well. Look for the Bowen Island Blonde Ale and their special bitter, but, really keep your eyes pealed for their smooth Hemp Cream Ale and their Hemp Lager, made with hemp seeds in the mash along with the malted barley.

DIRECTIONS: From Highway 99, turn west at Function Junction onto Alpha Lake Road two kilometers south of the town of Whistler. Cross the railroad tracks, and the brewery is the second building on the right. (Note: There is also a road called Alta Lake Road heading west from 99 at the south end of town. These roads are not the same.)

Hours: Call ahead for a tour and tasting
Children: Yes
Food: No
Entertainment: No
Smoking: No
Payment: Interac, Visa, MC
Beer to go: Yes, bottles

High Mountain Brewing Company & Brewhouse

Established 1997

4355 Blackcomb Way • Whistler, B.C. V0N 1B4
(604) 905-2739 • www.markjamesgroup.com

Whistler and Blackcomb, twin ski areas a couple of hours due north of Vancouver, combine to create an opulent destination resort for powder hounds from every skiing nation on earth. You can ski right out the door of your condo onto the slopes—or, for that matter, down to the High Mountain Brewhouse!

Or better yet, make an evening of dinner and good locally brewed beers at the High Mountain Brewhouse. They offer early bird specials, but no matter when you plan to come, get a reservation, because this 300-seat restaurant fills up, especially during ski season. You can go the wood-fired pizza route, or perhaps just have a "small plate" such as oysters with chipotle salsa or curried veggie soup. Or, try the pastas, stirfries, or one of the wood-fired rotisserie entrées.

The building itself is striking, somewhat reminiscent of an alpine lodge, with a rustic elegance. Take advantage of one of the two patio seating areas when weather permits. Otherwise, the lofty beam-and-post interior offers split level dining in either a pub or restaurant atmosphere. The expansive architecture offers great views of the Ripley Manufacturing sixteen-hectoliter brewing system. There's an in-house bakery making good breads and desserts, and the pub offers televised sports.

Brewmaster Pete Kis-Toth's standard lineup of brews includes some from each branch of the beer family tree. North American interpretations of traditional British ales are the headliners, with Twin Peaks Pale Ale (rich and smooth), Big Wolf Bitter, (crisp at the finish), Dirty Miner Stout, and Frank's Nut brown Ale (named for B.C.'s famed Frank Appleton, High Mountain's start-up consultant). On the cold-fermented side, the Brewhouse serves up Lifty Lager and Northern Light Lager. Seasonal offerings include a Bavarian hefeweizen and a dunkelweizen, a cherry beer, an apricot-honey beer, and the wildly popular hemp ale.

Hours: 11:30 a.m.–Midnight Sunday–Thursday, 11:30 a.m.–1 a.m. Friday and Saturday
Children: Yes, in the restaurant
Food: Upscale pub fare, wood-fired pizza and rotisserie
Entertainment: Live DJ on weekends, 15 TV screens with sports events, pool table
Smoking: Yes, in the pub
Payment: Visa, MC, AmEx, ATM on premise
Beer to go: Yes, bottles

DIRECTIONS: From Highway 99, enter Whistler and pass Village Gate Boulevard. Turn right on Lorimar Road, then take a right on Black Comb Way. The brewpub is in the shopping center on Black Comb Way, with underground parking available.

Coquitlam Brewing Company

Established 1999

1163 Pine Tree Way • Coquitlam, B.C. V3B 8A9
(604) 552-2337

The Coquitlam Brewing Company is a prime example of B.C.'s new wave of upscale restaurant/brewpubs. Located in a retail destination development within this Vancouver bedroom community, it offers either restaurant or nouveau-lounge "pub" atmosphere. The brewpub has glass and wood curves that wrap around extensive seating areas, creating refuges from the crowds of shoppers. Pin lights descend from an ultra-modern faux drop ceiling, while the tables sport a stylized Egyptian grain sheaf motif.

A glass-encased brewhouse (ten-hectoliter, Northern Manufacturing) separates the restaurant in the front from the pub in the rear; an additional glassed-off room of tanks is in the back corner. On the pub side, a curved bar serving liquor and hot drinks uses the brewhouse as a backdrop—a functional division from the restaurant.

The menu offers a full range of salads and appetizers, as well as entrées ranging from rotisserie turkey to Italian thin crust pizza and jambalaya. Given the eclectic assortment, let your appetite be your guide—choose between a grilled vegetable wrap or a grilled New York steak. Many items include the brewpub's beers in the recipes.

Don Moore, formerly of Okanagan Spring Brewery and Tree Brewing, set up the brewery and formulated its high quality beers. He makes "simple beers with complexity" that are unfiltered, of a distinctly British style, and often feature grain bills of nine or ten different malts. Standards include a session-style British brown, a pale ale with a hint of citrus, an ESB with a ramped-up hop profile, and Honey Coriander Cream Ale, which is slightly spiced to provide a cleansing finish to the taste. Seasonals include a Vienna Märzen in the spring, a wheat in the summer, a stout in the fall, and a spiced Christmas ale for the cold months.

Hours: 11 a.m.–midnight Sunday–Thursday, 11 a.m.–1 a.m. Friday and Saturday
Children: Yes, in the restaurant
Food: Pizza, rotisserie entrées, seafood
Entertainment: Occasional special events
Smoking: Yes, in the pub and a section of the restaurant
Payment: Visa, MC, AmEx, Interac
Beer to go: No

DIRECTIONS: From Highway 1, take the exit immediately north of the Port Mann Bridge onto Highway 7 East to Port Coquitlam. Continue as Highway 7 becomes an arterial retail strip, crosses Lougheed Highway, then becomes Pine Tree Way. Continue a few blocks to Lincoln Street and turn right. You are now in front of the Coquitlam Center mall; the brewery is at the far corner of the building. Parking is available above the brewery via a ramp immediately past the brewery's entrance.

Mission Springs Brewing Company

Established 1996

7160 Oliver Street (at Lougheed Highway) • Mission, B.C. V2V 6K5
Information: (604) 820-1009 •Reservations: (604) 504-4200

If you're passing this way, Mission Springs Brewing Company makes for a fun pit stop. This roadhouse entered the brewing scene in 1996, and is now a must-stop for good beer and great ambiance. What began as an automotive theme (an antique pickup truck serves as their logo—the same truck that's mounted overhead in the restaurant), has evolved into a rowdy array of antique knick-knacks and memorabilia. However, the brewing system (Newlands Manufacturing, 11 hectoliter) is housed out of sight.

Take your pick from the pub (with pool tables and TV screens) or the restaurant (with the stuffed bear and antique tools). Or, perhaps you'll opt for one of the patios that offer a beautiful view of the mighty Fraser River.

There's a full bar, complete with espresso machine; the pub and restaurant menus are supplemented with seasonal menus and many special menus. The restaurant prides itself on its use of all fresh foods and its in-house, from-scratch bakery.

Brewer Stefan Arnason uses his three open fermenters creatively to offer a wide range of beers, from a Honey Cream Ale to an Oatmeal Stout. Try the creamy, faintly licoricey stout on a nitro beer engine; or stick with something off their fifteen cold taps—the Nut Brown Ale is a good choice; other options include a Blonde Draft Ale and an IPA, as well as a seasonal or two. If you're buying bottled beer to go from the retail store, enjoy the labels' fun slogans, such as the Nut Brown Ale's "So full of malty goodness, it hurts."

DIRECTIONS: From Highway 1, take the McCallum Road exit just north of Abbotsford. From the junction of Highway 7 and Highway 11, follow Highway 11 North and cross the Mission Bridge over the Fraser River. Turn west onto Lougheed Highway. The brewpub is a few miles down the Lougheed Highway on the river side of the road, next door to the RCMP station.

Hours: Pub, 11 a.m.–midnight Sunday–Thursday, 11 a.m.–1 a.m. Friday and Saturday; restaurant, 11 a.m.–11 p.m. Sunday–Thursday, 11 a.m.–3 a.m. Friday and Saturday; retail store, 9 a.m.–11 p.m. daily
Children: Yes, in the restaurant
Food: Full menus in both pub and restaurant
Entertainment: Beach volleyball courts, pool tables, big screen TV, DJ five nights a week, live music two nights a month
Smoking: Yes, in the pub and part of the Rrestaurant
Payment: Interac, Visa, MC
Beer to go: Yes, bottles

Okanagan Valley Brew Tour

The Okanagan Valley has the makings for an excellent multiple-brewery tour. Situated in the rainshadow of the Cascades, the Okanagan Valley is dry and sunny most of the year. The region offers several ski slopes, the expansive and picturesque Okanagan Lake, stunning mountain vistas, and endless fruit orchards. Come here for fun in the sun or the snow, and enjoy a plethora of craft beers up and down the long valley.

Your first stop should rightfully be the Ridge Brewing Company and Westridge Motor Inn, in Osoyoos, the southern gateway to the Okanagan Valley. This watering hole serves as an oasis in the arid landscape. With a full-service motel on the property as well, the Ridge can prove to be a welcome stop from either of the main highways in the area.

A short drive north through stark brown and orange canyonlands brings the thirsty tourist to the town of Penticton. Located at the southern end of Okanagan Lake, this is a summer tourist town for folks from Vancouver in search of a beach getaway. The first stop here for the brew enthusiast is The Tin Whistle. This is a microbrewery designed for visitors, with taps for tasting right out front, and the whole brewhouse—bottling and kegging facilities—all in the same room. Tours begin with each walk-in group. Penticton is also home to one brewpub and one restaurant/brewery combination. The Barley Mill Pub, a fixture of Penticton, popular with both the locals and the vacationers, has multiple seating areas to suit your mood.

Continue north on your brew tour to the northern shores of Okanagan Lake, where you'll find the town of Kelowna (a First Nations name for the grizzly bear). This is a charming city, where you can delight in waterfront walks along the lakeshore. Or, try a short hike at the edge of town, and enjoy a view of the expansive lake. Kelowna offers the craft beer enthusiast tasting opportunities and retail stores at both Tree Brewing Company and at Granville Island Brewing Company's production facility. Tree Brewing also offers regular tours, so check their schedule. For a brewpub and bowling lanes experience, the Zone Entertainment Group will soon be opening another property in Kelowna similar to their Big River brewpub on the Lower Mainland.

The next town up the valley is Vernon, home of Okanagan Spring Brewery. "OK Spring," as it's known locally, is one of B.C.'s largest microbreweries, producing both its own widely recognized line of beers, as well as the recently acquired Shaftebury label. The brewery is housed in a set of unassuming warehouses near Vernon's city center and offers tours (call ahead) and a retail store. The brewery recently remodeled and expanded is well worth the stop for a peek at the German-style, horizontal conditioning tanks.

Continuing north past Vernon, the valley climbs upward into majestic mountain terrain, and the road splits. Either direction leads to a microbrewery—east is Mount Begbie Brewing in Revelstoke, and west is Bear Brewing in Kamloops.

Either of these production-oriented breweries makes a good final stop, as a conclusion to your brew tour of the Okanagan Valley.

Ridge Brewing Company Brew Pub/ Family Restaurant/Hotel

Established 1998

PO Box 431 • Junction of Highway 3 and Highway 97
Osoyoos, B.C. V0H 1V0
Ridge Brew Pub: (250) 495-7679 • Westridge Motor Inn: (800) 977-8711

On the Canadian side of the Highway 97 border-crossing is a lake called Osoyoos with a town by the same name on its shores. This First Nations name means "the narrows" or "meeting place," and refers to a bottleneck in the middle of the lake. Highway 3 also comes through Osoyoos, descending the slopes of the Cascade Mountains from Manning and Cathedral Provincial Parks. To the north on Highway 97 is the lake country of B.C.'s Okanagan Valley; to the south, the Okanagan River makes its way into Eastern Washington.

The Osoyoos area retains much of its agricultural heritage from a century-and-a-half of cattle ranches and orchards. The warm climate attracts many urbanites escaping from the congestion of B.C.'s Lower Mainland. The Ridge Brewing Company sits at the main crossroads of Osoyoos, along with a motel facility that dates from the 1970s, but was remodeled as part of the brewpub venture in 1997. Given its prime location, it is poised to serve travelers with the winning combination of good food, beer, and lodging.

The lodging facilities are neat and tidy motel-type rooms. It is a classic motor inn in many respects, with standard room configurations, an outdoor swimming pool, and cement patio area, as well as a Jacuzzi/sauna. It also offers a game room, rental movies, and prepared packages for golf or ski outings. (Mount Baldy is forty-five minutes away, reached by a regular shuttle bus running to and from Osoyoos.)

The brewpub is a spiffy new building with a Southwest theme playing off this region's naturally arid terrain. A mission-like bell tower beckons thirsty wayfarers off the byways to partake of some refreshing food and beverages. Hop vines growing up bright, white plaster walls, and a faux dry creek bed remind you

Hours: Ridge Brew Pub, 11 a.m.–1 a.m. daily
Children: Yes, in the restaurant
Food: Eclectic international cuisine in the brewpub
Entertainment: Ridge Brew Pub, live music on weekends, TV sports events and regular pools, pull-tabs and pool table; Westridge Motor Inn, golf and ski packages, game room, outdoor swimming pool, movies
Smoking: Yes, in the pub
Payment: Interac/Debit, Visa, MC, AmEx, Diners Club
Beer to go: Yes, bottles

of your parched throat as you slip into the cool interior. The establishment offers a sports bar pub area and a handsome restaurant dining room. The overall feel is a modern one of stainless steel, marble, and fir.

The restaurant is centered around a large gas fireplace, with tiered seating areas of rustic softwood and a glass wall allowing a full view of the shiny brewhouse (ten-hectoliter, Pacific Brewers). Folks relax in this snug-like dining room and sip unfiltered craft beers and sample foods of a variety of ethnicities. The appetizer list includes the likes of a crab quesadilla, a cured-meats platter, and escargot. The dinner menu spans salads and soups (a Santa Fe wrap and corn chowder, for example) and heartier fare such as baked penne ragout and blackened fish.

Chris Johnson moonlights as brewer here, making the long trek from Buckerfield's Brewery in Victoria (see Swans Suite Hotel, page 191) to brew at the Ridge. In addition to several guest taps, the pub keeps the Ridge's three standard English-style ales on tap: a blonde that's very light and a bit buttery; a bitter that's nutty, with a deep malty hue; and a nut brown that's true-to-style. Seasonals have included a stout and fruit ales made with local fruit, as well as a couple of lagers.

Though the entire brewpub is a smoking area, its high-volume air circulating system makes the atmosphere tolerable for non-smokers. The Ridge's brewpub also sports a state-of-the-art, in-house sound system, with multiple environment room controls to separately set the mood for the pub, the restaurant, and the banquet room downstairs. This makes for pleasant live music enjoyment on the weekends, when you can expect to find a pianist or even a band.

If you're looking for something to do during your stay, the pub area is a sports fan's heaven, with 'pool' opportunities, and multiple screens to catch a game's every nuance. Or, why not take a jaunt out of town up to Lake Kliluk near Keremeos; called "Spotted Lake" because of its high concentration of minerals, it is renowned for its healing properties.

DIRECTIONS: This brewpub/hotel sits on a small bluff overlooking the junction of Highway 3 and Highway 97. From Highway 3 turn south into the parking lot; go behind the motel to get to the brewpub.

Tin Whistle Brewing Company

Established 1995

954 W Eckhardt Avenue • Penticton, B.C. V2A 2C1
(250) 770-1122

Tin Whistle is a cottage brewery set in an Old West-style building and designed as a tourist attraction. Penticton is a hot spot for summer tourists from the Vancouver area with its miles of lakeshore and abundant watersport opportunities. The Tin Whistle's entire brewing operation is set up in a small space for viewing from the front walk-in area, which doubles as a retail store.

The brewery was named for the first old locomotive to run on the Kettle Valley Railroad, which served the area in the early twentieth century. Photos of this old railway adorn the walls of the brewery. The brewhouse was designed by the legendary brewery consultant Frank Appleton (who happens to live in the hills outside of Penticton), and built by Ripley Stainless from neighboring Summerland, B.C. The beers are filtered, and are distributed throughout the Okanagan Valley, the Lower Mainland, Vancouver Island, and Alberta.

The brewing company offers five ales, all named for indigenous wildlife and all geared toward the tourist's palate, qualifying as "cross-over" beers for the microbrew novice. Coyote Ale is a light-bodied golden, while Black Widow Dark is a robust ale with plenty of chocolate malts and a fair amount of hops. Rattlesnake Extra Special Bitter has some frontal hop boldness; Killer Bee is a dark ale, smooth from the added honey. Peaches 'n Cream uses Okanagan Valley peaches and apricots, along with four malts for a rich, creamy treat.

DIRECTIONS: Highway 97 becomes Eckhardt Avenue as it enters town. The brewery is at the south end of town, just before the last stoplight, in front of the golf course.

Hours: Retail Store, winter 11 a.m.–5 p.m. Monday–Saturday; summer 11 a.m.–7 p.m. daily; brewery tours daily
Children: Yes
Food: No
Entertainment: No
Smoking: No
Payment: Interac, Visa, MC
Beer to go: Yes, bottles

Barley Mill Brewpub

Established 1998

2460 Skaha Lake Road • Penticton, B.C. V2A 6E9
(250) 493-8000

Penticton is a summer vacation destination for those seeking to escape the damp grayness of British Columbia's Lower Mainland. It's nice to know that after a day of basking in the rays on Okanagan Lake, fishing, windsurfing, or whatever floats your boat, there's a brewpub waiting in downtown Penticton.

The Barley Mill Pub is in a quasi-Tudor-style building with high ceilings and nice woodwork—perfectly suited to the Barley Mill's British theme. Walking up to the front of the building you might think you were in grand old England, as you pass the classic lamp post standing amidst neatly trimmed hedges around the pub, which has the air of a country estate.

The downstairs pub originally opened in 1983, while a second pub-space and the brewing operation upstairs were added in the late 1990s. There are fully stocked bars both upstairs and down, in addition to the fresh house ales and lagers. Upstairs. you'll find pool and darts; a pool table is downstairs.

They serve from their full menu in both the upstairs and downstairs areas. If it's pub fare you want, you can choose between pizza and burgers, or select from a list of about twenty sandwiches. There's also a Southwestern cuisine section, as well as steaks, seafood, and other favorites such as teriyaki chicken and the tostada salad.

Brewer Ray Huson, long-time homebrewer, met the developers who created the Barley Mill while bartending at a local golf course. He's now at the controls of a ten-hectoliter brewing system by Specific Mechanical, brewing several standard ales and one lager. On a given day at the pub, you're sure to find Appaloosa Lager, a Canadian-style lager that's aged a full two months. You'll also find the thirst-quenching Cayuse Wheat Lite Ale, the award-winning Palomino Pale Ale, and Nite Mare Brown Ale, a classic English brown. You might also catch Filly Light, a low-alcohol, low-gravity lager that's good on hot Okanagan afternoons. Seasonal brews tend to be fruit ales—using Okanagan Valley cherries, raspberries and other fruits.

Hours: 11 a.m.–1 a.m. Monday–Saturday, 11 a.m.–midnight Sunday
Children: No
Food: Pub fare, steaks and seafood
Entertainment: Pool, steel-tip darts, occasional live music
Smoking: Yes, in a smoking section
Payment: Interac, Visa/Mc, AmEx
Beer to go: Yes, bottles

DIRECTIONS: From Highway 97, turn East on Skaha Lake Road. The brewpub is about a mile down Skaha Lake Road on the right, just after Galt Avenue.

Tree Brewing Company

Established 1996

1083 Richter Street • Kelowna, B.C. V1Y 2K6
(250) 860-8836

Kelowna, home of the Tree Brewing Company, is situated on Okanagan Lake, roughly in the center of the lake's east shore. The town makes a great destination for fishing and boating of all sorts in the warmer months, and is close to a few different ski areas for winter fun. Tree Brewing, Kelowna's first local microbrewery, has grown rapidly through the 1990s, so that its bottles are available throughout the province's liquor store system and widely distributed on draft throughout British Columbia's Interior and Lower Mainland.

The brewery, located in downtown Kelowna, features a beautiful tasting bar (for tour groups) and a retail store selling cold beer and plenty of souvenirs. The 20,000-hectoliter annual-capacity brewery is comprised of various pieces of used equipment, including a collection of grundies and European-made horizontal conditioning tanks.

Hours: Retail Store: 10 a.m.–5:30 p.m. Monday–Saturday; Brewery Tours: Summer: Noon, 2 p.m., 4 p.m. Wednesday–Saturday; winter: call ahead to arrange a tour.
Children: Yes
Food: No
Entertainment: No
Smoking: No
Payment: Checks, Visa, MC
Beer to go: Yes, bottles

Brewmaster David Brown is a graduate of the prestigious Siebel Institute in Chicago, Illinois. He uses whole hop cones instead of pellets, unusual for a B.C. brewery of Tree's size; many brewers believe whole hops lend fuller, more pronounced flavors than pellets. His beers have been winning awards, so seek out Tree's distinctive brews in their equally distinctive, artistically painted packaging.

Tree's standard beer line includes a red ale, an amber ale, and a classic English-style pale ale, brewed with five different malts, and hopped with both Noble Goldings and classic New World hops. When the northwesterlies turn British Columbia cold, and you need a warming nip, seek out their Mid-Winter Ale which is spiced, potent, and very smooth.

DIRECTIONS: From Highway 97, after crossing the bridge over the lake into the heart of town, turn west on Richter Street. Follow Richter about 15 blocks to the large building on the right containing Granville Island Brewing, Calona Wines and, further down the street, Tree Brewing.

Okanagan Spring Brewery

Established 1985

2801 27th Avenue • Vernon, B.C. V1T 1T5
(250) 542-2337

Okanagan Spring was inland B.C.'s first microbrewery. Founded by the German immigrants Buko von Krosigk and Jakob Tobler, along with Tobler's sons, "OK Spring" as it's widely known, has grown to become a regional brewery, and is now part of the publicly traded Sleeman conglomerate.

The Okanagan Spring Brewery in Vernon now also produces the Shaftebury line of craft beers, acquired in 1999. Shaftebury was founded in East Vancouver in 1987 by Tim Wittig and Paul Beaton, two college students waiting tables and wondering what to do next. Neither had a brewing background, so they hired Spinnakers' original brewer, John Mitchell, and never looked back. In their first decade of business, they grew Shaftebury into a major player in the craft beer business.

Shaftebury beers are generally mild and malty, and include a slightly sweet and light-bodied Honey Pale Ale, a lightly hopped Rainforest Amber Ale, and the enigmatic, dark-colored Cream Ale, with a nutty flavor from some dark-roasted malt. Rounding out the Shaftebury line are a hefeweizen and a hemp ale. On your tour, look for the three enormous lager tanks built sideways into a wall, another German tradition put into practice. Okanagan Spring's beer lines are distributed on draft all around British Columbia, and in bottles and cans throughout Western Canada, as well as some limited markets in the U.S.

Their standard Okanagan line consists of a Pilsner and a premium lager; their Extra Special Pale Ale (one of the best selling beers in B.C.), their Honey Blonde Ale, and a bottle-conditioned Old English Porter that is quite good, with subtle nut and molasses nuances. Look for the Saint Patrick's Stout in March, and a traditional-style hefeweizen made with sixty percent wheat in the summer, followed by Autumn Red, a full-bodied ale.

Hours: Brewery tours Monday, Wednesday, Friday 1 p.m. and 3 p.m., or call to arrange one; retail store, 9 a.m.–5 p.m. Monday–Friday
Children: Yes
Food: No
Entertainment: No
Smoking: No
Payment: Visa, MC
Beer to go: Yes, bottles

DIRECTIONS: From Highway 97, turn east on 28th Avenue and drive three blocks. The brewery is on your right.

Bear Brewing Company

Established 1995

975-B Notre Dame Drive • Kamloops, B.C. V2C 5P8
(250) 851-2543

Bear Brewing is a straightforward microbrewery, with no tasting room or retail store, but with tours provided to interested visitors. Situated in the town of Kamloops, this micro is penetrating the heart of the interior North American commercial beer culture with good, true-to-style craft beers.

Partner/brewer Dave Beardsell holds a degree in microbiology and was formally trained in brewing at Doemen's, in Munich, and at the Brewing Research Institute, in Nutfield, England. After working for Okanagan Spring Brewery, he teamed up with fellow craft beer enthusiast Brian Keast to start Bear Brewing.

Beardsell incorporated many of the tricks he learned in England and Germany into the Bear Brewing venture. The brewing system is all self-designed, including a German-style mash tun in addition to a English-style mash/lauter tun. He imitated Yorkshire stone open-fermentation vessels with concrete tanks that are chilled prior to adding the wort and pitching the yeast. This is quite a departure from the conventional modern stainless steel fermentation tanks.

The three Bear Brewing standards are Brown Bear Ale (a Northern English-style brown, full-bodied with lots of chocolate malt), Black Bear (a dark mild type made with black currants and blackberries—their most popular beer), and Polar Bear Lager (a creamy, Czech-style lager). Bear also brews the house beers on contract for Earl's Restaurant chain, which has locations throughout Canada, as well as a few in the U.S. The most popular of this line of contract brews is the Albino Rhino, a pale ale.

DIRECTIONS: From Highway 1, take the northern-most City Center exit and turn west on Notre Dame Drive. Follow Notre Dame until it begins to curve uphill. The brewery is on the left.

Hours: Call ahead to arrange a tour
Children: Yes
Food: No
Entertainment: No
Smoking: No
Payment: Checks
Beer to go: Yes, draft

Buffalo Brewing Company

Established 1997

611 Brunswick Street • Prince George, B.C. V2L 2B9
(250) 564-7100

If you're in Prince George, then you know that Northern British Columbia is a rugged area. Quite mountainous, with some windswept plains and a few major rivers carving their way toward the sea, this land is still mostly wild. Prince George offers all the necessary comforts, though, including a good brewpub whose name invokes the wildness of the landscape.

The Buffalo Brewing Company offers family dining, with beer for the grown-ups. If you can, time your visit for the Sunday pizza and beer specials. The pizzas are gourmet, with combinations such as spicy prawns, roasted peppers, garlic and hot sauce, or roma tomatoes, basil, roasted garlic, and feta. They also offer steaks, ribs, and burgers, as well as various pastas and roasted chicken dishes.

On one side of the establishment is a full service pub, while the other side sports a restaurant with its own bar. Both bars offer special house cocktails and TV sports events on televisions built right into the bar. Young kids under seven eat free. Look for a coming sister establishment, or two, opening soon in other parts of Western Canada.

Buffalo Brewing Company is an alehouse, with five or so of their dozen standard ales on tap at any given time. Look for 54/40 Gold Ale, Star Fire Amber Ale, Hef's Wheat Beer, and Jacknife Brown Ale. You'll also find a porter or a stout: Spruce City Porter, made with dark sweet cherries and Canadian maple syrup, or Double Eagle Stout—a dry stout with lingering flavors of bittersweet chocolate. Brewer Ron Bradley, formerly of Bowen Island Brewing Company, also offers seasonals such as a hefeweizen, a red ale, and a raspberry hemp ale, with ten percent hemp seed in the grist.

DIRECTIONS: From Highway 97, turn onto Queensway into City Center. Turn onto Brunswick Street; the brewpub is several blocks down Brunswick on your right.

Hours: Restaurant, 11:30 a.m.–9:30 p.m. daily; pub, 11:30 a.m.–midnight Sunday–Thursday, 11:30 a.m.–1 a.m. Friday and Saturday
Children: Yes, in the restaurant
Food: Northwest cuisine
Entertainment: Occasional live music
Smoking: Yes, in the pub
Payment: Interac, Visa, MC, AmEx, Discover
Beer to go: Yes, draft

Mount Begbie Brewing Company

Established 1996

201-C Victoria Road E • Revelstoke, B.C. V0E 2S0
(250) 837-2756

Revelstoke lies amidst the splendor of wild British Columbia, at the foot of both the Monashee Mountains and the Canadian Rockies, and at the intersection of the Columbia and Illecillewaet Rivers. A mile up the road is Mount Revelstoke National Park, and a few miles farther is Canada's Glacier National Park. There's even a pair of small ski areas nearby to try out, or plan a trek to nearby Mount Begbie's three peaks—there's a relatively easy hike to a glacier.

The small town can now proudly boast about a hometown craft brewery making quality beers. A young couple named Bart and Tracey Larson dived into the commercial brewing scene in the mid-'90s and set up shop here in Revelstoke.

Mount Begbie's filtered beers can be characterized as West Canadian interpretations of both British and German ales. First, there's Begbie Cream Ale; as with some other modern Canadian cream ales, it is reminiscent of a British mild. Then there's the Alpine Amber Ale, with lots of crystal malt and a complex hop profile that gives it an interesting kick at the end. Third is the Tall Timber Ale, a caramely take on the classic nut brown style. Finally, there's High Country Kölsch that's fairly true to this rare German style.

If you're anywhere nearby—from the Okanagan Valley to the Rockies—look for Mount Begbie's striking tap-handles or bottle packages. The bottles sport a variety of antique photos from the Wild West history of the region, and the hand-painted tap-handles often include some handsome wood burl content. If you're coming to Revelstoke, Tracey and Bart will be happy to have you—but it's best to call ahead to make an appointment. You'll get a chance to taste a fresh draft ale in the crow's nest office overlooking the seven-barrel brewhouse.

Hours: Summer, noon–5 p.m. Monday–Friday, 11 a.m.–2 p.m. Saturday or call for appointment; winter, call ahead to arrange a tour
Children: Yes
Food: No
Entertainment: No
Smoking: No
Payment: Cash only
Beer to go: Yes, draft

DIRECTIONS: From Highway 1, take the Victoria Street exit just north of the Trans Canada Highway Bridge over the Columbia River. Follow Victoria east as it skirts the edge of town, then starts to curve south along the railroad tracks. The brewery is on your right just past the cross street of Orton Avenue.

Nelson Brewing Company

Established 1991

512 Latimer Street • Nelson, B.C. V1L 4T9
(250) 352-3582

You'll find the bohemian town of Nelson, B.C. nestled at the foot of the majestic Kootenay Range. Whether you've been hiking in the Kootenays or skiing at Whitewater Hill, Nelson makes the ideal homebase. With its picturesque mountain scenery, richly artistic community, and beautiful homes dating to the beginning of the 1900s, Nelson is a delightful stop. Consider staying at the Heritage Inn downtown, where Mike's Place, upstairs, pours all of Nelson Brewing Company's current draft beers.

Nelson Brewing Company is a reincarnation of the town's old brewery of the same name, which operated from 1894 until 1955. Owner/brewer Paddy Glenny re-established the brewery in 1990, at its original location. It's easy to find—right across the street from the striking firehouse used in the classic Hollywood movie, "Roxanne."

Paddy Glenny, who ran a brewery for over a decade in Oxford, England, designed and installed the twenty-hectoliter brewhouse system, and refurbished the 1960s bottling line. Nelson Brewing is now sending out bottled and kegged beer to the East and West Kootenays, as well as to the Okanagan Valley and B.C.'s Lower Mainland.

The folks in Nelson support their local brewery. They're proud to have great, local beers such as Nelson's best-seller, Old Brewery Ale, a true-to-style British pale ale, lightly hopped. Nelson Afterdark (a classic dark mild, with rich malt nuances), Nelson Strong Ale (a six percent alcohol/volume IPA), and Valhalla Gold (a classic Canadian-style cream ale) round out the standard lineup. You're also likely to find a dry stout, approximating the original Guinness, but a bit stronger.

Hours: Call ahead to arrange a tour
Children: Yes
Food: No
Entertainment: No
Smoking: No
Payment: No retail sales
Beer to go: No

DIRECTIONS: As you pull into Nelson, Highway 3 and Highway 6 become Baker. Turn uphill onto Ward Street and proceed to Latimer Street. The brewery is the large Victorian industrial-style building on the corner of Ward and Latimer, just uphill from the classic firehouse.

Windermere Valley Brewing Company

Established 1996

Invermere Industrial Park • Invermere, B.C. V0A 1K0
(250) 342-3247

The Windermere Valley is truly one of the more breathtaking places in North America. The Canadian Rockies thrust skyward as abruptly and impressively as do the Colorado Rockies, and the mighty Columbia River begins its journey in this wide valley, pouring forth from a pair of long lakes, Windermere and Columbia. What's more, flanking the west side of the valley, facing the Rockies, is another mountain range, the Purcells.

This is a vacation area for Calgary and its hinterlands, and the throngs come in search of sunshine, lake recreation, or skiing. Amidst all this splendor is the small town of Invermere, on Windermere Lake. Just to keep you on your toes, there's a town on the other side of the lake named Windermere, but Windermere Valley Brewing is in Invermere. Got it?

Hours: Call ahead to arrange a tour
Children: Yes
Food: No
Entertainment: No
Smoking: Yes
Payment: N/A
Beer to go: No

Jay Regitnig, a self-taught brewer, started Windermere Valley Brewing as a one-man operation, and continues in much the same capacity. His brewery is in a small warehouse space at the edge of town; he'll be glad to give you a tour and tasting any day if he's available, but just call ahead to make sure he's not off delivering some more kegs. You'd see a ten-hectoliter brewhouse made by DME (of Prince Edward Island) in a modest, built-to-spec light industrial building.

His beers are available on tap throughout Eastern and Central B.C., including tap handles at Panorama and Fairmount, two of the four ski areas in the immediate Windermere vicinity. Regitnig makes two standard brews: Valley Gold (a smooth blonde ale brewed with fifty percent wheat) and Valley Copper (an approachable amber ale with nice hoppy highlights). He dabbles in seasonal beer releases as well, including a high-gravity winter ale.

DIRECTIONS: Call for directions

GLOSSARY

The following glossary of brewing terms is by no means exhaustive, but none-theless it provides an ample introduction to all aspects of brewing and beer-drinking terminology. A discriminating palate is an educated one, and know-ing style origins and traditional characteristics can help provide frames of refer-ence when ordering beer in a pub or restaurant. This becomes increasingly useful as North America's Pacific Northwestern beer culture matures, and breweries in-troduce more intricately formulated beers founded on styles and traditions less widely known in the New World, than, say, a British pale ale.

For many, a tour of the actual brewhouse of a favorite microbrewery or brewpub is a necessary part of a complete visit; boning up on terms such as "lauter tun" and "bright tank" will make such a tour a more enriching experience. This glossary also comes in handy for sorting through issues such as how a beer's "original gravity" measurements derive from its "mash" process and how its "specific gravity" relates to its measurement in degrees "Plato."

abbey ale: A traditional Belgian style of top-fermented beer, usually bottle-conditioned, me-dium to full in body, strong in alcohol content, often with candy sugar added in the boil for added strength and flavor complexity. See also *Belgian ale, Trappist ale.*

acidic: A flavor descriptor indicating sourness or bitterness, often from infection in the beer by lactic or acetic acid, though occasionally describing an acceptable quality, as with some Belgian ales and German wheat beers.

ale: A general term used for any beer that is brewed using a top-fermenting yeast at fermen-tation temperatures above 58° F/14.5° C. It distinguishes a beer from being a lager, and generally indicates a beer with assertive aromas and flavors, and prominent hop-ping levels. See also *top-fermenting yeasts, altbier, lager.*

ale lagering: See *cold-conditioning.*

alehouse: A tavern or pub which specializes in serving a wide selection of craft-brewed beers on draft. See also *pub.*

alkalinity: Water hardness as measured for beer-style formulation.

altbier: (also called *Düsseldorfer alt* or just *alt* ("old" in German.) A traditional German style of top-fermented beer originating in Düsseldorf. It is coppery to dark in color, with medium body, rich maltiness and medium hopping levels, and is cold-conditioned.

amber ale: A widely varying North American ale style that is golden to rust in color, medium to full-bodied, often with a focus on malt flavors. See also *mild ale, pale ale, session ale.*

American ale: See *cream ale.*

apparent extract: The measure of the gravity of a finished beer, including the alcohol-to-suspended solid ratio. See also *real extract, extract.*

aroma (also called *nose* or *bouquet*): The initial stage of taste, yielding first impressions through the sense of smell. Depending on the beer style, aroma can be predominantly malty, hoppy, fruity, yeasty, alcoholic, or a mixture of these.

aromatic hops (also called *finishing hops*): Hops added to the sweet wort late in the boil to provide hop aromas to the beer. See also *bittering hops.*

astringency (also called *huskiness*): A flavor descriptor used to indicate a harsh, dry taste or sensation likened to chewing grape skins, often the result of over-sparging the mash and extracting phenol compounds. Sometimes the term is used to refer to high hopping rates and/or excessive carbonation. See also *bitterness.*

attenuation: The degree to which beer has fermented, usually expressed as a percentage of extraction of available fermentable sugars.

balance: A flavor descriptor used to indicate the relationship among flavor constituents in beer, including malts and other grains, hops, yeast, and alcohol. When a beer is "well-balanced," no single flavor constituent is more strongly represented in the taste than the others, particularly regarding the malt-hop ratio.

Balling: See *Plato.*

Bamburger: See *rauchbier.*

barley wine (also, *barleywine*): A traditional English-style ale that is ruby to brown in color, heavy in body and high in alcohol content, often quite sweet or estery, but sometimes with a bitter finish. Barley wines are so-named because of their unparalleled potency, and are often aged for years.

barrel, imperial (bbl imp), U.S. (bbl): The standard cask equaling two kegs (traditionally wooden but now often metal) used for storing and selling beer; used as a volume measurement for vessels larger than one barrel.

beer engine: A faucet device invented in the 1700s that allows the bartender to pull beer straight from a conditioning cask, resulting in a delicately carbonated glass of beer. This is the traditional handpump used in British pubs. See also *tap, real ale.*

beer style: In the broad spectrum of beers, there are regionally and internationally accepted categories of beer styles, most originating from cultural traditions, and many even from specific cities. The American Homebrewers Association recognizes twenty-one major styles and sixty-eight total styles. Beers brewed intentionally to match the accepted parameters of a recognized beer style are said to be "brewed to" or "true to" style. See also *beer type.*

beer type: Beers resembling other beers within a recognized style, without the intent of the brewer, are said to be of that style's "type." See also *beer style.*

Belgian ale: Beer is the national drink of Belgium in much the same way that wine is of France. If the term Belgian ale is used nonspecifically, it likely means abbey ale, but traditionally was used for a copper-colored draft ale that is well-balanced in bitterness and body.

best (ale): A traditional British prefix attached to an ale name denoting it as the brewery's proudest offering of that variety (e.g., best bitter, best brown). Usually a "best" version of a house beer is somewhat bolder in flavor, body and/or strength. See also *bitter ale.*

bitter ale: A traditional English-style ale that is light-bodied and light in strength, with high hopping levels, this beer was commonly the draft equivalent of the bottled pale ale; the quintessential "real ale."

bittering hops: Hops added to the sweet wort early during the boil to offset the sweetness of the malts, providing bitterness and flavors. See also *aroma, hops.*

bitter(ness:) A flavor descriptor used to indicate a sharp taste that can be almost a biting or puckering sensation, primarily produced in beer with the addition of hops during the boil, wherein the malt sweetness is balanced by the hops. See also *dry, hoppy, sweet.*

black-and-tan: See *entire.*

blonde ale: A modern North American style of top-fermented beer, very light in body, straw-colored, and often including some wheat in the mash. This style was known widely as cream ale prior to Prohibition. See also *cream ale.*

bock: A traditional German-style bottom-fermented beer that is often copper to dark in color (though sometimes as pale as straw), strong in alcohol, medium to high in gravity, usually malty. "Bock" means "goat" in many Germanic languages, and thus most bock beers bear the name or the image of a goat.

body (also called *chewiness*): A descriptor used to indicate the perceived fullness in the mouth or thickness of the liquid. Technically, body is attributable to the suspension of dextrins and proteins present in the finished brew, controlled by grain to water ratio and attenuation due to temperature during the brewing process.

bottle-conditioned: Carbonated by a secondary fermentation occurring in the bottle by means of the addition of a small amount of yeast and/or fermentable sugars at the time of bottling.

bottom-fermenting yeasts: Yeasts that usually ferment at lower temperatures than top-fermenting yeasts, and take their name from the fact that they are most visibly active in the bottom portion of the fermentation vessel. Traditionally, these are the varieties of yeasts used for making lagers. See also *lager, top-fermenting.*

break: The coagulation of proteins and other material that flocculates and precipitates out of the brew, thus enhancing beer clarity.

brew: To make beer from malt and other ingredients by means of steeping, boiling and fermentation. The term is used in the vernacular as a synonym for beer. See also *boil, mash.*

brewery tap (also called a *tap-room*): A drinking establishment that serves beers brewed on premise in an adjoining craft brewery which primarily supplies other retail beer outlets. Brewpubs differ in that their beers are served primarily on-premise, while tasting rooms tend to be less full-service than brewery taps. See also *brewpub, tasting room.*

brewhouse: The place in a brewery where the preparation of the wort occurs, referring primarily to the brewing equipment, including the mash tun, lauter tun, and kettle. The term has also now entered the vernacular as a synonym for brewpub.

brewpub (also called *homebrew house*): A food and beverage establishment that is the sole or primary retail outlet for beers brewed on premise, often also serving food in a restaurant atmosphere; usually connotes on-premise beer sales greater than fifty percent of total brewery production. See also *brewery tap, pub, tasting room.*

bright tank: A brewery vessel used for storing a finished beer that is ready for disbursement into kegs or bottles.

British ale: Britain produces a tremendous selection of ales, and is the birthplace of the "real ale" movement, which is widely credited with inspiring the world-wide craft beer resurgence. If the term British ale is used nonspecifically, it is likely to mean "bitter" or "pale ale," but may also be used to specify a beer made with British ingredients or using a single temperature infusion mash. See also *bitter, pale ale, real ale.*

brown ale: (also called *brown beer*) A traditional English-style ale that is medium brown and opaque in color, light to medium in strength, with low hopping levels and sweet malt flavors. This beer was traditionally the bottled equivalent of the draft dark mild ale. See also *mild ale, Belgian ale.*

Brussels lace: The residual thin white foam that clings to the side of the glass in a lacy pattern as some beers are consumed; usually associated with beers that have extremely fine foam characteristics, dense heads, or high gravity.

California common beer (also called *steam beer*): A traditional North American style of beer made with a bottom-fermenting yeast but fermented at ale (high) temperatures, these beers feature caramel malt flavors and are light-bodied and medium in strength. Today it is the proprietary name of the flagship beer of the Anchor Brewing Company of San Francisco. See also *cream ale.*

Campaign for Real Ale (CAMRA): Founded in 1971 in England, the popular British grassroots consumer movement to save "real ale" from extinction in the face of the overwhelming worldwide popularity of lagers. The campaign is widely credited with saving many British breweries from closure, and also with inspiring the microbrewing renaissance that has become a global phenomenon. See also *real ale.*

carbonation: The dissolution of a gas, especially carbon dioxide, in a liquid, as in yeast's release of carbon dioxide into beer.

cask-conditioning: The process of ale fermentation wherein the secondary fermentation occurs in the cask from which it will be served. This can be accomplished either by transferring the beer to the cask just before it is completely "fermented out," or by the more traditional means of krausening. Cask-conditioned ales are served at cellar temperature (about 55° F or 13° C) using a beer engine, or by a gravity-flow tap, with a very light level of carbonation. See also *krausening, real ale.*

cellar: The place in the brewery where the fermentation of the beer occurs (whether a basement cellar or not), along with the casking, kegging, and/or bottling of the finished product, and its subsequent storage. See also *real ale.*

chewiness: See *body.*

chill haze (also called *protein haze, opaqueness*): A haziness consisting of particulates that coalesce in beer when it is chilled, typically to temperatures below 45° F or 7° C, and usually disappearing when the beer warms. This product defect does not affect flavor.

Christmas beers: Relatively modern incarnations of the British and European tradition of brewing strong, full-bodied ales for the cold winter months. This tradition, particularly strong in England and Belgium, often includes adding spices such as nutmeg, cinnamon, or even orange zest to the brew. See also *old ale.*

clarifiers (also called *finings*): Any substance used to help yeast and unfermented proteins settle out of beer once fermentation is complete for the prevention of chill haze.

clarity: The quality of clearness in beer that is the absence of chill haze or particulates in general in a finished beer.

cold tower: See *tap.*

cold-conditioning (also called *ale lagering*): A method of finishing a beer's fermentation, in which the beer is stored at cold temperatures. This tends to lend the finished product a smoother, creamier consistency. See also *lager.*

cold-filtering: A substitute for filtration in which the finished beer is chilled and the yeast particulates are allowed to precipitate out of solution.

conditioning: The process of maturing beer wherein fermentation is completed and carbonation is achieved; the final stage in preparation of the final product.

conditioning tank: (also called *maturation tank* or *lagering tank*) A brewery vessel used for maturing a beer after fermentation to give the finished product time to completely "ferment out," and to develop flavor nuances, robust body, and sufficient carbonation.

continental dark lager: See *Münchener.*

continental light lager: See *Pils(e)ner.*

conversion (also called starch *conversion*): The process of malt enzymes changing grain starch molecules into fermentable sugar molecules during the mash.

cottage brewery: A small craft brewery, commonly one producing 10,000 barrels or less annually.

cracker: See *mill.*

craft brewery: A catch-all term for any size brewery that produces hand-crafted beers in relatively small batches without adjuncts in the grist, and without pasteurization of the finished beer.

cream ale (also called *sparkling ale* or *American ale*): A traditional North American style of beer that is light-bodied and well-carbonated, medium in strength, and very smooth and malty with low hopping levels. Generally, this is a beer that is brewed as an ale (at high temperatures) but then aged and conditioned as a lager. Originally, the term "cream ale" was used to refer to a different style—what is today called a golden (blonde) ale. See also *California common beer.*

cross-over beers: Craft beers brewed primarily to appeal to consumers accustomed to megabrewery pale lagers. The term is applied to a variety of light-bodied and light-colored ales and lagers.

Czech Pilsner (also called *Bohemian Pilsner*): The cities of Plzeň and České Budějovice in the Bohemia region of the Czech Republic gave birth to two of the original golden lagers, which are still made there. The names live on internationally—Budweiser with a single proprietary usage in North America, Pilsner as the definitive hoppy golden lager-style name. See also *German lager*, *Pilsner*.

dark lager: See *Münchener*.

doppelbock: Literally, "double bock," this beer is stronger, often darker than a regular bock, and usually named using the suffix "-ator." See also *bock*.

Dortmunder: A German style of bottom-fermented beer named for its city of origin, that is straw to golden in color, well-balanced or on the malty side, light in body, and medium to high in alcohol content. In Germany, these beers are known as "export" beers.

draft (draught): Beer served by tap or beer engine from keg or cask, as distinct from bottled; dispensed using carbon dioxide, nitrogen, air, etc. The British form (literally, "drawn") is usually used to describe beer dispensed from a beer engine or a gravity-flow tap, as distinct from a cold tap. See also *beer engine*, *tap*.

dry(ness): A flavor descriptor used to characterize beer that lacks a cloying aftertaste or that is generally not sweet; often associated with hop characteristics and/or bitterness. See also *bitterness*, *hoppiness*, *sweetness*.

dry hops: Hops that are added to the beer in the conditioning tank or cask, as distinct from aromatic and bittering hops which are added during the boil prior to fermentation. Dry-hopping adds additional hop aroma and flavor, but not more bitterness.

dunkel: A German term (literally "dark") used to designate beers as darker versions of Established styles; e.g., a dunkel weizen is a dark weizen (wheat beer). Alone, the term is often used specifically to refer to Münchener-style beer. See also *Münchener*, *helles*.

dunkelweizen: See *weizen*.

Düsseldorfer: See *altbier*.

entire: An old term, originally referring to the combination of the first, middle, and last runnings into one batch of beer. It came to mean a mixture of beers ordered by customers at a beer bar, such as the black-and-tan, a mix of a light colored beer (typically a Pilsner) and a dark colored beer (typically a porter or stout).

enzymes: Organic compounds (technically proteins) that act as catalysts in several reactions crucial to brewing, notably the conversion of malt starches into fermentable sugars.

esters: Compounds present in beer as byproducts of fermentation, specifically the oxidation of alcohol. They lend fruity aromas and flavors, particularly at the onset, and finish of a taste. See also *fruitiness*.

export: A descriptor used to designate different styles of beer; in northern Europe and Canada, an "export" is a premium lager beer, in Germany it is the local name for the Dortmunder style, and a Scottish export is a heavy, strong ale. Generally an "export" has higher gravity, higher alcohol content and/or more hops than the domestic version of the brew. See also *stout, Scotch ale, India pale ale*.

extra special bitter (ESB): See *bitter ale and best (ale)*.

extract: Solids such as dextrins dissolved in wort or beer; literally, solids that are "extracted" from the grain during the process of the mash, then suspended in the solution of the beer. See also *specific gravity*.

fermenter: A brewery vessel in which the yeast is pitched into the wort and fermentation results. A variety of vessels are used, either open (traditionally for ales) or closed (traditionally for lagers).

filtration: The process of removing yeast and unfermented protein particles that cause chill haze in unfiltered beer, as well as unwanted micro-organisms. Modern breweries usually filter beer by forcing it through a dense medium such as diatomaceous earth.

final gravity (also called *terminal gravity*): A measurement of the density, or "specific gravity" of a beer after fermentation. This figure, compared with the original gravity figure, yields a final measure of the degree of fermentation, compared with the potential of the fermentables present in the wort. See also *extract, original gravity, specific gravity*.

finish: The final stage of taste, yielding final impressions and often most characterized by hops or yeast flavors.

flagship beer: A brewery's best-selling and/or most widely recognized, and popular, beer; usually a brewery's first beer on the market and often their hallmark offering.

fruitiness: A flavor descriptor used to indicate aromas and flavors in beer reminiscent of specific fruits, such as bananas, pineapples, and apricots; usually associated with ales and higher fermentation temperatures and often caused by esters. See also *esters*.

German lager: If the term German lager is used nonspecifically, it is likely referring to the German version of the classic Czech (Bohemian) Pilsner. The typical German Pilsner is paler, smoother, less hoppy but with a drier finish than the Czech Pilsner style. See also *bock, Czech Pilsner, Dortmunder, Märzen, Münchener, Pilsner, Vienna*.

golden ale: See *blonde ale*.

grain bill: The recipe of grains to be used for a brew.

graininess: A flavor descriptor used to indicate aromas and flavors in beer reminiscent of raw grain or cereal, acceptable only at low levels.

grand cru: A Belgian lambic that is aged unblended, is medium in body and strong in alcohol, often with pronounced oak highlights and other flavor complexities.

gravity: See *specific gravity*.

gravity dispense (also called *gravity flow*): The traditional method for dispensing cask-conditioned ale, usually by setting the cask directly on the bar with a simple spigot for pouring.

grist: Milled (usually coarsely) malt and/or other grains to be used for brewing.

grist case: (also called *grist hopper*) A brewery vessel in which the malt and/or grains are stored prior to the mash, usually above the mash tun.

grundy: A small brewery vessel used as a conditioning tank, or in some cases other types of tanks; in fact, inventive brewers have converted these vessels into every type of brewery vessel, from kettles to serving tanks.

hand-crafted: Beer making on a small scale, with the use of only choice ingredients in small batch brewing, and the adherence to the goal of not compromising quality in the name of quantity.

head: The foam on the surface of a poured glass of beer or on a fermenter of wort. On a glass of beer, fineness and sustainedness are the desired criteria.

heat exchanger: A device that, following the boil, quickly chills the wort to fermentation temperature so the yeast can be pitched as quickly as possible, preventing infection by invading micro-organisms prior to the start of fermentation.

heavy ale: A traditional Scottish style of ale that is ruby to brown in color, hearty in body, and medium to strong in alcohol. See also *Scotch ale, light ale, wee heavy*.

hefe: The German word for yeast, this term is sometimes used as a prefix to indicate that the beer is bottle- or cask-conditioned, and has yeast present in the finished beer.

hefe weizen (or *hefeweizen*): A traditional style of top-fermented beer originating in the Bavaria region of Germany, made with a significant percentage of wheat in the grist, and with more of the special wheat-beer yeast added for the final conditioning—usually bottle-conditioning, but sometimes cask-conditioning. Literally "yeast wheat," the term hefe weizen is applied to a broad category of wheat beers in North America, including many fruit flavored wheat beers. See also *kristall weizen, weizenbier*.

helles: A German term, literally "brightness/clearness," used to designate beers as lighter versions of Established styles; e.g. a helles bock is a light bock. See also *Münchener*.

hops (humulus lupulus): An aromatic vine of the mulberry family whose female flower cones are dried and used to spice and clarify beer as well as preserve it. A member of the morning glory family, and a close relative of cannabis, the hop plant is grown extensively in the Pacific Northwest. See also *noble hops*.

hoppy/hoppiness: A flavor descriptor used to indicate aromas, flavors, and/or bitterness derived from the addition of hop cones, pellets or extracts in the process of beer making. See also *bitterness, dry, sweetness*.

huskiness: See *astringency*.

India pale ale (IPA): A substyle of pale ale, IPAs traditionally were higher alcohol, highly hopped pale ales, casked and shipped to India with dry hops steeping as preservatives. Modern Pacific Northwest IPAs emulate the old-time hop characteristics with very high hopping levels, and prevalent dry-hopping in various pale ales and IPAs. See *pale ale*.

international bitterness units (IBUs): An analytical measurement of the bittering compounds present in a beer due to the addition of hops. Roughly 12 to 15 IBUs (where most domestic North American lagers fall) is the threshold for tasting hop bitterness, while anything over 25 IBUs is considered bitter.

keg (also called a *half-barrel*): A metal vessel with a volume equal to a half-barrel or fifteen and one half U.S. gallons. It is used for serving beer under pressure.

kellerbier: A traditional German bottom-fermented beer that is light in body and color, low in carbonation, highly hopped, and unfiltered.

kettle (also called a *copper*): A brewery vessel in which the wort is boiled with hops following the mash process and prior to fermentation.

Kölschbier: A traditional top-fermented beer style from Cologne, Germany, that is light gold in color, malty with estery or lactic flavor highlights, but crisp in mouthfeel. The term Kölsch is a closely regulated style name in Germany.

krausening: The process of finishing a beer's fermentation by adding a small portion of fresh, fermenting wort; this is the true method for creating "real ale," or a cask-conditioned ale. See also *cask-conditioning, real ale.*

kristall weizen: A traditional German style of top-fermented beer made with a significant percentage of wheat in the grist. Literally, "crystal wheat," a kristall weizen is a filtered wheat beer without yeast present in the served beverage, as distinct from hefe weizen's yeasty character. See also *hefe weizen, weizenbier.*

lactic: A descriptor used for the sourness associated with beer infected by the *lactobacillus* bacteria, an undesirable infection except in the unique case of lambic beers.

lager: From German *lagern,* "to store." When used as a noun, it is a beer bottom-fermented at colder temperatures than an ales. "Lager" is not a style of beer, but rather a method of production, yielding beers that are clear and smooth. See also *cold-conditioning.*

lagering tank: See *conditioning tank.*

lambic: A traditional Belgian style of top-fermented beer, straw to brown in color, medium in strength, very malty, with complex, wine-like flavors that usually include an acidic tartness or sourness. These beers are produced via spontaneous fermentation from specific strains of airborne yeasts and bacteria found only in the Senne Valley, where they are exclusively made and defined by legal descriptions. See also *Trappist.*

lauter tun (also called a *lauter tub*): A brewery vessel in which the malt and/or grains are separated from the sweet wort following the mash process and prior to the boil.

light ale: A traditional British variant of a bitter ale, with lower alcohol content than a standard bitter. In the U.S., the term is applied to a beer with light body. In Scotland, the term designates a ruby-colored ale of medium body. See also *bitter ale, light beer, Scotch ale.*

light beer: A North American term for any beer with low alcohol content. See also *light ale.*

lightstruck: A descriptor used for beer damaged by exposure to the ultraviolet light of the sun or an artificial light source. See also *skunkiness.*

Maibock: A strong bock traditionally brewed in the spring as the last brew before hot summer months. See *bock.*

malt: Barley or other grain which has been soaked, allowed to germinate, then dried and/or roasted via kilning. Germination allows the development of enzymes which lead to starch conversion in the mash and subsequently to the production of sweet wort. See also *pale malt, specialty malt.*

malt extracts: Concentrated syrup or powder made by evaporating sweet wort; used as the primary ingredient for beer making by many homebrewers, and by a few breweries.

malty: A flavor descriptor used to indicate sweet grain flavors in beer that are hearty, like breads, or sweeter, like molasses, honey or treacle. The term is usually used as these flavors relate to, or dominate over, hoppiness. See also *bitterness, dryness, hoppiness.*

Märzenbier (also *Octoberfest*): A traditional German style of bottom-fermented beer that is amber to brown in color, medium in body and strength, and well balanced between malt and hops. The name derives from the month of March, which was the last safe month for brewing prior to the hot weather of the summer. *Märzenbiers* were traditionally stored and consumed over the summer, and the *Märzenbier* that remained at the end of the summer was consumed in a fall Octoberfest festival. See also *saison.*

mash: A mixing of milled malt and/or other grains and hot water where the starch conversion process occurs. The mash process in its simplest form generally consists of three main stages: mash-in (the mixing of the milled malt and/or grains with hot water), starch conversion, and mash-out (a final heating of the mash to maximize the starch conversion process and produce a clearer wort).

mash tun: A brewery vessel in which the mash process occurs.

maturation tank: See *conditioning tank.*

mead: A fermented beverage made primarily from honey. Usually light in body, sweet and crisp, mead is somewhere between beer and sparkling wine.

megabrewery: A very large brewery whose beer is nationally or internationally distributed, and commonly producing 500,000 barrels or more annually.

metallic: A flavor descriptor used for beer flavors akin to tin or blood, often caused by overexposure to metal.

microbrewery: A moderate-sized craft brewery, commonly one producing 20,000 barrels or less annually.

mild ale: A traditional English-style ale that is typically amber in color (often called a "dark mild"), light in strength with low hopping levels, this beer was commonly the draft equivalent of the bottled brown ale. The name "mild" distinguishes these malty ales from the hoppy "bitters." See also *bitter, brown ale.*

mill (also called a *grain cracker* or just *cracker*): A brewery device used for cracking malt and other grains, in preparation for the mash.

mouthfeel: The sensory qualities associated with a beverage other than taste, including body and carbonation.

Münchener (also called *continental dark lager*): A traditional German lager style originating in Munich, that is medium-dark brown in color, with a palate that is malty, though not outright sweet in its accent of the malts. In Munich this style is specified as dunkel. See also *helles, dunkel.*

nitrogen dispense (also called *nitro*): The use of nitrogen, rather than carbon dioxide or air, to move beer from the keg to tap. Nitrogen lends the draft beer a distinct creamy texture without the addition of the gassy flavor often associated with carbon dioxide; it is most often used to pour stouts.

noble hops: Hop varieties with superior aroma and flavor potential; includes such classic varieties as Saaz (Czech Republic), East Kent Goldings (U.K.), Spalt (Germany), and Lublin (Poland). See also *hops*.

nut brown: This substyle of brown ale is achieved when malt combinations are used to produce nutty flavors. See also *brown ale*.

off flavor: A test descriptor describing any of various flavors resulting from problems in the fermentation or storage process, including sulferish, mediciny (phenolic), corny, and buttery. See also *skunkiness*.

Oktoberfest: See *Märzenbier*.

old(e) ale (also called *strong ale, winter warmer*): A traditional English-style ale that is ruby to brown in color, medium to strong in alcohol, and malty These beers are often aged for years in the bottle or cask with rich flavors maturing from their balanced malts and hops, but the name "old" refers to the pre-lager style of warm (top) fermentation used. See *also altbier, barley wine, ale, wee heavy, strong ale*.

opaqueness: See *chill haze*.

original gravity (OG) (also called *starting gravity*): An analytical measurement of the density, or "specific gravity" of the wort prior to fermentation. High original gravity indicates that a beer will be full-bodied and strong, but a final gravity reading is needed to measure alcohol content. See *also extract, final gravity, specific gravity*.

oxidation: The exposure of beer to oxygen during the brewing or cellaring processes, especially at warm temperatures. Oxidation can give beer off aromas or flavors akin to wet cardboard or cheap wine.

pale ale: A traditional English-style ale, "pale" can be a confusing descriptor, since this style ranges from golden to dark copper in color. Pales are usually well-hopped and medium-bodied, with North American versions being especially hoppy. Hoppiness and robust body are even more pronounced in the substyle India pale ale (IPA). See also *bitter, dry hops*.

pale malt (also called *two-row malt*): The primary ingredient for most craft-brewed beer, as distinct from a combination of pale malt and adjuncts like corn and rice as the base for most megabrewed beers. Pale malt is so known because it is lightly roasted when compared with most of the specialty malts use to create nuances of flavor and richness of body. See also *specialty malt*.

pasteurization: A method of enhancing shelf-life, at the cost of product freshness, by heating finished beer to a high enough temperature, for a long enough period of time, to kill any beer-spoiling bacteria present.

phenolic: See *off flavor*.

Pils(e)ner (also called *pils, continental light lager*): A traditional Czech style of bottom-fermented beer originating in the Czech cities of Plzeň and České, Budějovice. These beers are very pale to straw in color, on the light side in body and very well-clarified, with floral, hoppy aromas and flavors. See also *Czech Pilsner, German lager.*

pitch: To add yeast to wort, thereby beginning the fermentation process.

Plato (also called *Balling,* its predecessor)*:* A measurement, expressed in degrees, of the total fermentable and unfermentable sugars present in the wort prior to fermentation.

pony keg (also called a *quarter-barrel:* A vessel, typically metal and consisting of a half-keg, used for serving beer under pressure, usually using carbon-dioxide, nitrogen, or a mixture of the two.

porter: A traditional British style of top-fermented beer, widely varying in color, body, and hopping levels, but categorized into two broad substyles: brown porter and robust porter. Brown porters are medium to dark brown in color (sometimes with a ruby hue), light to medium in body, with malty sweetness and some balancing hop character. Robust porters are black in color, with chocolatey and roasty (even charcoal-like) flavors, with medium to high hop levels. See also *entire, stout.*

premium (lager): A beer that is a brewery's proudest offering of that style, usually American Pilsner; generally used by megabreweries to refer to a beer that has fewer adjuncts and higher quality malt than their standard offering of that type. See also *best ale.*

primary fermentation: The initial stage of fermentation, characterized by very active yeast, converting the wort's sugars into alcohol and carbon dioxide. See also *secondary fermentation.*

prime: To add sugar to beer just before bottling or kegging, thereby restarting fermentation to achieve natural carbonation in the final vessel.

Prohibition: The prevention, by law, of the manufacture and sale of alcoholic beverages was adopted by both Canada and the United States at the beginning of the 1920s, and was repealed in 1933. Prohibition put an end to the neighborhood brewpub in America, until they reappeared on the West Coast in the early 1980s.

pub: Short for public house, a neighborhood food and beverage establishment, usually connoting draft beers and sandwich fare; often an integral community gathering place, hence the original name, "public house." See also *alehouse, brewpub, tied house.*

rack: To transfer beer from one vessel to another, as in the case of transferring from primary to secondary fermentation, thereby removing the bulk of the yeast sediment by leaving it behind.

rauchbier: (also called Bamburger) A traditional German style of bottom-fermented beer, originating in the Northern Bavarian city of Bamburg. Literally "smoke beer," these beers contain a portion of malts that are kilned over beechwood fires, lending an unmistakable smokiness to the finished beer.

real ale: A term popularized by CAMRA (CAMpaign for Real Ale, which also see) and applied to signify characteristics such as cask-conditioning and served-on-draught; usually also connoting ale that is hand-crafted in small batches using quality, natural ingredients; fresh and unpasteurized. "Real" ale is live ale, with the fermentation by the yeast reaching its peak in the cask from which the ale is served. See also *beer engine, hand-crafted.*

real extract: The measure of the gravity of a finished beer, not including the alcohol in the volume to suspended solid ratio. See also *apparent extract, extract.*

red ale: This term is used for two very different beers: the Belgian red ale and the Irish red ale. The Belgian beer is a tart or even sour beer brewed with multiple yeast strains, as with many Belgian beers. The Irish ale is a slightly malty, strong beer, often with buttery or fruity flavor highlights. See also *Belgian ale.*

Reinheitsgebot: The most celebrated of the Old World's historic laws governing beer making, this was a 1516 Bavarian "purity" law restricting brewing ingredients to malted barley, hops, water, and yeast (added upon its discovery in the 1880s)—except in the cases of Germany's various wheat beer styles.

roggenbier (literally, "rye beer"): A traditional German and Scandinavian style of beer that includes some rye in the grist. Sahti, an alcoholic beverage of Estonia and Finland, is made with rye and oats and flavored with juniper. See also *rye.*

ropiness: Body descriptor used for the gummy coagulations caused by certain spoilage bacteria, lending the beer a thickness or sliminess.

running ale: An ale brewed to be consumed immediately. See also *stock ale.*

runnings: The wort collected following the sparge, in preparation for the boil.

rye beer: See *roggenbier.*

saison: (also called *sezoen*): A traditional Belgian/French style of top-fermented beer that is pale in color and opaque, well carbonated, and slightly sour, with citrusy and fruity malt flavor highlights. Saisons traditionally vary in strength from "children's" (low) up through "family" and "double" to "royal," these strongest being only medium in relative strength. See also *Märzenbier.*

schwarzbier: A traditional German style of bottom-fermented beer, literally "black beer," that is dark brown to black in color, medium in strength, full-bodied, and balanced in bitterness with roasty malt or bitter chocolate flavors; roughly a lager equivalent of porter or stout.

Scotch ale: A traditional Scottish style of top-fermented beer that is ruby to brown in color, medium to heavy in strength and body, and low to medium in hopping levels; often with a similar flavor profile to Scotch whisky, or with toffee or butterscotch flavor highlights. See also *Scottish ale, export.*

Scottish ale: A traditional Scottish style that is roughly an equivalent of the English bitter; generally lighter-colored, lighter-bodied, and lower in alcohol content than a Scotch ale, but usually with equivalent or higher hopping levels. See also *Scotch ale.*

secondary fermentation: The latter stage of fermentation, characterized by a slowing of yeast's conversion of the wort's sugars into alcohol and carbon dioxide, and by a settling of suspended solids increasing the beer's clarity. See also *primary fermentation.*

serving tank: A brewery vessel used to dispense a finished beer directly to a tap, thereby eliminating the step of kegging.

session ale: A traditional British term for ale styles that are well-suited to "sessions" involving multiple pints traditionally consumed during business meals; usually used for beers that are medium-bodied, lightly hopped, and moderate in alcohol content. See also *amber ale.*

skunkiness: A descriptor used for the aroma, and sometimes flavor, of beer that has been infected or damaged, particularly beer that has been lightstruck (which see also).

small ale: A light-bodied and/or light strength ale, often specifically a secondary beer made from the secondary runnings from a mash, after the primary runnings are used to make a strong ale. See also *strong ale.*

soapiness: A flavor descriptor used for beer aromas and flavors akin to soap. Generally, this is caused when beer is not racked out of the primary fermenter before the yeast begins metabolizing the dead cells of their kindred, a process known as "autolysis."

sparge: To rinse the mashed malt and/or grains with hot water in order to maximize the extraction of sugars into the resulting sweet wort. The remaining grains are called "sparged," or "spent grains."

specialty malt: Any malt added to the grist along with the primary malt (usually pale two-row), typically more thoroughly roasted than two-row, including such classic malts as crystal (a.k.a. caramel), common in pale and amber ales, and chocolate and black patent, common in porters and stouts. See also *Pale Malt.*

specific gravity (also called *present gravity* or just *gravity*): An analytical measurement of the density of a beer in terms of suspended solids in the wort prior to fermentation, compared with suspended unfermentable solids in the finished beer. See also *extract, original gravity, final gravity.*

stability: The overall condition of finished beer prior to consumption, especially with regard to freshness and clarity. Biological stability refers to the freshness, or the absence of spoilage. Colloidal stability refers to non-biological clarity, or the absence of chill haze or other opacity.

steam beer: See *California common beer.*

steinbier: A traditional German type of beer, whose name (literally, "stone beer") refers to the method of production: boiling the wort by adding heated stones.

stock ale: An ale brewed to hold in stock, either as inventory or to age. The term is sometimes used for an ale that is hearty and made to be consumed with food. See also *running ale.*

stout: A traditional British style of ale with a very full-body and dark to black color. Evolved from porter (originally the name was "stout porter," referring to the hearty body), there are several varieties of stouts. The quintessential international stout is a dry Irish stout that is assertively bitter with roasty or coffee-like flavors. Sometimes a strong stout is given a strength rating by number of "X's," on a roughly one to five X scale, in which one X is the least strong. See also *barley wine, export, porter.*

strength: The potency of a beer due to its alcohol content. Various systems are used to measure strength. In the U.S., alcohol content is measured by percent by weight (abw = alcohol by weight, e.g., 3.2 percent abw beer is that percent by weight).

strike: The addition of hot water to milled malt at the start of the mash.

strong ale (also called *old ale*): A traditional Belgian style of ale that is ruby in color, medium in body, with high alcohol content and low hopping levels. In Britain the term is sometimes used synonymously with "old ale," but traditionally referred to the beer made from the first runnings of a mash. See also *barley wine, old ale, small ale, wee heavy.*

sulfuricness: A taste descriptor used for the off-flavors and aromas caused by certain yeast strains and released as a byproduct of their fermentation processes, which can be very subtle or pronounced. The byproduct is dimethyl sulfide (DMS), and is usually likened to the smell of sulfur or a burning match, but also to the flavor of cooked vegetables or even rotten egg in extreme cases.

sweet(ness): A flavor descriptor that indicates sugary, malty or honey flavors in beer; usually as these flavors relate to or dominate over bitterness. See also *bitterness, dryness, hoppiness.*

sweet wort: The liquid created during the mashing process, consisting of malted-barley sugars, enzymes, and other compounds suspended in water. See also *wort.*

tap: Standard dispensing device used for serving draft beer, wherein carbon dioxide, or a mixture of CO_2 and nitrogen, is forced into the keg under pressure to expel the beer and to prevent oxidation. The term is also used occasionally as short-hand for brewery tap.

tap room: See brewery tap.

tasting room: A drinking establishment that serves beers brewed on-premise in an adjoining craft brewery which primarily supplies other retail beer outlets. Some tasting rooms allow the actual purchase of draft beer for consumption on premise, while other breweries must provide only tastes, and might sell bottled beers in an adjoining retail store area. See also *brewpub, brewery tap.*

terminal gravity: See *final gravity.*

tied house: A pub or brewery tap room that is literally "tied" to a brewery through special, often exclusive, contractual arrangements or outright ownership of the pub by the brewing company. See also *pub, brewery tap, Prohibition.*

top-fermenting yeasts: Yeasts that usually ferment at higher temperatures than bottom-fermenting yeasts and take their name from the fact that they are most visibly active in the top portion of the fermentation vessel. See also *ale, bottom-fermenting.*

Trappist ale: A traditional Belgian style of top-fermented beer, usually bottle-conditioned, medium to full in body, strong in alcohol content, often with candy sugar added in the boil for added strength and flavor complexity. This term is used exclusively by six official Trappist monastic breweries, five in Belgium and one in the Netherlands. See also *abbey ale, Belgian ale.*

Vienna: A traditional Austrian-style, bottom-fermented beer that is coppery or reddish-brown in color, light to medium in body, light in strength, with a balanced flavor profile leaning toward maltiness, often with roasty undertones; similar to *Märzenbier/Oktoberfest,* but lighter in body and strength.

wee heavy: A traditional Scottish-style ale that is ruby to near black in color, medium to strong in alcohol and medium to thick in body. This style is similar to English old ale (though generally sweeter) and barley wine (though generally less potent). See also *Scotch ale, barley wine, old ale, strong ale.*

weiss(e)bier: A traditional German-style beer originating in Berlin and Bavaria. Literally, "white beer," it contains some wheat in addition to the malted barley, and often with strong esters reminiscent of banana or clove. See also *wit, and weizenbier.*

weizenbier: A German designation, literally "wheat beer," used for a widely varying style of beer originating in Bavaria and in the Baden-Württemberg area. Generally, weizenbiers are medium-bodied, though a dunkelweizen is medium to heavy in body and color. In North America, the term "weizen" is used loosely for any beer made with yeast, sometimes opaque or clear, sometimes with strong wheat flavor or with fairly typical ale characteristics. See also *weissbier.*

wheat beer: A modern American style of top-fermented beer containing a high percentage of wheat in the mash. The style was popularized in the Pacific Northwest and is often served with a lemon slice and/or called hefeweizen, though it lacks the Bavarian style's assertive yeast esters. See also *hefeweizen, weizenbier.*

wild beer: Beer containing carbon dioxide that has broken free from solution.

winter warmer: See *Christmas beers, old ale.*

wit(te): A traditional Belgian-style ale literally meaning "white," very light in color and body, cloudy, very lightly hopped, usually quite sweet, and often spiced with coriander and curacao orange peel. See also *weissbier.*

wort (also called *bitter wort*): The liquid created by boiling the sweet wort with hops (and any clarifying agents used) in preparation for fermentation; the primary ingredient of the finished brew. See also *sweet wort.*

yeasts (brewers'): Relatively large micro-organisms whose metabolic consumption of sugars and subsequent release of alcohol and carbon dioxide constitute the process known as fermentation. Often referred to as one of the four ingredients of beer (water, grain, and hops being the others), yeast is technically an agent and is not generally intended for consumption in the final product.

yeasty: A flavor descriptor used for the distinctive aromas and flavors caused by the presence of yeast in the finished beer; also used for the off-flavors caused by over-exposure of actively fermenting yeast to the sediment of spent yeast during a prolonged fermentation.

APPENDICES

PACIFIC NORTHWEST ALEHOUSES

As with the list of Seattle Alehouses (see page 111), this sample list of alehouses of the Pacfic Northwest is far from complete. But it does give you many ideas for where to find craft beer throughout the region, including pubs, taverns, restaurants, and nightclubs. All of the following establishments offer at least ten craft beers on-tap at any given time—which means you're bound to find a craft beer to your liking, wherever you are in Oregon, Washington or British Columbia even if the town you're in doesn't sport its own brewery yet!

OREGON

NORTHWEST PIZZA & PASTA, 1585 Siskyou Boulevard, Ashland, OR (541) 488-2080
    Pizza and pasta restaurant with 20-plus craft beers on tap

MCKENZIE'S RESTAURANT AND BAR, 1033 Bond Street, Bend, OR (541) 388-3891
    American cuisine restaurant with 10-plus craft beers on tap

BOMBS AWAY CAFÉ, 2527 Monroe Street, Corvallis, OR (541) 757-7221
    Mexican restaurant with 10-plus craft beers on tap

THE FOX & FIRKIN, 202 SW 1st Street, Corvallis, OR (541) 753-8533
    British pub with 10-plus craft beers on tap and 27 total, upscale pub fare

SQUIRRELS TAVERN, 100 SW 2nd Street, Corvallis, OR (541) 753-8057
Tavern with 12-plus craft beers on tap, pub grub, live music

SUDS 'N' SUDS, 1035 NW King Boulevard, Corvallis, OR (541) 758-5200
Pub with attached laundry room, with 30-plus craft beers on tap, basic bar snacks

SAM BOND'S GARAGE, Blair & 4th Avenue, Eugene, OR, 97401 (541) 431-6603
Pub with 10-plus beers on tap, live music every night

BJ'S PIZZA, 1600 Coburg Road #4 -and- 3540 W 11th Avenue, Eugene, OR
(541) 342-6114 -and- (541) 687-2423
Chain Italian fare restaurant serving craft beers from one of their two Northwest brewing locations as well as guest taps

BJ'S PIZZA, 345 NW Burnside, Gresham, OR (503) 667-7851
Chain Italian fare restaurant serving craft beers from one of their two Northwest brewing locations as well as guest taps

GEMINI PUB, 456 N State Street, Lake Oswego, OR (503) 994-7238
Neighborhood pub with 15-plus craft beers on tap, pool, pub fare, live music

GRUB STREET GRILL, 35 N Central Avenue, Medford, OR (541) 779-2635
Family oriented restaurant and bar with 10-plus craft beers on tap

BOGART'S NORTHWEST, 406 N 14th Street, Portland, OR (503) 222-4986
Pub with 25-plus craft beers on tap and a great bottle selection

CAPTAIN ANKENY'S WELL, 50 SW 3rd Avenue, Portland, OR (503) 223-1375
Pub with 15-plus craft beers on tap, Italian fare, eclectic crowd

COYOTE'S PUB, 2809 NE Sandy Boulevard, Portland, OR (503) 234-8573
Pub with 25-plus craft beers on tap, extensive pub burger menu

DUBLIN PUB, 6821 NW Beaverton-Hillside Highway, Portland, OR (503) 297-2889
Irish pub with live folk music and 100-plus beers on tap, younger crowd

GALWAY'S PUB, 3728 NE Sandy Boulevard, Portland, OR (503) 281-5464
Irish pub with 12-plus craft beers on tap

HAWTHORNE STREET ALE HOUSE, 3632 SE Hawthorne, Portland, OR
(503) 233-6540
BridgePort Brewing Company's ales featured with 15-plus craft beers

HIGGINS, 1239 SW Broadway, Portland (503) 222-9070
Restaurant with 12-plus craft beers on tap including Belgians, upscale menu, large selection of bottled Belgian beers

HORSE BRASS PUB, 4534 SE Belmont, Portland, OR (503) 232-2202
Traditional English pub with 35-plus craft beers on tap, cask-conditioned ales, English fare; where the McMenamins, the Widmers and the Ponzis of BridgePort hatched the Oregon microbrewing revolution

KELL'S IRISH PUB, 112 SW 2nd Avenue, Portland, OR (503) 227-4057
Irish-Anglo fare, 10-plus craft beers on tap, unsurpassed whiskey and scotch selection; sister establishment of pub by the same name in downtown Seattle

LAURELTHIRST, 2958 NE Glisan Street, Portland, OR (503) 232-2202
Funky English-type pub with15-plus craft beers on tap, veggie and healthy menu, breakfast, live music

McDUFF'S, 1635 SE 7th, Portland, OR (503) 234-2337
Pub with 12-plus craft beers on tap, lots of domestics, pub fare

MICKEY FINN'S BREWPUBS; 4336 SE Woodstock Boulevard, Portland, OR (503) 788-6073; 12066 SE Sunnyside Road, Portland, OR (503) 698-6073; 1339 NW Flanders, Portland, OR (206) 222-5910
Pubs with 20-plus craft beers on tap, non-smoking, pub fare

MOUNT TABOR THEATRE AND PUB, 4811 SE Hawthorne Street, Portland OR (503) 238-1646
Rustic non-McMenamins theater-pub with 15-plus craft beers on tap, pub fare and pizzas, live music, pool

THE PILSNER ROOM, 0309 SW Montgomery, Portland, OR (503) 220-1865
Upscale restaurant with 20-plus craft beers on tap

PRODUCE ROW CAFÉ, 204 SW Oak, Portland, OR (503) 232-8355
Funky beer bar with 20-plus craft beers on tap, large selection of bottled beers; one of original owners co-founded McMenamins

RED STAR TAVERN AND ROAST HOUSE, 503 SW Alder Street, Portland, OR (503) 222-0005
Tavern with 12 all-craft beers on tap, menu specializes in roasted and grilled meats

THE ROSE & RAINDROP, 532 SE Grand, Portland, OR (503) 232-6996
Upscale British pub with 25-plus craft beers on tap, British fare

THE SNAKE & WEASEL, 1720 SE Twelfth, Portland, OR (503) 232-8338
Neighborhood pub with 10-plus craft beers on tap, eclectic crowd, healthy snacks, live music, house beers by local breweries, beer tasting club

TWILIGHT ROOM, 5242 N Lombard, Portland, OR (503) 283-5091
Graffiti-enriched pub with 12-plus craft beers on tap, pub fare

Oregon Bottled-Beer Retail Shops

Belmont Station, 4520 SE Belmont, Portland, OR (503) 232-8538
Next to Horse Brass, shipping available

Burlingame Grocery, 8502 Terwilliger, Portland, OR (503) 246-0711
Perhaps the best selection in the Pacific Northwest

Washington

Harbour Public House, 231 Parfitt Way SW, Bainbridge, WA (206) 842-0969
Neighborhood pub with 10-plus craft beers on tap, fireplace, deck

Billy McHale's, 4065 Factoria Boulevard, Bellevue, WA (425) 746-1138
Restaurant/bar chain with 10-plus craft beers on tap; TV sports, video games

New Jake O'Shaugnessy's, 401 Bellevue Square, Bellevue, WA (425) 455-5559
Restaurant in Bellevue Square Mall with 20-plus craft beers on tap, full menu; original Jake's in Queen Anne has become a Larry's Market supermarket

Archer Alehouse, 1212 10th Street, Bellingham, WA (360) 647-7002
English-style pub with 12-plus craft beers on tap including Belgians; non-smoking, steel-tip darts, great bottled Belgian and other European beer selection

Beaver Inn, 1315 N State Street, Bellingham, WA (360) 733-3460
Tavern with 15-plus craft beers on tap and pool tables

The Black Cat/Le Chat Noir, 1200 Harris Avenue (upstairs), Bellingham, WA (360) 733-6136
Restaurant and bar with 10-plus craft beers on tap, full bar, steaks and seafood menu

The Calumet, 113 E Magnolia Street, Bellingham, WA (360) 733-3331
Upscale restaurant with 10-plus craft beers on tap, live jazz, eclectic Northwest cuisine

Grandstands Beer Emporium, 113 Grand Avenue, Bellingham, WA (360) 671-3080
Tavern with 15-plus craft beers on tap, sandwich menu and pool tables

Stanello's Restaurant, 1514 Twelfth Street, Bellingham, WA (360) 676-1304
Italian restaurant and sports-oriented bar with 12-plus craft beers on tap

Up & Up Tavern, 1234 N State Street, Bellingham, WA (360) 733-9739
Tavern with 15-plus craft beers on tap, pool tables, live Celtic and rock music

VILLAGE INN PUB & EATERY, 3020 Northwest Avenue, Bellingham, WA (360) 734-2490
Pub with 12-plus craft beers on tap, pool tables, pull-tabs, pub fare

CANYON'S RESTAURANT AND TAP ROOM, 22010 17th Avenue SE, Bothell, WA (425) 485-3288
Full menu restaurant with 15-plus craft beers on tap, American fare, patio seating

GOOCHI'S, 104 E Woodin Avenue, Chelan, WA (509) 682-2436
Pub with 30-plus craft beers on tap

TOBY'S TAVERN, 8 NW Front Street, Coupeville, WA (360) 678-4222
Large, water-view tavern with 10-plus craft beers on tap, pool tables

GOLDIE'S IN EDMONDS, 180 Sunset Avenue, Edmonds, WA (425) 778-7466
Restaurant and bar with 10-plus craft beers on tap

RORY'S OF EDMONDS, 105 Main Street, Edmonds, WA (425) 778-3433
Restaurant and tavern with 20-plus craft beers on tap; darts and video golf games

MINT, 1608 Cole Street, Enumclaw, WA (206) 825-8361
Full menu pub with 20-plus craft beers on tap; excellent selection of Pacific Rim Brewing Company's beers on tap

EVERETT ROASTER AND ALE HOUSE, 3105 Pine Street, Everett, WA (425) 339-2000
Restaurant with 15-plus craft beers on tap, grilled and roasted meats, sister establishment to Kirkland and Sharpe's Roasters

JAKE'S ALES, 2318 SW 336th Street, Federal Way, WA (253) 927-1288
Large pub with 30-plus craft beers on tap, pub fare, darts

BILLY MCHALE'S, 1800 S 320th, Federal Way, WA (253) 839-4200
Restaurant/bar chain with 10-plus craft beers on tap; TV sports, video games

LOLLIE'S BROILER & PUB, 32925 1st Avenue S, Federal Way, WA (253) 838-5929
Strip mall pub with 20-plus craft beers on tap, good pub fare, trivia

CHARLIE O'S, 5114 Pt. Fosdick Drive, Gig Harbor, WA (253) 851-1050
Pub with 10-plus craft beers on tap, good limited pub fare, pool and video games

TIDES TAVERN, 2925 Harborview Drive, Gig Harbor, WA (253) 858-3982
Restaurant/pub overlooking Gig Harbor with 10-plus craft beers on tap, deck seating, full menu; 3 house beers brewed by Harmon Brewing Company

THE ROOST, 120 NW Gilman Boulevard, Issaquah, WA (425) 392-5550
Family restaurant with 12-plus craft beers on tap; servers dressed like roosters

PONY KEG, 8535 S 212th Street, Kent, WA (253) 395-8022
   Tavern with 10-plus craft beers on tap, pool tables and video games

KIRKLAND ROASTER, 111 Central Way, Kirkland, WA (425) 827-4400
   Restaurant/pub with 20-plus craft beers on tap, roasted meats; was adjoined to
the old Hale's Brewery in Kirkland; sister pub to SeaTac Sharpe's Roaster

ROSE HILL ALEHOUSE, 12859 NE 85th Street, Kirkland, WA (425) 828-9712
   Restaurant/pub with 25-plus craft beers on tap, good pub fare; pool and darts,
shuffleboard; features a contract brew IPA made by Northwest BrewW‰orks

DOGHOUSE, 230 1st Street Langley, WA (360) 221-9825
   Pub with 12-plus craft beers on tap, pool table

LAKE WASHINGTON GRILL HOUSE & TAPROOM, 6161 NE 175th Street,
Kenmore, WA, (425) 486-3313
   Restaurant/alehouse overlooking Lake Washington with 20-plus craft beers
on tap

MAWELL'S, Marysville, WA (360) 653-3581
   Restaurant with 10-plus craft beers on tap

MILTON TAVERN, 7320 Pacific Highway E, Milton, WA (206) 922-3340
   Non-smoking saloon with 30-plus craft beers on tap

BILLY MCHALE'S, 15210 Redmond Way, Redmond, WA (425) 881-0316
   Restaurant/bar chain with 10-plus craft beers on tap; TV sports, video games

FOXY'S PUB, 944 Harrington NE, Renton, WA (425) 228-7950
   Pub with 15-plus craft beers on tap, pub fare, live music; "where smokers are
welcome"

LAZY BEE PUB & EATERY, 739 Rainier Avenue S, Renton, WA (425) 255-7423
   Neighborhood pub with 10-plus craft beers on tap, pub fare and pizzas

WHISTLE STOP ALE HOUSE, 340 Burnett Avenue S, Renton, WA (425) 277-3039
   Pub with grilled sandwiches and10-plus craft beers on tap

THE CABIN, Richmond Beach Drive, Richmond Beach, WA (206) 542-1177
   Funky neighborhood tavern with patio and 10-plus craft beers on tap, pool
tables, snug

THE BRICK TAVERN, 1 Pennsylvania Street, Roslyn, WA (509) 649-2643
   Shown in the TV series "Northern Exposure" with 10-plus craft beers on tap

C.J. BORGS, SeaTac International Airport, SeaTac, WA (206) 433-5024
   Pub in the airport with 10-plus craft beers on tap

Sharp's Roaster & Alehouse, 18427 Pacific Highway S, SeaTac, WA (206) 241-5744

Restaurant with full menu of roasted meats and 20-plus craft beers on tap, just south of the SeaTac airport

Fred's Rivertown Ale House, 1114 1st Street, Snohomish, WA (360) 568-5820

Pub with 25-plus craftbeers on tap; house beers by Diamond Knot Brewing Company

Ale House Pub & Eatery, 2122 Mildred Street W, Tacoma, WA (206) 565-9367

Sports bar with 45-plus craft beers on tap

Katie Downs Tavern and Eatery, 3211 Ruston Way, Tacoma, WA (253) 756-0771

Upscale pub overlooking the Sound with 12-plus craft beers on tap, pub fare and pizza

The Spar Beer Parlour, 2121 N 30th, Tacoma, WA (253) 627-8215

Open since 1913 with 12-plus craft beers on tap, pub fare; world map covered in currency brought in by visitors

The Swiss, 1904 Jefferson, Tacoma, WA (206) 572-2821

Pub with full menu and 30-plus craft beers on tap

R.P. McMurphy's at the Academy, 400 E Evergreen Boulevard, Vancouver, WA (360) 695-9211

Restaurant/pub with 30-plus craft beers on tap, darts; live music Wednesdays–Saturdays, open mike Wednesdays

R.P. McMurphy's at Cascade Park, 316 SE 123rd Avenue, Vancouver, WA (360) 253-4355

Restaurant/pub with 30-plus craft beers on tap, darts; live music Fridays–Saturdays, live comedy Wednesdays

British Columbia

Fogg 'n Suds; 7090 Lougheed Hwy., Burnaby, B.C. (604) 421-7837
Restaurant (chain) with 10-plus craft beers on tap, large selection of bottled beers

Fogg 'n Suds, 45300 Luckakuck Way, Chilliwack, B.C. (250) 824-9961
Restaurant (chain) with 10-plus craft beers on tap, large selection of bottled beers

FOGG 'N SUDS, 577 Victoria Street, Kamloops, B.C. (250) 851-2030
Restaurant (chain) with 10-plus craft beers on tap, large selection of bottled beers

FOGG 'N SUDS, 1816 Bowen Road, Nanaimo, B.C. (250) 754-7837
Restaurant (chain) with 10-plus craft beers on tap, large selection of bottled beers

HERITAGE INN/THE LIBRARY PUB/MIKE'S PLACE PUB, 422 Vernon Street,
Nelson, B.C. (250) 352-5331
Hotel with two pubs and a nightclub in it; great Nelson Brewing Company
selection at each venue, especially Mike's Place upstairs, where all the Nelson brews
are always on-tap, along with several other craft beers

RAVEN PUB, 1052 Deer Cove Road, North Vancouver, B.C. (604) 929-3834
Old World-style pub with 20-plus craft beers on tap

FOGG 'N SUDS, 200-500 W Broadway, Vancouver, B.C. (604) 872-3377
Restaurant (chain) with 10-plus craft beers on tap, large selection of bottled beers

THE 604, Vancouver, B.C. (604) 739-8131
Restaurant/lounge with 10-plus craft beers on tap, live DJ seven nights

O'DOULES RESTAURANT & BAR, 1300 Robson, Vancouver, B.C. (604) 684-8461
Lounge and restaurant with 10-plus craft beers on tap; live jazz Thursday–
Saturdays, live opera Sundays

SHARK CLUB, 180 W Georgia Street, Vancouver, B.C. (604) 687-4275
Night club with 15-plus craft beers on tap; lots of pool tables upstairs, live DJ on
weekends

CHRISTIE'S CARRIAGE HOUSE, 1739 Fort Street, Victoria, B.C. (250) 598-5333
Elegantly restored, Queen Anne-style building with 25-plus craft beers on tap,
live music, trivia game night; "largest selection of craft beers in B.C."

STICKY WICKET/STRATHCONA HOTEL, 919 Douglas Street, Victoria, B.C.
(250) 383-7137, (800) 663-7476, www.strathconahotel.com
Five bars all with varying craft brews on-tap, full menu; pool, billiards, snooker,
steel-tip darts, rooftop volleyball

FOGG 'N SUDS, 2569 Dobbin Road, Westbank, B.C. (250) 707-3644
Restaurant (chain) with 10-plus craft beers on tap, large selection of bottled beers

RECOMMENDED READING

There is a wealth of resource information on beer, brewing, and beer culture. The following short list gives you a starting place in the area that interests you. A little searching will yield a wealth of books, periodicals, and web-sites in each of the categories.

BEERS AND BEER STYLES

Jackson, Michael, et. al. *The Beer Companion: America's Microbreweries and Classic Beers from Europe.* Philadelphia, PA: Running Press, 1993.

Smith, Gregg. *The Beer Enthusiast's Guide: Tasting & Judging Beers from Around the World.* Pownal, VT: Storey Communications, 1993.

BREWPUBS, PUBS, AND TAVERNS

Harper, Timothy and Garrett Oliver. *The Good Beer Book: The Ultimate Guide to the Most Distinctive Breweries, the Greatest Bars and Pubs, and the Best Beers.* New York, NY: Berkley Publishing, 1997.

Hieronymus, Stan and Daria Labinsky. *Beer Travelers Guide.* Durham, NC: All About Beer Magazine, 1995.

Lewis, Ashton. *How to Open a Brewpub or Microbrewery.* Davis, CA: American Brewers Guild, 1992.

BREWING AND HOMEBREWING

Miller, Dave. *Dave Miller's Homebrewing Guide.* Pownal, VT: Storey Communications, 1995.

Mosher, Randy. *The Brewer's Companion: Being a Complete Compendium of Brewing Knowledge.* Seattle, WA: Alephenalia Publications, 1994.

Papazian, Charlie. *The Home Brewer's Companion: The Essential Handbook.* New York, NY: Avon Books, 1994.

BREWING HISTORY

Meier, Gary and Gloria Meier. *Brewed in the Pacific Northwest: A History of Beer Making in Oregon and Washington.* Seattle, WA: Fjord Press, 1991. Seattle, WA

Smith, Gregg. *Beer: A History of Suds and Civilization from Mesopotamia to Microbreweries.* New York, NY: Avon Books, 1995.

BEER AND BREWING PERIODICALS

All About Beer "America's Foremost Beer Publication." 1627 Marion Ave.; Durham, NC 27705; (919) 490-0589 or (800) 977-2337; www.allaboutbeer.com

Brew Your Own "The How-To Homebrew Beer Magazine." PO Box 1504; Martinez, CA 94553-0504; (510) 372-6002; www.byo.com

BrewPub Magazine. PO Box 2473; Martinez, CA 94553; (530) 758-4596 or (800) 900-7594; www.brewpubmag.com

Celebrator Beer News. 20958 Corsair Blvd.; PO Box 375; Hayward, CA 94543; (510) 670-0121 or (800) 430-2337; www.celebrator.com

Northwest Beer Notes. 223 Independence Way; Cashmere, WA 98815; (509) 782-1147; www.beernotes.com/northwest

Zymurgy. American Homebrewers' Association; PO Box 1510; Boulder, CO 80306-1510; (303) 546-6514; www.beertown.org/AHA/aha.htm

INDEX

A

Admiral Pub 119
Alameda Brewhouse 49
Ale House Pub & Eatery 248
Alki Tavern 119
Anchor Steam Brewing Company 9
Archer Alehouse 150, 245
Athenian Inn 116
Atomic Ale Brewpub & Eatery 159, 165
Attic Alehouse & Eatery 114

B

Bad Albert's Tap and Grill 112
Bagdad Theater & Pub 55, 83
Ballard Firehouse Food & Beverage Co.
Ballard Grill & Alehouse 112
Bank Brewing Company 18
Barley Brown's Brewpub 78
Barley Mill Brewpub 83, 213, 218
Bay Front Public House 19
Bayou Brewing Company 170
Bear Brewing Company 213–221
Beaver Inn 245
beer styles 11–12
beer to go, defined 14
Bell Tower Brewhouse 88
Belltown Pub 111, 116
Belmont Station 245
Bend Brewing Company 74
Big Horn Breweries 104–105
Big Horn Brewery/Ram Restaurant 41
Big Horse Brewing Company 69
Big House Brewing 160, 168
Big River Brewing Company 180, 196
Big Star 119
Big Time Brewery & Alehouse 121
BigRidge Brewing Company 182, 196
Bill's Tavern & Brewhouse 23
Billy McHale's 245, 246, 247
BJ's Pizza, Grill and Brewery 50, 243
Black Cat, The 245
Black Rabbit Restaurant and Bar 67
Blue Moon Tavern 111, 114
Blue Moon Tavern & Grill 79, 83
Blue Pine Brewpub 25, 30

Blue Star 115
Bogart's Northwest 243
Bohemian Café 112, 116
Bombs Away Café 242
Bottleworks 119
Boundary Bay Brewery & Bistro 150, 155
Brew Club 188
Brew Garden, The 159
Brew Tour, Eugene 33; Greater Puget Sound
    95–96; McMenamins 55–56; Okanagan
    Valley 213; Southern Oregon 25–26;
    Washington's "Fourth Corner" 150
Brewer's on the Bay 20
brewhouse, defined 10
brewing process 12–13
brewpub, defined 10
Brick Tavern 247
Bricks Broadview Grill 115
BridgePort Brewing Company 45, 51, 79
bright tank 13
Brooklyn Seafood, Steak & Oyster House
    117
Buckaroo 112
Buckerfield's Brewery 183
Buffalo Brewing Company 222
Burlingame Grocery 245

C

C.J. Borgs 247
Cabin, The 247
Caldera Brewing 17, 25
Calumet, The 245
Canyon's Restaurant and Tap Room 246
Capital Steak House 188
Captain Ankeny's Well 243
Captains City Brewing Company 95, 111, 147
Casa U-Betcha 117
Cascade Lakes Brewing Company 73
Cascade Microbrewery & Public Firehouse
    42
Charlie O's 246
children, defined 14
Christie's Carriage House 184, 249
CI Shenanigans Seafood & Chop House
    104–105
CI Shenanigans, Spokane 104–105

College Inn Pub 111, 115
Columbia Brewery 45
Comet Tavern 117
Concordia Brewery at Kennedy School 81
Conor Byrnes Pub 112
contract brewing 11
Cooper's Alehouse 115
Coquitlam Brewing Company 196, 211
Corcoran Glassworks 68
Cornelius Pass Roadhouse Brewery 81
Courtyard Restaurant 57
Coyote's Pub 243
craft brewery, defined 10
Creek Brewery, The 196, 198–199
Crocodile Café 117
Crosswalk Tavern 115
Crystal Ballroom 80, 84
Crystal Brewery 81
Cypress Room 58

D

Dad Watson's 55, 82
Danté's 115
Deluxe Bar & Grill 117
Deschutes Brewery & Public House 75
Detention Bar 58
Diamond Knot Brewing Company &
    Alehouse 95, 145
Dix BBQ & Brewery 196, 200
Doc Maynard's 117
Doghouse 247
Dublin Pub 243
Dubliner 113
Duchess Tavern 115
Duke's Greenlake Chowder House 113

E

Eagle Brewing Company 95, 146
East 19th Street Café 83
Edgefield Gardens 68
Edgefield Lodge/Brewery 17, 82, 84
Edgefield Manor 80
Edgefield Wine Cellar and Tasting Room
    67–68
Ellersick Brewing Company 144
Elliot Glacier Public House 71
Elliott Bay Brewery & Pub 122
Elysian Brewing Company & Public House
    123
Elysian Brewing Company/GameWorks 124
Engine House No. 9 Restaurant & Brewery
    109

entertainment, defined 14
establishment, defined 14
Eugene Brewpub Scene 33
Everett Roaster and Ale House 246

F

F.X. McRory's 117
Fiddler's Inn 115
Fish Brewing Company 94, 96
Floyd's Place Beer & BBQ 113, 117
Flying Pig Brewing Company 150, 152
Fogg 'n Suds 248, 249
food, defined 14
Forecasters Brewpub 136
Fort Spokane Brewery 171
Fox & Firkin, The 242
Foxy's Pub 247
Fred's Rivertown Ale House 248
Front Street Ale House 95, 149
Full Sail at River Place 51
Full Sail Brewing Company-Hood River 70
Fulton Pub & Brewery 55, 81

G

Gallagher's Where-U-Brew 143
Galway's Pub 243
GameWorks 124
Gemini Pub 243
George and the Dragon Pub 113
Globe Tavern 115
Golden Valley Brewery Pub & Restaurant 44
Goldie's in Edmonds 246
Goochi's 246
Gordon Biersch Brewing Company 125
Grady's 115
Grandstands Beer Emporium 245
Grant's Brewery Pub 162
Granville Island Brewing Company 196,
    201, 213
Granville Island Hotel 196, 198–199
Greater Puget Sound Brew Tour 95–96
Greater Trumps 83
Green Lake Alehouse 113
Greenway Pub 79, 83
Grub Street Grill 243

H

Hair of the Dog Brewing Company 52
Hale's Ales 126
Harbour Canoe Club Brewhouse, Restau-
    rant, Marina 183, 186
Harbour Public House 245

Harmon Pub & Brewery 96, 107
Hawthorne Street Ale House 243
Hazel Dell Brewpub 89
Headquarters for the International Association of Rogues 20
Heads Up Brewing Company 96, 98
Heritage Inn 249
Higgins 243
High Mountain Brewing Company & Brewhouse 196, 210
High Street Brewery & Café 33, 81
Highland Pub & Brewery 81
Hillsdale Brewery & Pub 55, 79, 82
Hilltop Alehouse 113
homebrewing, legalized 9
Hood Canal Brewery 99
Hop Scotch 117
Hopvine 117
Horse Brass Pub 45, 244
Horseshoe Bay Brewing 9
Hotel Oregon 83, 84
hours, defined 14
Howe Sound Inn & Brewing Company 207–208
Howie's on Front Street 25
Hoyt's Pub 113
Hugo's Brew Club 183, 187–188

I

Ice Harbor Brewing Company 159–160, 167
Icehouse 67
International Association of Rogues 20
Islander Pub and Grill 119
Issaquah Brewing Company 137

J

J&M Café 112, 117
Jake's Ales 246
Jazz Alley 117
Jersey's All American Sports Bar 118
Jody Maroni's Sausage Kingdom 66
John Barleycorns 82

K

Katie Downs Tavern and Eatery 248
Kell's Irish Pub 111, 118, 244
Kinkora 118
Kirkland Roaster 247

L

La Boheme Tavern 113
La Conner Brewing Company 150, 153

Lake Chelan's Deep Water Brewing & Public House 176
Lake Washington Grill House & Taproom 247
Lakewood Ram & Big Horn Brewery 104–105
Latona Pub 113
Laurelthirst 244
Lazy Bee Pub & Eatery 247
Le Chat Noir, The 245
Leavenworth Brewery 173
Leschi Lake Café 115
Library Pub, The 249
Lighthouse Brewing Company 81, 194
Little Red Shed 67
Lollie's Broiler & Pub 246
Longwood Brewpub 195
Lucky Labrador Brewing Company 54
Lunar Brewing Company 127

M

Mac & Jack's Brewery 141
Mad Dog Alehouse 115
Magnolia Hotel 183, 187–188
Maple Leaf Grill 116
Marin Brewing Company 107
Maritime Pacific Brewing Company 128
Market Street Pub 84
Mawell's 247
Maxwell's Brewery & Pub 95, 101–102
McCormick & Schmick's 118
McCormick & Schmick's Harborside Restaurant 51
McDuff's 244
McKenzie's Restaurant and Bar 242
McMenamins 79–80
McMenamins Brew Tour 55–56
McMenamins, Boons Treasury 84; West Linn 82; Edgefield Brewery 67–68; Kennedy School 55, 57, 80, 84; Broadway 84; on the Columbia 82; Pubs & Breweries 17, 33, 45, 79–80; St. Johns Pub 84; Tavern 83; Cedar Hills 82; Corvallis 83; Mall 205 84; Mill Creek 82; Murray 81; Oregon City 83; Roy Street 82; Sherwood 84; Sunnyside 82
Merchants Café 118
Methow Valley Brewing Company 175
Mia & Pia's Pizzeria & Brewhouse 76
Mickey Finn's Brewpubse 244
microbrewery, defined 10
Mike's Place Pub 249

Mill Creek Brewpub 160, 168
Milton Tavern 247
Mint 246
Mission Springs Brewing Company 212
Mission Theater & Pub 55, 79, 83
Mona Lizza Ristorante 33, 36
Monkey Pub 116
Mount Begbie Brewing Company 213, 214, 223
Mount Tabor Theatre and Pub 244
Mt. Angel Brewing Company 43
Mt. Hood Brewing Company 72
Murphy's Pub 116

N

Nelson Brewing Company 224
New Jake O'Shaugnessy's 245
Nickerson Street Saloon 113
Nor'Wester 17
North Cascades Brewing Company 150
North Fork Brewery/Pizza/Beer Shrine 150, 158
Northern Lights Brewing Company 169
Northwest Brewhouse & Grill 142
Northwest Brew-Wërks 140
Northwest Pizza & Pasta 242

O

O'Doules Restaurant & Bar 249
Oak Harbor Pub & Brewery 148
Oak Hills Brewpub 82
Okanagan Spring Brewery 213–220
Okanagan Valley Brew Tour 213–214
Old Lompoc Tavern and Brewery 59
Old Market Pub & Brewery 60
Old Peculiar 113
Old World Deli 39
Old World Pub & Brewery 61
Olympic Club 55, 80, 82
Orchard Street Brewery 150, 156
Oregon Brewers Guild 15, 45
Oregon Hotel 80
Oregon Shakespeare Festival 25
Oregon Trader Brewing Company 40
Oregon Trail 39
Osprey Brewpub 25, 28
Oxford Hotel 80

P

Pacific Alehouse 112
Pacific Crest Brewing Company 129
Pacific Inn Pub 116

Pacific Northwest Alehouses 242–249
Pacific Rim Brewing Company 24, 130
Park Pub 114
payment, defined 14
Pelican Pub & Brewery, The 22
Peppers Mexican Restaurant 94
Philadelphia's Steaks & Hoagies 62
Pike Brewing Company 131
Pike Place Market 111
Pilsner Room 244
Pioneer Square 112
Pioneer Square Saloon 118
Pony Keg 247
Port Townsend Brewing Company 95, 100
Portland 45
Portland Brewing Company 45, 63
Powerhouse Restaurant & Brewery 96, 110
Powerstation Pub & Theater 84
Produce Row Café 244
Prohibition 9
Puyallup Ram & Big Horn Brewery 104–105
Pyramid Ales/Pyramid Brewery & Alehouse 132
Pyramid Brewery, Inc. 10

Q

Queen Anne Thriftway 119

R

R&B Brewing Company 196, 202
R.P. McMurphy's, at Cascade Park 248; at the Academy 248
Raccoon Lodge and Brewpub 47
Rainbow Inn 111, 116
Raleigh Hills Pub 83
Ram International 104–105
Ram Restaurant 41
Ram Restaurant & Big Horn Brewery 96
Ram's Head, The 83
Rattlesnake Mountain Brewing Company 159, 166
Raven Pub 249
Ray's Boathouse 114
RC's Billiards, Brew and Eatery 118
Reading Gaol 114
Red Dawg Brewpub 92
Red Door Alehouse 114
Red Star Tavern and Roast House 244
Redhook Ale Brewery 9, 10, 136
Ridge Brewing Company Brew Pub/Family Restaurant/Hotel 213, 215–216
Riley's Pizza 95, 146

Ringlers Annex 84
Riverwood Pub 82
Roanoke Park Place Tavern 118
Roanoke Tavern 119
Rock Bottom Restaurant & Brewery 64, 133
Rock Creek Tavern 83
Rock Pasta Brick Oven Pizza & Brewery 108
Rock Wood-Fired Pizza & Brewery 108
RockSport 119
Rogue Ales 19, 20, 137
Rogue Ales Bay Front Public House 19
Romper Room 118
Roost, The 246
Rory's 116
Rory's of Edmonds 246
Rose & Raindrop, The 244
Rose Hill Alehouse 247
Roseburg Station 26, 82
Roslyn Brewing Company 161
Russell Brewing Company 181

S

Sailfish Bar & Grill 139
Sailor Hägar's Brewpub 196, 206
Sailor Tavern 184
Salmon Creek Brewery & Pub 90
Sam Bond's Garage 243
San Juan Brewing Company 95, 149
Santa Fe Café 116
Saxer Brewing Company 48
Scuttlebutt Brewing Company 150, 151
Seattle Alehouse Scene 111–112
Seattle Ram Café 104–105
Seventh Street Brew House 73
74th Street Alehouse 112
Shark Club 249
Sharp's Roaster & Alehouse 248
Siletz Brewing Company 21
Silver City Brewing Company 95, 97
Siskiyou Brewing 17
Siskiyou Pub 25
Six Arms 55, 83
Six Degrees 114
604, The 249
Skagit River Brewing Company 150, 154
Sloop, The 114
Small Brewers Big Beer Festival 26
smoking, defined 14
Snake & Weasel, The 244
Snipes Mountain Microbrewery & Restaurant 159, 163
Snoqualmie Falls Brewing Company 138

Solicitor's Corner Restaurant and Bar 172
Sound Brewery & Smokehouse 96, 103
Southern Oregon Brew Tour 25–26
Spar Beer Parlour 248
Spencer's Restaurant & Brewhouse 33, 38
Spinnakers Brewpub & Guesthouse 183–184, 189–190
Spokane Ram & Big Horn Brewery 104–105
Squirrels Tavern 243
St. John's Pub 55
Standing Stone Brewing Company 25, 27
Stanello's Restaurant 245
SteamWorks Brewing Company 196, 203
Steelhead Brewing Company 33, 35
Sticky Wicket/Strathcona Hotel 249
Storm Brewing Company 196, 204
Strathcona Hotel 184
Stumbling Monk 119
Suds 'n' Suds 243
Sully's Snow Goose 114
Swans Suite Hotel & Brewpub 183, 191–192
Sweetwater Brewing Company 172
Swiss, The 248

T

T.S. McHugh's 114
Tacoma Ram & Big Horn Brewery 104–105
Tapps Brewing Company 135
Teddy's Tavern 116
Terminal Gravity Brewing Company 17, 77
terminology 10–11
Thompson Brewery & Pub 82
Tides Tavern 246
Tin Whistle Brewing Company 213, 217
Tir Na Nog Brewpub 104–105, 134
Toby's Tavern 246
Tree Brewing Company 213–219
Triangle Tavern 114
Tugboat Brewing Company 65
Twilight Room 244
Twin Rivers Brewing Company 139

U

Umpqua Brewing Company 26, 32
Unicorn 111
Up & Up Tavern 245

V

Vancouver Island Brewing Company 184, 193
Vancouver, B.C. 196
Victoria's Charms 183–184

Village Inn Pub & Eatery 246
Vintage Bistro 91
Virginia Inn Tavern 111, 118
Von's 118

W

Walkabout Brewing Company 17, 25
Washington's "Fourth Corner" Brew Tour
150
Water Street Hotel 95, 101–102
Wedgwood Alehouse & Café 116
West Brothers Bar-B-Que 36
West Brothers Brewery 33, 36
Westridge Motor Inn 213
Wet Dog Café 24
Whatcom Brewery 150, 157
Whidbey Island Brewing Company 148
Whistle Stop Ale House 247
Whistler Brewing Company 9, 209

White Eagle 84
Whitstran Brewing Company 159, 164
Widmer Brewing & Gasthaus 66
Wild Duck Brewery, The 33, 37
Wild River Brewing & Pizza Company 25–
26, 29, 31
Wild River Publick House 29
Wind River Brewing Company 88
Windermere Valley Brewing Company 225
Winthrop Brewing Company 174
Woodland Park Pub 111
Workshop Pub 95
Wyatt's Eatery & Brewhouse 40

Y

Yakima Brewing Company 9, 159, 162
Yakima Valley Brew Tour 159–160
Yaletown Brewing Company 196, 205
Youngs Brewing Company 93

ABOUT THE AUTHORS

HUDSON DODD, an erstwhile homebrewer, lives in Bellingham, Washington, with his wife, Mary Kurlinski, and their cats, Jester and Periwinkle. Hudson is a wilderness conservation activist and works for the Northwest Ecosystem Alliance, while continuing his search for the perfect porter on the weekends
.

MATTHEW LATTERELL currently serves as Assistant Dean for Information Technology at the University of Oregon School of Law and in his spare time provides technology support to regional nonprofit organizations. A tremendous fan of Northwest hops, Matthew believes that "bitter is always better."

INA ZUCKER recently graduated from Law School and is pursuing a career in environmental law. She spends much of her time at the LocoMotive, an upscale vegetarian restaurant she and her family own in Eugene, Oregon, yet still finds time to enjoy the eclectic flavors of regional red ales.